I AM PITTS:

MEMOIRS OF AN AMERICAN PATRIOT

DEXTER M. PITTS

CONTENTS

DISCLAIMER

This Book is not sponsored, endorsed or written with the permission of the U.S. Army, The Louisville Metropolitan Police Department, The Sahuarita Police Department or the United States Border Patrol. The stories and opinions within this book are solely that of the author and based on his personal experiences. This book was not written to reflect or be an official representation of the above mentioned organizations. This book also contains some strong language that some might find offensive.

DEDICATION

This book is dedicated to my mother, Idella Pitts. Thank you for the values, morals, and many life lessons you taught me and for loving me unconditionally. Most of all, thank you for introducing Jesus Christ into my life. Because of the discipline you instilled in me, the standards you set before me, and the accountability you required of me, I am the man I am today because of you.

To the men and women of the United States Military whom I served with directly, those who shed their blood in defense of America with me and those who paid the ultimate sacrifice so that we may live free.

To the men and women of law enforcement who wear the uniform every day to protect and serve their community and this country.

To my wife Christina: You have stood by my side through the years and have loved me through my roughest times and have prayed me out of many dark days. Without your love and your support, this book would not have been possible.

Lastly, to my children Brooklynn and Dexter (DJ): I pray that when you are both old enough to read this book and comprehend the stories within that you will be inspired by the life that I have lived and learn from my many mistakes. I pray that you find your own way and meaning in your own lives and that you follow Jesus Christ's example. But I also pray that you both experience many hardships and failures in life. It is the hardships and failures you encounter in your lives that will make you tougher, stronger, better and grow you into the leaders that not only your families need, but our country. There is nothing to be gained in comfort. It is only in the discomfort of life that you will find yourselves, your purpose, and your own identity.

How did I get to this point in such a short amount of time? How did I go from being a beloved Purple Heart veteran who had appeared on the HBO documentary "Alive Day Memories: Home from Iraq," to being an extra in the Spike Lee Joint movie "Miracle at St. Anna"? How did I overcome my war wounds to achieve my dream of becoming a Louisville Metro Police Officer and marrying into one of the most influential and powerful families in Louisville, Kentucky to praying for death at the hands of a criminal on a random traffic stop? A decade later, I stand on the other side of the pandemonium that once had a stronghold on my life. I can honestly say that I am living the American dream. I have joy and fulfillment in my everyday life, and I try not to take that for granted because I still remember what it was like when both were non-existent in my life.

When I started writing my memoirs in 2014, American started to undergo a radical transformation following the police killing of Michael Brown in Ferguson, Missouri in August of 2014. This transformation led to the polarization of our once united country based on trivial matters such as skin color, binary politics, and identity politics. It was hard to believe that 13 years prior, Americans stood arm in arm as a united front under the guise of the American flag in the wake of the 9/11 attacks. My country that I loved and cherished so much, the country that I shed blood for and narrowly lost my life for was fading away before my eyes. The good name of America and all its great accomplishments since its inception were now being overshadowed by the missteps of its founders and its dark past.

Yes, America does have a troubled and turbulent history with its treatment of black people and those who did not have white skin. There is no denying that. That part of history cannot be ignored or swept under the rug. When the U.S. Constitution was written in 1787 and ratified in 1788, "We the People" did not apply to my African ancestors. All white men were created equal, while all others were left out of the picture and the conversation of life, liberty, and the pursuit of happiness. America was not a great place for my predecessors; however, America has shown its greatness as it has evolved from a land hostile to those with melanin in their skin to a welcoming and beautiful nation composed of an assortment of people with different skin colors, cultures, and religions from across the world. America is not a perfect country and there are still many issues that linger, but America has continuously changed its tone towards minorities and has progressed and started to live up to its mantra of freedom for all.

Due to me being a rather large black man, I have experienced racism and prejudice firsthand. I have been unjustly followed by loss prevention in stores and given "really good customer service" because of how I look. I have been stopped and detained by the police for looking suspicious or matching the description and was released. I have walked past people sitting in their vehicle and heard them lock the door as they looked at me with fear. With my presence alone, I have terrified people pumping gas by simply saying hello to them. But make no mistake. I am not a victim. I do not want your pity or apologies. Those individual's negative perception of me because of the color of my skin has not kept me from achieving the American dream. Because what truly matters is how I see myself and what I believe I can accomplish; so why should I be offended? A few negative encounters with small, minded people does not speak for all of America. Therefore, I still proclaim that I am proud to be an American and proud to call America home.

America is now under fire from within and is being torn apart internally by its own citizens and its elected officials. Those same citizens and elected representatives who live freely and comfortably under the blanket of freedom provided to them by the U.S. Constitution, have now weaponized that freedom, the U.S. Constitution and America's past to attack, dishonor and dismantle the land that provided it to them. I have watched as American pride, patriotism and the American way of life has been unjustly mislabeled as racist, bigoted, and intolerant. From my position on the frontlines of America in the trenches as a black police officer, I have seen this falsehood uncontrollably spread across the country and poison the minds of America's next generation. To them, the American dream never died because they believe it never existed. Or they believe it is real, but it is not within their reach because of the color of their skin, white supremacy, systematic racism, and oppression from a country that was not built for them.

I soon found myself caught in the middle of dulling factions on each side of the political aisle and being forced to choose where my loyalty and allegiance resided. I had to choose which all-inclusive box complete with the labels already attached and preloaded ideals, beliefs, and identity that I wanted to be stuffed in to be given a voice. There was no option for being a reasonable and mutual party. It was either or. Are you a black or are you an American? Are you black or are you blue (a cop)? Are you a Republican or a Democrat? Are you a liberal or conservative? Do Black Lives Matter or do All Lives Matter? The battle lines had been drawn in the sand. After choosing what camp you belonged to in this fight, you had to get on social media and make a post swearing your allegiance to your faction and spend countless hours engaging in social media debates and fights that accomplished nothing with people you will never meet and who have zero impact on your life.

I was confident in who I was as a person at this point in my life. I had my own identity. I was an American. Yes, I am black man. But I do not derive my identity, beliefs, politics, or my character from the color of my skin. The only colors that I pledge my allegiance to are red, white, and blue. My allegiance is to my country and the U.S. Constitution, not a political party or a specific group of people. When I watched the Twin Towers fall in 2001, it was not white America, black America, Hispanic America, or Asian America that was specifically attacked. America as a whole was attacked, and when I enlisted into the U.S. Army as an infantryman to go and fight against America's enemies, I did it for all Americans. I still possess that same attitude and belief now as a police officer. When someone calls 911 for help, I do not care about the color of their skin, their sexual orientation, their political inclinations, social economic status, their immigration status, or their religious beliefs. I only care about providing them the best service I can and helping them in their time of need.

I have always been a very open and accepting person and willing to hear other people's opinions and gain understanding of their point of view. However, when I started to vocalize my beliefs that were rooted in conservatism and Christianity, I felt as though I was not afforded the same opportunity to have my voice be heard. I always seemed to be the dissenting black voice when it came to the emotional and controversial topic of being black in America. And this did not sit well with many of my black co-workers, black friends, black church members, family members and the black community in general.

The moment I stepped out of line, and expressed an individual thought based on my life's experiences that did not align with the black agenda and the black community, my voice was instantly silenced. My black card was immediately cancelled, and I was shouted down.

"You sellout!" "Race traitor!" "Uncle Tom!" "Coon!" "You self-hating negro!"

I was exiled from the black community because I did not cosign and support all things black. I refused to buy into the black victim mentality and use the race card to advance my life. I had already traveled down that road in my past and it did me no favors.

Growing up dark skinned, I always felt victimized, attacked, and judged because of how dark my skin is. It was never white people taunting and terrorizing me. The mistreatment and rebuke that seemed to constantly rain down on me during my adolescent years was always at the hands of people who looked like me. I never saw myself as a victim of systematic racism and oppression from white people. There was no threat of evil, racist, white men who were out to get me.

In 2014, I grew weary and frustrated constantly trying to explain, defend and argue my beliefs. It was a draining and daunting task. And to make matters worse, I felt alone as a black conservative. I was constantly under attack and on the defensive. So instead of engaging in never-ending debates, I felt compelled to write my memoirs in hopes that people would come to understand me and why I feel the way I do and view certain topics and respect me as my own man with my own opinion. With that in mind, I started writing. However, when I started writing, I wrote from a place of anger, frustration, rejection, and revenge. My words took aim at the black community and all its shortcomings. I wanted the black community to accept responsibility for its ill treatment of me growing up and as a black police officer. I also took aim at all the people in my life who caused me much grief and pain. I wanted to shame them and hold them accountable for the things they did and said to me before the masses.

While it felt great unleashing years of hurt and pain onto my keyboard, I started to realize that I was going about this the wrong way. I had grown and developed spiritually, mentally, and emotionally past the hurt, frustration and anger that once controlled my life. I came to the realization that if I continued writing with malice in my heart that I would only end up hurting, shaming, and offending an entire community of people that were not solely responsible for all my pain and suffering. I decided to change course and started writing from my heart with love hoping to achieve understanding, healing, and compassion and forgiveness.

While my main objective with sharing my life's story was to help people understand who Dexter Pitts is, I also want those who choose to read this book to see that the black experience in America is not one size fits all. If you listen to the media and buy into everything you see on TV and social media, you will truly believe that America is a dangerous place for black people due to racist police and evil white people. You would believe that black people are being hunted down and killed for sport and bragging rights by evil white police officers. The truth is that there has never been a better time to be black in America. America has been good to me and my family. And in return, I live my life according to JFK's famous saying, "Ask not what your country can do for you, but what you can do for your country."

America has afforded me the opportunity to work hard, provide a comfortable life for my family and achieve my life goals and dreams. I am not trying to anyone convince anyone that racism, oppressions, prejudice, and discrimination are not real in America. As I previously described a few of my personal encounters, they are very real factors and can affect black people in various degrees and they should be addressed. Despite those issues and those who subscribe to such an archaic belief system, all those obstacles can still be overcome. Some of us might have to fight longer and harder than others due to our life's circumstances, but if you stay focused and persist you will break through that barrier and take control of your life, your destiny and achieve your version of the American dream.

There are many military books being published today by popular military veterans, many of which come from the Special Forces community. They are my idols. There is nothing I enjoy more than reading their amazing stories of courage and sacrifice while under fire. Even though I love their stories and I aspired to be like them while I served, I never attained that title. Most veterans and civilians cannot identify with Navy SEAL training, Special Forces training, being in a Ranger Battalions or going to war and narrowly escaping with your life. But what everyone can identify with is struggle.

For most of my life, I have struggled to find my own identity. I have always been the person who people counted out and never expected much out of. I am a true underdog. Always counted out, looked down upon and cast aside. Despite the deck being stacked against me, I still managed to fight my way to achieve the American dream. I have never been the best at anything or the all-knowing expert in any area. I can be best described as average. At times, even being average felt like a struggle. I have always had to work harder and put in more effort and more hours than the average person to be successful. I was not born with any special talents or attributes. I do not come from a wealthy family. Nothing has ever been given to me. Everything I have and all that I have accomplished has been by way of my Pitts principles: personal responsibility, integrity, trustworthy, tenacity and selflessness.

[1]

FAMILY FAITH AND FEAR

BLACKIE, spook, midnight, crispy, tar baby, ugly, Kingsford, darkie, black ass. You hear these insults, and you can almost picture a scene from a movie based in the 1950s during the Jim Crow era somewhere in the Deep South; this was far from that scene. This was just another day in Radcliff, Kentucky, and me riding the bus to school in the seventh grade, being taunted by the other black kids for being too dark-skinned. Before this, my life was seemingly perfect growing up in Fort Knox, where I spent many years. Growing up in the military, my race and the color of my skin were never an issue. Diversity was the norm for all of us, and it was not forced, but that was not the reality I lived in anymore.

As I sat on the bus crying from the verbal beating I was taking, my mind thought back to all the pleasant memories and the comforts that Fort Knox provided me. Oh, how I wished I could snap my fingers and travel back in time to escape the hell that my thirteen-year-old life had become. I would lay in my bed at night and cry myself to sleep, thinking about what life used to be.

In reality, what I was experiencing was nothing compared to what my parents experienced growing up in the age of Jim Crow in the Mississippi Delta in Bolivar County. My parents and grandparents knew real racism, discrimination, and prejudice. Not like the "racism" people love to complain and whine about today. Whites only and colored only signs painted on windows and hanging over bathroom doors and water fountains. The countless talks about growing up black in Mississippi always stuck with me. The stories I remember the most are my mother's stories about working in the cotton fields and picking cotton for extra money.

Growing up in the military was an awesome experience. I loved when my mother would take my sister and me to visit our dad at the motor pool. He would let us climb around on the tanks and play inside. I loved the sights, smells, and sounds of the motor pool. I would hear my dad's soldiers firing up the mighty turbine engine on the M1 Abrahams tanks, and the smell of burning diesel would pollute the air. I would then watch in amazement as the massive war machines would roll out of their assigned bay.

Fort Knox, Kentucky, was the closest thing to living in a utopia that you could find in America. Endless games of tackle football, basketball, and playing war in the woods with my friends until the streetlights came on were everyday occurrences during the summer. Even better was the 4th of July fair that would come to Fort Knox every year. After a long day of eating junk food, games, and rides, I would curl up under my mother's arms and watch the spectacular firework display as we celebrated America's independence.

Once a year, during the summer, we would drive down south to Mississippi to visit our family. My cousins lived deep in the country on a plantation. We would load up on fireworks and converge in the freshly plowed cotton fields far away from adult supervision on the property that spanned into the distant horizon. We divided up into teams, split the fireworks between each team, and went to war shooting roman candles and bottle rockets at each other. We would get so entranced in these battles that we would build forts out of metal scraps and old wood lying around. Then, after all the fireworks were expended, we would lay in the plantation fields and stare at the stars in the night sky for hours.

Having a father who was a U.S. Army Sergeant First Class (E-7) meant regimentation and zero room for excuses. Discipline and respect were demanded. It was yes sir, no sir, yes ma'am, no ma'am. Failing to do so resulted in the back of my dad's hand colliding with my face or my dad flicking me in the back of the neck with his solid fingers. Being an old-school southern black man, I love you rarely came from my father's mouth. He expected us to know that he loved us by putting food on the table and clothes on our backs.

My dad was a man of very few words, but the times he did speak and pour into me were pivotal. I was oblivious to racism and discrimination growing up in the military. I never experienced them personally, but I can still remember my first encounter with a bigot.

My father and I were somewhere deep in Tennessee when both my father and I became hungry. My father decided to pull off at the next truck station to calm our hunger pains. As we walked into the store, my father found the nearest bathroom while I went up to the counter to look over the menu. An older white gentleman was behind the counter. I can still see his long gray beard and matching gray hair. I had never seen anyone look at me with such discontent, but I was oblivious.

"Sir, may I have a cheeseburger and fries, please?" I politely asked.

"We don't have anything for you to eat here," he said to me grumpily.

My father emerged from the bathroom and joined me at the counter, and I told him what the man behind the counter had said. My father had a look of suspicion on his face.

"Get in the car, Dexter. Let's go," my father said calmly.

My father knew something I did not know. I was innocent and unsuspecting. As we were walking out of the store, I looked around and saw other people eating and noticed that everyone there was white, except us.

Confusion and shock set in. My young and innocent mind was trying to make sense of what had just happened. As we walked back to the truck, I turned to my dad for answers.

My father went on to explain to me how there are hateful people in this world that would hate you for something as simple as the color of your skin. He taught me there was no need to get upset at someone's ignorance and that I should not waste my time and energy trying to figure them out. It was this very incident and the very moment that my father laid a solid foundation in my life about racism and discrimination. He also explained to me how there were people who would use the color of their skin as an excuse for their bad decisions and all their failures in life when the truth is, they are lazy and lack character.

"Drop down and give me ten push-ups first." "You are going to have to put in some work if you want that." My father would say in response to some of my requests.

"He is your son, not one of your soldiers!" My mom would chime in.

Mothers are special. There is something about a mother's touch and words that make you feel as though there is nothing more important in the world than you. My mother was the most loving, caring, and sweetest person you could have ever met. She loved the Lord, and she adored both my sister and me. She worked hard to ensure that we had nice things because she was denied such things growing up on a farm as 1 of 19 children, and she did not want that for us.

She was a woman who did her best to live according to the Holy Bible and ensured that my sister and I abided by its teachings. Words cannot explain the depth of love and respect I had for my mom. I was a mama's boy, and I am not ashamed to admit it. If you had a mother like mine, you would have been a mama's boy also. I spent most of my time with my mom because my dad was usually away in the field training or out on the road driving trucks. She was always there for sporting events, school events, heartbreaks, and failures. She was there to catch my tears when the other kids were picking on me or when things didn't work out for me.

She was always there to comfort and support me, but she was also there to issue punishment and corrective training, and she did it well. Just as she did not hold back on loving me, she did not hold out on punishing me either. It was a fine balancing act, and she had learned how to master it. I loved and cherished her while at the same time fearing and revering her.

Like most marriages, my parents had their fair share of problems. When you bring two different personalities together as one, you can expect problems. They were like oil and water; they did not mix; however, they found a way to make it work for almost 28 years. Now that I am older and have been divorced and married more times than I want to admit, I look back at some of the marital disputes in my parent's marriage, and I can see how unhealthy and dysfunctional things were. Despite their issues, my sister and I still had a great upbringing even though we witnessed some unforgettable encounters between our parents.

Being a southern black family, we took our Pentecostal beliefs seriously. Anytime the church doors were open, and there was an event, the Pitts family was there. There was shouting, jumping, people climbing and walking over the pews, running laps around the church, catching the Holy Spirit, speaking in tongues, and faith healings.

Of all the things I learned from church, I learned to fear God. I did not fear Him out of reverence or love. I feared Him because I viewed Him as the mean old man in the sky that did not want me to have any fun. And if I did anything fun that made him angry, he was going to send me to hell. Fear seemed to be the driving force behind everything at our church, but it seemed even more so when it came to the youth group.

A traveling Christian group of entertainers who used puppets to teach us about God, sin, and hell came to perform for us at the church one evening. The only thing I remembered from the entire event was a puppet that kept screaming.

"You going to lie! You are going to die! Then you are going to fry!" The puppet yelled repeatedly.

I was terrified and traumatized beyond reason. When I went to bed that night, I had a horrific dream that I had died and gone to hell, and the puppet was screaming at me the entire time as I jumped up and down, screaming from being burned in hell's flames!

"I told you, Dexter! You lied! You died! Now you are going to fry! I told you, Dexter! Why didn't you listen, Dexter!" The puppet yelled at me.

I awoke from my dream, screaming at the top of my lungs, and ran to my parent's room, but the door was locked. I kicked and punched on the door until my mom came out of the room and comforted me. I was drenched in sweat and tears, and I stayed awake the rest of the night too afraid to go back to bed. As if that was not enough, the doom, gloom, and fear of the man in the sky continued.

Our pastor held an impromptu church service where we watched a documentary about music and how it was all satanic. I can still hear the pastor's words echoing in my mind.

"If you listen to rap music and rock and roll, you're going to hell! This stuff is no good, folks. By allowing your family to listen to this stuff, you are subjecting your family to the powers of evil."

The video showed a man playing a vinyl record backward which projected a satanic message in it. I looked over at my parents, and I knew what was coming next. Our family went home that night, and my father went berserks. He went into my room and my sister's room and grabbed up all our entertainment that was not Christian, and tossed them into the trash. I did not have a lot of cassette tapes or CDs, but the ones I did have I loved dearly. My Michael Jackson, "Moon Walker" VHS and Soul for Real "Candy Rain" cassette tapes were my prized possessions. He destroyed them right before my eyes.

Everything we did had to revolve around church and God. If it was not of God, we were not really allowed to partake in it. My mother was extremely religious, but she also realized that we were kids and wanted and needed to have some fun. When our dad was away, she would let us make our own decisions and choose our own fate as opposed to always dictating to us. I was grateful for my mother's discretion. She was hard, but she was fair. She gave us just enough rope to hang ourselves, but also enough to where she could reel us in if we got out of hand.

[2]

DARK SKIN DRAMA

My parents separated after my sixth-grade year, and I moved to Milwaukee with my mom and sister. We lived there for a year with my mom's family while she and my dad worked things out. Then, in the fall of 1997, my parents reunited, and we moved back to Kentucky. My dad retired from the army after 20 years of service and decided to settle in Radcliff, Kentucky, where we would start our lives all over again, and I would attend Radcliff Middle School.

I was not one to make trouble. I was a shy kid and did my best to avoid conflict, but it always seemed to find me. My fight or flight response was to run automatically, cry and find my mom. I could only take so much, and I would eventually get tired of running and crying, and I would feel backed into a corner. And that was when I would lash out violently.

I was involved in my fair share of fights when I was younger, and I won most of them, but I still did not enjoy having to fight. I desired peace more than anything. I just wanted to get along with everyone and be friends. From seeing my parents' bicker and fight to some crazy arguments and fights with my sister and being picked on by some older kids on Fort Knox, I had endured my fair share of conflict and stress, but none of those incidents prepared me for the storm coming my way.

I rode the bus to school many times in my adolescent years, and I never had a problem. But this was not the utopian society of Fort Knox I previously experienced. Things were a lot different. In the rear of the bus sat a group of black kids who all lived in a low-income apartment complex a few streets over from where I lived. I had never met them before, but I saw them as potential new friends in my innocent and unsuspecting mind. They, on the other hand, saw weakness, fear, and someone they could beat up.

"Man, you are black as hell! Look at how black he is!"

"Dang! That nigga is black as hell. And he ugly too!"

I could feel the fear and anxiety in me rising. I was terrified and paralyzed with fear. I just sat in my seat, staring straight ahead. I wanted to run, but I had nowhere to run. I could feel the wells of my eyes start to swell with tears.

"We are going to call your black ass spook because you are so black you are pretty much a ghost! You can sneak up on people at night and spook them!"

Laughter radiated from the rear of the bus at my expense. I never felt so alone and afraid.

"No way! We going to call this nigga midnight! This dude is so black he looks like 12 AM!"

"What's wrong blackie? Are you about to cry? This crispy ass nigga is about to cry!"

Tears slowly marched down my face, and it was a death sentence. The insults and taunting increased upon seeing my tears. The bus finally came to a stop, and everyone unloaded and went into the school. I sat on the bus for a moment, trying to calm down and wipe my face. The verbal bashing was over for now, but I could not calm down because I knew that I had to return to the bus after school to get home.

The only thing I can remember about that day at school was the fear and anxiety that followed me the entire day. Usually when I was at school, time seemed as though it would pass very slowly, but not today. Today, time felt as though it was stuck in fast-forward. Every time I looked at the clock, my heart would get heavier and heavier. With every minute that ticked by, my heart rate increased. I was so stressed out and worried that I didn't even eat lunch. When I heard the final bell ring to signal the end of the school day, I felt a dark and heavy presence come over me.

As I made my way down the hall to the awaiting buses, my feet felt heavy, like I was wearing cement shoes. I'm sure if anyone was watching me, they could probably see my heart beating in my chest through my shirt. I got onto the bus, but I didn't see the other kids. Maybe they were not getting on the bus, I thought to myself. I sat down in my seat and waited. I could hear loud talking and laughter from outside of the bus. One by one, the kids got onto the bus, and I was in their crosshairs directly in their line of fire once again.

"Midnight is back y'all! And this nigga is still black and ugly!" one of them yelled as they took time berating me one by one.

I was aware of my skin color, but I was never truly aware of how dark my skin was. It was never a factor before, and it never had any bearing or outcome on my friendships or how I felt about myself. Now it was evident to me; I was different. I sat in my room in the dark, replaying the day over in my mind. I could still hear their laughs and jokes haunting and torturing my mind as they echoed in my head. It was like they were in my room with me.

The stress and fear were so overpowering that I had no desire to eat or talk to anyone. My mind and emotions were so scrambled that I didn't even think to do my homework. I sat in my room in the darkness. The only light present in my room was the light from my alarm clock, which struck more fear in me because I realized that I would be at the mercy of this group again in a few hours.

This cycle of bullying carried on for weeks and only grew more intense and their attacks bolder. The leaders of this pack were Terrell and Rhonda. Terrell was a grade below me. He was short and fat and tried his hardest to make me fight him. Ronda was the loudest and meanest of the entire group. I was bigger than all of the kids bullying me, but I was outnumbered.

Christmas of that same year my parents gifted me with one of my most prized possessions: a black and orange FUBU (For Us by Us) baseball jersey and a matching jacket. I was in love! I could hardly wait to wear it to school to show it off. Maybe it would impress the kids on the bus, and they would think I was cool and leave me alone.

"Nice jacket," Terrell said to me as he walked past me on the bus.

They all made their way to the back of the bus and sat down quietly. There was a very light conversation amongst them, but nothing was said to me or about me. For the first time in weeks, they had left me alone. I thought to myself that maybe it was over. Perhaps they saw my jacket and assumed that I was cool now because I had this high-priced, name-brand jacket and that they would leave me alone from here on out.

I stepped off the bus at school and walked down the hall to my first class of the day with my head held high. I felt like a new man. It was like I was starting a fresh chapter in my life and that my suffering at their hands was finally over. School was perfect that day. Everyone complimented me on how much they loved my jacket. A few people asked to wear it, and I gladly let them in hopes of being accepted and being viewed as one of the cool kids in school.

They say the man makes the clothes; the clothes don't make the man. Well, that statement did not apply to me on this day. My clothes made me. My jacket made me feel like I was a superstar.

The last bell rang for the day, and I walked out to the awaiting buses anxiety-free. My guard was down, and I was relaxed. The evil crew of juvenile thugs got on the bus right after me and headed to the back of the bus.

I sat in my seat, nestled in my jacket, ready to go home. As the bus traveled down the streets of Radcliff dropping kids at every stop, I started to get hot and decided to take my jacket off and put it in the seat next to me. As I sat in my seat, Terrell reached over, snatched my jacket, and ran to the back of the bus. I stood up in anger, ready to go and get my jacket back. I saw all of them looking at me, daring me to come and get it. I sat back down in my seat, and the fear and darkness that I assumed was gone crept back into my life and deflated the imaginary world that I constructed that day.

I walked through the front door of our home with my face covered in tears. I ran straight past my mother and went straight to my room as I had done for so many weeks. My mother could tell that something was wrong. She also noticed that I did not have my jacket and approached me to investigate.

"Boy! Where is your jacket!" She questioned me with staunchness.

I hesitated to answer. I looked up and saw my mother's face transition from one of love, concern, and compassion to one of frustration. I was afraid of the monsters on the bus that harassed me, but they were nothing compared to the wrath of Idella Pitts.

"Boy, you better answer me! Where is your jacket!"

The tone of her voice made my spine quake in terror. I didn't want to tell her because I was embarrassed and ashamed of letting the kids on the bus bully me. I fought through the tears and proceeded to tell my mother what I had been experiencing the past few weeks and how Terrell had taken my jacket. I could see a fire spark in her eyes.

"Do you know how hard I worked to get you that jacket! And you are just going to let someone take it! Oh, no! Get in the car! We are going to get that jacket back right now!" She scolded me.

My mom stormed off to her room, and I could hear the jingle of her keys as she walked back towards me.

"Let's go! Now!" She demanded.

We got into the car, and I guided her to the apartment complex where my jacket was being held captive. We got out of the car and headed up to the complex. I had no clue which apartment Terrell lived in, but that didn't matter to my mother. She was a determined woman and was going to bang on every door in the complex until she found out which apartment housed my FUBU jacket.

My mom knocked on every door until she found the right one.

"My son says that your son Terrell took his jacket from him on the bus today."

The lady, whom I presumed was Terrell's mother, greeted us with a look of annoyance and frustration. It was like she had done this before and was all used to this routine.

"Terrell, do you have this boy's jacket?"

Terrell emerged from the rear of the apartment and made quick eye contact with me, but he didn't say anything. His mom did all the talking.

She questioned Terrell once more, "Do you have this boy's jacket? Yes or no?"

Terrell was silent and did not answer. He disappeared back into the apartment and appeared with my jacket in hand. He handed me my jacket and disappeared once more without saying another word. There was no apology or any further exchange of dialogue between any of us. They closed the door and went back into the privacy of their smoked engulfed apartment, and we descended the stairs back into my mother's car.

The potent smell of cigarette smoke had attached to my jacket. I looked at my jacket with disgust. You would have figured that I was happy to have it back, but I wasn't. The jacket was now tainted in my eyes; it was a painful reminder of my misery. The luster and allure had been stolen along with my jacket.

The fire in my mom's eyes from earlier had subsided, and I felt safe in her presence. She reassured me that I would be okay because I was a child of God, and no one messes with God's children. She then placed her hands on my head and prayed over me, asking God to protect me and give me the courage to stand up to those bullying me.

"You are never alone. God is always with you, baby. Now do me one favor. Stop sitting in the back of the bus and sit towards the front, far away from those kids. And stand up for yourself. Don't let them push you around." My mom encouraged me.

I was comforted and reassured by my mother's words and prayers. I felt recharged and ready for whatever might come the next day. I went to sleep that night with peace of mind for the first time, but that only lasted until I made my way back onto the school bus. As I sat in the front of the school bus, I looked back and noticed the evil brood staring at me. I exited the bus and headed to my class. As I walked down the hall to class, one of them shouted out to me.

"We are going to jack your blacktail up later, you snitch! Just wait and see!"

I sat in class panicked and worried. Word about my impending doom spread quickly.

"What did you do to make them so mad at you, Dexter? They are telling everyone they are going to jump you." My other classmates inquired all day.

I trembled on the inside at the news that I had received from the other kids at school. I instantly started to pray to ask God to make them go away. When I got back onto the bus that afternoon, I sat in the front of the bus again. I waited for Terrell and the other kids to come onto the bus, but only a few of them got onto the bus, minus Terrell. One of them walked past me and said to me in a low tone.

"You are dead in the morning!" One of them said to me as they walked past me.

That night at home, I could hear my mother's words from the other day swimming around in my head. "Stand up for yourself. Don't let them push you around."

I took those words to heart, and I started to prepare for combat. I had reached that point where I felt cornered. I was tired of running and crying.

Before going to bed that night, I went to the garage and headed straight for my dad's toolbox. I grabbed a box cutter and took it to my room. I took my chain link I used to lock my bike and sat it next to my backpack. I then took a pool ball from my dresser and placed it into one of my tube socks.

I arose at the sound of my alarm with an intense focus. My game face was officially on. I got dressed and placed the box cutter in my left pocket, the pool ball and sock in my right jacket pocket, and I draped my bike chain around my neck and hid it under my t-shirt. The metal links sat cold against my skin. The bike chain was heavy and uncomfortable, but that did not matter to me. It was a necessary tool for me to wage war against my mortal enemies that morning. Before walking to the bus stop, I got down on my knees and prayed to God, asking for his protection before the battle.

As I walked to the bus stop, I went over all the different scenarios in my head about how this epic battle would ignite. I envisioned myself thrashing each one of them. I was ready to inflict copious amounts of pain. I was not simply out for revenge. I was out for blood, and I was ready to spill theirs all over the floor of the bus. They had created a monster.

I stepped onto the bus, but this time, I didn't sit in the front. I sat in the middle of the bus, hoping to taunt them and lure them in. I wanted them to attack me so that I could make the bloody and violent visions I had a reality. I sat down in my seat and was ready to fight. My left hand tightly gripped the box cutter, and my right hand had a firm grip on my tube sock.

Terrell, Ronda, and their crew walked onto the bus, and my blood pressure skyrocketed. This was it. It was time to bring the pain. As they got closer to me, I gripped my weapons tighter. My fight or flight response had switched from flight into fighting overdrive.

"Maybe I should attack them first and catch them off guard?" I thought to myself.

The group of kids walked straight past me, and they didn't say a word to me. They didn't even make eye contact with me. I sat hunkered down in my seat, waiting for them to attack me from the rear, but the attack never came. The bus arrived at school, and they walked past me again and didn't say anything. I was so confused, and I was let down. I was sure that they were coming for me. The message that was delivered to me the other day was loud and clear. What changed? The bus ride home was a repeat of that morning. Not talk, no eye contact, nothing. Maybe this was a part of their plan? Maybe they were waiting to ambush me when I least expected it.

Days passed, and still no attack. The days turned into weeks, and they still had not attempted to fight me. It was unexplainable to me. Over the next few weeks, the violent crew of misfits was disbanded one by one. Terrell was kicked out of school for his troublesome behavior. Rhonda's apartment complex burned down, and she was forced to move, which meant that she had to catch a different bus. And just like that, the leaders of the pack who had become the bane of my existence were no more.

Did God hear my prayers and come to my rescue? I do not know what it was, but I was just happy that they were out of my life. Although my ordeal with Terrell, Ronda, and their crew was over, I still had to endure teasing and name-calling at the hands of others at school. I would walk down the halls of school, and random kids would shout stuff at me like blackie, darkie, or charcoal.

"Hey, Dexter! How in the hell did you get so black?"

I had zero self-confidence, and my self-esteem was at an all-time low. After class one day, I walked out into the hall and heard tons of laughter. I wondered what was going on. Someone approached me and said,

"They were joking on you so hard in class today. Someone compared you to a black hole during the astronomy lesson today."

An entire hallway full of kids, and they were all laughing at me. I lowered my head, went into the bathroom, sat in the stall, and cried. In another incident, I walked into class and on my desk was a piece of paper. Someone had taken a black sharpie and made a smiling face and colored it in with the sharpie. At the top of the paper was my name. On the bottom of the paper were the words "tar baby."

I would go home and look at myself in the mirror and hate my own reflection. I hated myself for being dark-skinned. I was mad at God for making me dark-skinned. If I could have done anything to not be dark-skinned, I would have done it. All I wanted was to be accepted. I was never mean to anyone. I didn't deserve to be treated the way I was.

On the one hand, a lot of the black kids were making fun of me for being dark-skinned, but on the other hand, they were also making fun of me for "acting white." I was constantly reminded that I was a dork and that I was not cool because of my "whiteish behavior."

"Why do you talk like that?" "Why do you dress like that?" "Why do you act like that?" "Can you all believe that he actually likes that song? That's white people's music."

I had no identity or a sense of community and belonging. I had friends, but I felt like a drifter.

My mother did not have very dark skin. Her skin was a beautiful golden-brown color. Her skin was perfect in my eyes. I wanted my skin to look like hers. I really believed that if I had skin that looked like hers that my life would be different. I would look at my mom's pictures from when she was younger. Her skin was much darker in her earlier pictures. One day I asked my mom what happened to make her skin lighter. She explained to me how she bleached her skin.

While shopping with my mother at Wal-Mart one evening, she showed me a product called "Black and White Bleaching Creaming." My mom purchased the product for me and taught me how to apply it to my skin. I was so excited about this product and believed that it was going to give me a new life. Maybe this way the girls would start to notice me, and the other black kids would stop making fun of me for having dark skin and accept me. I would apply the cream in the morning before school, during school, and right before I went to bed. However, I stopped using it after some time because I did not see any change in my skin tone. I had grown to believe that having dark skin meant that I would never be good enough or handsome enough for anyone.

My 8th-grade year was ending soon. The black jokes and teasing kept coming with no end in sight. Day in and day out, for most of the school year, there was someone laughing at me. I could feel the strife and anger building up in me over the months. I suppressed all my emotions and anger daily. I kept everything bottled up and pressed down inside of me. I could feel myself being backed into a corner again and being forced to lash out. I was growing more and more frustrated being the source of laughter at Radcliff Middle School.

As I sat working on my project for my Humanities class, I heard chatter coming from the other side of the room. I looked up and saw a group of black kids laughing and pointing at me. As usual, I would sit and take it. I was bigger than most of the kids in my class, but they could see past my size and see that I was a wimp. I had taken their abuse so long, and they knew that I was not going to do or say anything, but that was not the case on this day. A surge of anger and adrenaline rushed through my veins. I had reached that point of no return again. The No. 2 pencil that I was holding in my hand snapped in half. I rose to my feet, and I was drunk with rage, and I climbed onto the table.

"You all got something to say to me!" I yelled across the room while looking down on everyone.

The room fell silent, and all eyes were on me. The group pointing and laughing at me hushed, and their jaws dropped.

"The next person to laugh at me, point at me or say anything to me is getting knocked out! Try me! I dare you!" I shouted as I continued on with my rant.

As I stood on top of the desk hovering over my classmates, I saw fear in their eyes for the first time as they glanced at me perched over them. I was the alpha male. I was bigger than most of them, and I could easily rip them in half if I wanted to. I was too big and too strong to be letting people victimize me and have so much power and control over me. The bell rang a short time later, and class was over.

As I walked out of class and into the hallway, I felt different. The other kids looked at me differently. It wasn't just my imagination either. Things were different.

For the rest of the school year, no one laughed at me or said anything to me directly. I suppose my message had been received. Anyone who messed with me was going to suffer the consequences.

[3]

THE FRIED CHICKEN BANDIT

SCHOOL WAS a necessary evil in my life. It was something that I did not enjoy, but I knew that I had to do it. It was a struggle for me from the very beginning. I was never a top student and I didn't expect to be. I was a B and C student at best, and I struggled to make B's. I was not a dumb kid. I just never applied myself or put in the needed effort. I was lazy. I would do just enough to get by and to keep my mother satisfied.

Because I would do just enough to get by, I often conjured up my mom's undivided attention in a not so good way. She was constantly getting on me about my grades and how important it was for me to have an education so that I could have options in life. The words of wisdom and encouragement that she constantly spoke to me fell on deaf ears. She had high expectations for me and a lot of hope for my future. She wanted nothing more than to see me graduate and make something of myself.

Going into my sophomore year, my desire to play football vanished. Quitting the football team at the start of the season caught the attention of Coach Webb, the teams wide-receiver coach who intercepted me in the student parking lot after learning that I quit the team.

"You are a quitter! No one likes a quitter. You are not going to accomplish anything in life because you like to quit! You are letting your teammates down!"

I didn't say anything to Coach Webb. I walked off nonchalantly, but his words pierced my soul. Once those words were spoken to me, deep down inside of me I knew that I had to prove him and anyone else who thought that I was a quitter wrong. I did not see myself as a quitter. I viewed it as me reprioritizing things in my life and shifting my focus and attention to something that I enjoyed.

During my sophomore year, I sat at a table in the library along with my other classmates day dreaming as I listened to an army recruiter's sales pitch. I grew up in the military and I wanted nothing to do with it. I had zero interest in ever joining the service.

After he was through giving us his speech on how awesome life in the army was, he passed out test booklets so that my entire class could take the ASVAB (Armed Services Vocational Aptitude Battery). I wanted to revolt and not take the test, because I knew that it was pointless to me. So, I cracked open the book and proceeded to start answering the questions. A few minutes into the test I decided that I did not want to waste my time, so I started filling in random answers to the multiple-choice questions without putting any sort of thought or effort into it. I just wanted to be done and go on with my day.

When I turned 16, my dad bought me my first car. It was a forest green, 1997 Chevy S-10 pickup truck. I was ecstatic to have my very own car, but there was one condition. I had to pay for the insurance and the gas. So, I set out to get my first job.

I entered the workforce my sophomore year so that I could have some money in my pocket. I had a few jobs here and there, but none that I liked. It was my job at Winn-Dixie that taught me one of my most important lessons I would ever learn.

I stocked shelves, swept, moped the floor, bagged groceries, and collected the carts from the parking lot. It was an easy, decent paying job and I got to work with my best friend Jeff. It was the perfect job for me, up until I ruined it trying to fit in, following the crowd and caving to peer pressure.

It was a hot summer day, and I was tired and thirsty from collecting the carts in the parking lot. I wanted something cold to drink, but I didn't have any money on me. I approached Jeff and asked him to loan me a dollar. Jeff replied.

"Just go and get whatever you want to drink, take it into the freezer and drink it. No one will care and no one will know. Everyone does it. It's not a big deal. We do it all the time."

I knew what Jeff was saying was wrong, but since everyone does it, it's not that big of a deal. We do it all the time. I walked back into the store and grabbed a cookie and crème Muscle Milk, walked into the freezer and chugged it down. And just like that, I had broken God's 8th commandment: Thou Shall Not Steal. Not only had I broken the commandment, I got comfortable doing so.

It started with drinks, then I progressed to candy and other pricey food items. The thought of getting caught never crossed my mind because it was so simple, however, as my mom always taught me, what's done in the dark always comes to the light.

Halfway into my shift I started to get hungry and decided to go to the deli and get me some fried chicken. I ordered a 3 piece with some sides. Instead of going to the freezer, I broke protocol and sat down in the break room. I didn't want my chicken to get cold, so I figured that the break room was good enough. No one was going to care anyway, right? It's just fried chicken. I sat in my chair savoring the golden fried goodness that was Winn-Dixie's fried chicken. Every bite seemed to get better. As I was about to start on my second piece of chicken, I heard the voice of Mr. Perry, my manager, questioned me from behind.

"Dexter, do you have a receipt for that?"

My heart stopped beating and I froze. I felt a cold chill go down my spine and the hairs on my body stood up. My appetite vanished in an instant and the chicken breast that was wedged between my fingers fell out of my hands and back into the box. I was caught red handed, but I was going to try and lie my way out of it. Before I could even formulate a lie in my mind Mr. Perry told me that he saw me get the fried chicken and not pay for it.

It was over. I was officially caught. I was sent home and told to come back the next day to learn my fate. As I walked into the store the following day, I could see that people were looking at me and staring. The news had spread that Dexter Pitts was a thief; he got caught stealing fried chicken from the deli. I walked into the security room to talk to Mr. Perry.

"Dexter, we really like you. Everyone here does. You are a good worker and you have always been very respectful. We thought about calling the police when you arrived here today to have you arrested for theft."

My heart stopped beating and I almost passed out when he mentioned the police.

"We are not going to do that. We are not going to press charges on you because we think you are a good kid who made a mistake, and we can tell that you regret what you have done. However, you will no longer be an employee here at Winn-Dixie. You violated our trust and our policy; therefore, we are terminating you effective immediately."

"Mom is going to kill me!" I thought to myself.

My parents had raised us to a certain standard and had high expectations of us, and I knew better than to do anything to embarrass our family. I knew that my mom was going to be terribly upset and disappointed at me. I got into my truck and drove home as slow as I could. My stomach was doing flips as I pulled into the driveway. I almost threw up in my car I was so nervous. I walked into the house and I was greeted by my loving, yet unsuspecting mom.

"What are you doing home so early? Aren't you supposed to be at work right now? She inquired.

It was the moment of truth. I braced myself for impact from my mom's fist.

"I got fired."

"Fired? What for?" She asked with a puzzled look on her face.

"For stealing," I said hesitantly.

"Stealing? What the hell did you steal, boy?"

"Fried chicken."

When I uttered the words fried chicken, I was sure that my mom was getting ready to rain down the wrath of God on me. Instead, all I heard was laughter followed by ridicule.

"Fried chicken! Of all the things to get fired for, your stupid, black ass got fired for stealing fried chicken! What is wrong with you boy? What were you thinking about? You know what! Don't even answer that! I don't even think I want to know!" My mom berated me.

To my surprise, my parents did not have to punish me. The guilt and shame I felt being caught stealing was punishment of its own. The fact I embarrassed and disgraced our last name left a lasting impression on me. I never wanted to feel that amount of shame again.

After my shameful exit from Winn-Dixie, I picked up a job bagging groceries at the Fort Knox Commissary. Not only did I have a new job, I met my first girlfriend while working there. Her name was Dede, and she was the prettiest girl I had ever seen. She was short, maybe five feet tall, and had long jet-black that reached down to the back of her knees. I learned that she was a Chamorro, from the island of Rota in the Mariana Islands.

It was a great feeling walking into school the first day of my junior year with one of the prettiest girls in town on my arm. My confidence and self-esteem skyrocketed, but as confident as I felt, I still had no clue what I wanted to do with my life. In a few years, I would be graduating high school and I had no plans or sense of direction. I was eager to find my calling in life, but little did I know that in the following months a burning desire to serve and defend my country would awaken within me.

[4]
YOU GOT THAT 9/11 FEELING

LIKE MOST YOUNG high school kids, I was unsure what I wanted to do with my life. Nothing appealed to me. I knew college was out of the question because my grades were not the best, and I scored low on my ACT.

On the morning of September 11, 2001, I arose from my bed in the early hours of the morning. As I got up out of my bed, the urge to lay back down and go back to sleep hit me hard. There was no skipping school for any reason in the Pitts house. If you were not at school, you better be sick or dead, and I was neither. My mother was scurrying about the house getting ready for work. Somehow, I convinced her that I was severely ill and not able to attend school that day. As she walked out the door to go to work, I laid back down and drifted back to sleep.

I awoke sometime later, turned on the news and watched the headlines scroll across the bottom of the television: "Two planes fly into the World Trade Center," "New York City Under Attack," "Plane crashes into the Pentagon," "America Under Attack," and "Terrorists Attack the United States."

I was glued to the television for hours. I looked at the clock it was around 3 PM. School would be out shortly, and my mom would be coming home from work soon. I sat in shock, watching the news replay the footage of the planes flying into the World Trade Centers and the Pentagon. My heart shuttered as I watched the Twin Towers collapsing. The images of people running through the streets trying to escape the cloud of dust and debris caused by the Twin Towers collapsing were seared into my memory. I was watching my generation's Pearl Harbor unfold before me.

In the aftermath of the attacks, Fort Knox was on full lockdown. I realized the true impact of 9/11 the following day as I pulled up to the Fort Knox entrance and saw a sea of cars waiting in line to be searched. Soldiers dressed in BDUs (battle dress utilities) carrying M-16 rifles stood guard. Bomb-sniffing dogs circled every vehicle, trying to gain access to the post. The one thing that stood out to me the most were the cement barricades that had been erected to protect the lives of soldiers and their families on the other side. The Fort Knox I knew and grew up in was gone. The America I knew was no more.

As I drove through Fort Knox, I could feel the heaviness of the recent events in the atmosphere. Walking into the commissary, you could see the look of stress and worry upon the faces of the military wives and family members who worked there. They all knew what was coming. They knew it was only a matter of time before they would have to kiss their husbands and wives goodbye as they went off to war. My friends and I chatted about the incident as we bagged groceries. The relaxed mood that usually accompanied my time working at the commissary was absent. There was no laughter or joking as we usually did.

Days had passed since the Twin Towers came tumbling down, and I was consumed with this history-making event. I rushed home after school every day to tune into the news to hear the latest updates. On September 14, 2001, I watched as President George W. Bush gave his famous bullhorn speech as he stood before the wreckage of the Twin Towers.

As I listened to President Bush give his speech in front of the remains of what was once the Twin Towers and chants of "U.S.A" from those in attendance flowed through my TV speakers, a surge of patriotism sparked to life within me. The urge to repay those who attacked my country took hold of me. It was now my patriotic duty to hunt down the cowards responsible for this unpardonable attack and deliver them into the hands of the grim reaper myself. I wanted revenge, and I wanted to rain down death, carnage, and unimaginable suffering upon those who were responsible.

Military service was embedded in my DNA all this time, but it had been lying dormant within me. As I watched the smoke billow from the rubble of the World Trade Center, I could see and hear my country calling out to me from the smokey wreckage.

In the wake of 9/11, America truly lived up to its name, the "United" States. Americas stood side by side, held each other's hands, and prayed together in unity. I never knew that such a bond could exist between people. American pride and patriotism swept over the country from coast to coast like a powerful current swallowing up everyone in its path. American flags waved in the wind all over town. Monikers outside of business displayed messages of encouragement, hope, love, and support for our country and our troops. There were no white, black, Hispanic, Asian, or any other individual identifiers. We were just Americans.

At school, there was always an abundance of military recruiters from every branch. Their tables were set up in the front of the cafeteria during lunch, and you could see the kids who had already made up their minds about joining the military because they would spend most of their lunchtime with their recruiter at the table. One of those kids was Deshon Otey. He was the oldest brother of my friends, Ronald and Dominique. Deshon had graduated in June of 2001 before the 9/11 attacks. Even before we were lured into the war on terrorism, Deshon always knew that he wanted to be a Marine. He was determined to earn his eagle globe and anchor and become one of the few and the proud.

After graduating from Marine boot camp, Deshon returned home to Radcliff for a few weeks on recruiting duty before shipping out to Marine Corps School of Infantry. I would see Deshon walking the halls of North Hardin in his dress blues, and he was beaming with pride. He was the perfect example of what it meant to be a Marine, and he exemplified it. He was only 5'5" inches tall, but he strutted with a confidence that made him eight feet tall. He would sit at the Marine Corps recruiting table in the cafeteria and talk with future Marine recruits about boot camp and his new life in the Marines.

The post 9/11 world was starting to take shape. Many of my friends who were planning to join the military knew what branch of service they wanted to join and what MOS (military occupational specialty) they wanted. I had no clue what branch of service I wanted to join or what I wanted to do in general. All I knew was that I wanted to get into the fight. It was in a dark movie theater up on the big screen where I discovered how I wanted to serve.

January of 2002, Director Ridley Scott released his latest movie "Black Hawk Down," which chronicled the events of the Battle of Mogadishu on October 3, 1993, in which the U.S. Army's 75th Ranger Regiment, Delta Force, and 160th SOAR (Special Operations Aviation Regiment) troops conducted a raid to catch a warlord. During the raid, two UH-60 black hawk helicopters were shot down, and the brave soldiers fought for 17 hours to rescue their fallen brothers. Soldiers from the 10th Mountain Division's Alpha Company 2-14 Infantry Regiment were called in to help with the rescue effort.

I gazed up at the movie screen in absolute amazement at the bravery and courage of the soldiers who were faced with overwhelming odds, yet they continued to fight. The symphony of combat: machine guns blazing, rifles crackling, and explosions sounded like music to my ears and screamed at the soldier within me. I was captivated by the idea of being a U.S. Army Airborne Ranger. My mind was made up, and I was now focused on becoming an airborne ranger.

The war on terror was in full swing, and U.S troops were engaged in combat against the Taliban and Al Qaeda in Afghanistan as part of Operation Enduring Freedom. My eagerness to become an airborne ranger grew as I watched videos of US troops fighting in the mountains of Afghanistan during Operation Anaconda on the nightly news. As excited as I was about wanting to join the army infantry and become an airborne ranger, there was still one obstacle in my way that I had to overcome: my mom. I was only 17, and there was no way my mom would agree to let me sign up and join the Army. So, I kept my plans to myself until I turned 18.

Upon telling my mom of my plans to join the Army and go and fight, she immediately shot down the idea and did everything she could to persuade me to change my mind. But there was nothing she nor anyone else could say to change my mind. This was the path I had chosen to pursue in life. I was her only son, her baby boy, and I was ready to go to war, and she was less than thrilled.

In November of 2002, I walked into the recruiting office in Elizabethtown to sign up to fight and kill terrorists. I came into that office on a mission to join the Army that day, and I did not waste time getting straight to the point.

"I want to be an airborne ranger," I insisted.

"I might be able to help you with that," Sergeant First Class Bennett replied.

There was one problem. Due to my previous carefree attitude about the military, I scored below what was needed to join.

My recruiter presented me with two options. I could retake the ASVAB, get a higher score, get an Airborne Ranger contract, and possibly a signing bonus. Or I could accept a point waiver, enlisted as an 11X (regular infantry) with no signing bonus.

"You can always go to airborne school and ranger school afterward." My recruiter convinced me.

Without hesitation, I accepted the waiver for the extra points. I did not want to wait to take the ASVAB test again, and I did not care about signing bonuses. This was not about the money. I wanted to fight.

After accepting the offer, he presented me with a list of duty stations: Korea, Germany, Fort Campbell, Kentucky, and Fort Drum, New York.

"Who is going to be first into the fight?" I asked.

"If you want to fight, the 10th Mountain Division is where you want to be."

"Well, that's where I want to go!"

I signed the paper and made it official. I would be joining the 10th Mountain Division, the military's most deployed unit.

I filled out a ton of paperwork that day and was sent home with an army backpack loaded with cool Army recruiting gear.

On November 16, 2002, I was officially sworn into the Delayed Entry Program at Louisville MEPS (Military Entrance Processing Station). I was another step closer to getting into the fight. I was given my official enlistment date for active duty: August 5, 2003. I was informed that I would be able to enlist as an E-3, Private First Class because I had two years of JROTC. In 9 months, I would be shipping off to infantry OSUT (One Station Unit Training) at Sand Hill in Fort Benning, Georgia, for 14 weeks to earn the right to call myself an infantryman. Nine months seemed more like nine years away because I was so eager. I needed all the time I could get because I was a fat body, and I did not meet the Army's height and weight standards, nor did I pass the body fat percentage tape test that morning. I was 5'11 and weighed about 280 pounds. In order to meet the Army's body fat percentage, I had to lose thirty pounds, and my recruiter was going to make sure that I lost the weight.

I went to the Fort Knox Military Clothing Store and purchased two U.S. Army Ranger running cadence CDs. I would take my Sony CD player with me on runs and sing along with the cadence as I ran through town. On weekends I would meet with my recruiter and other army recruits to do group PT (physical training), DC (drill and ceremony), and practice the other soldier tasks such as map reading and first aid. I also had plenty of help from my JROTC teacher, who was a retired Sergeant Major, Paul C. Gray. I was a 1st Sergeant in JROTC, and Sergeant Major Gray took me under his wings and shared with me all the knowledge he had gained in his 20 plus years of service in the Army. I was well on my way to becoming a soldier. The only thing I needed to do now was survive my senior year, graduate high school.

In the final weeks of 2002, the beating of war drums grew louder and louder as America was growing more and more frustrated with Saddam Hussein and his possible NBC (Nuclear, Biological, and Chemical) weapons program. America was ready to declare war on Iraq as troops amassed at the Iraq/Kuwait border. While my friends who graduated the year before me were preparing to take part in the historic invasion of Iraq, I was stuck in Radcliff doing homework.

When the war in Iraq kicked off, I would turn on the news and see American troops from the 1st Marine Division and the Army's 3rd Infantry Division (ID) steamrolling across the Iraqi desert, killing and destroying everything in their way. As I watched soldiers from the 3rd ID seize BIAP (Baghdad International Airport) on the news, I kept thinking to myself, "This sucks! I should be there! I am going to miss the entire war!"

On June 6, 2003, I walked across the stage to receive my diploma as rain poured down on us. After I tossed my graduation cap in the air and hugged and celebrated with my friends, I found my mom and my dad, and they both embraced me in their arms. I looked at my mom and noticed that she was crying. I was not sure if she was crying because she was proud of me or if it was because she knew that in less than two months, I would be leaving to join the Army and go fight in America's latest war.

I managed to stay disciplined and lost the weight required for me to be able to join the Army. I had dropped down to 250 pounds, and I felt as ready as ever. On August 5th, there was a knock at my parents' door. It was my recruiter ready to take me away to my new life.

"Are you ready?" He questioned me.

"Yes, Sir!"

I grabbed my bag and slung it over my shoulder, and turned to my mom to give her a hug. She held me tightly in her arms. Tighter than I had ever felt before. She had such a hold on me that I could feel her muscles quivering.

"I love you, baby. Take care of yourself, and remember to pray every day and read your Bible every chance you get. Remember, the Lord is always with you, always."

I kissed my mom on her cheek and tried to pull away, but she was not ready to let me go yet. When she was ready, she slowly released me from her grip. I looked her in the eyes, but I did not see any tears. I saw love, pride, and a look of concern and worry. I waved to my mom one last time as she stood at the front door as we pulled out the driveway. A gauntlet of emotions circulated throughout me. The day that I had been dreaming about had finally come. The first leg of my journey to becoming an airborne ranger had commenced.

[5]

DO YOU WANT TO BE A RANGER?

FROM THE MOMENT I set foot on Sandhill in Fort Benning, Georgia, I instantly regretted my decision to join the army. My lack of running skills, being a fat body, and being one of the three black recruits in the company garnished my drill sergeant's attention. Not only that, I was struggling to make the transition from civilian to soldier.

"A yo! Drill Sergeant!" I shouted, wanting to get my drill sergeant's attention for some assistance.

"A-Yo Drill Sergeant! A-Yo Drill Sergeant! Who the hell do you think you are talking to, private? Are we boys! Are we cool like that! Are we back home on the block chilling!? Start pushing!" Needless to say, I got my drill sergeant's attention.

I lost count of the number of push-ups I did or how long I got smoked, but when I was finally told to recover, my M16 rifle, which weighed 6.35 pounds, felt like it weighed a quarter ton. I had learned a valuable lesson. "A-Yo drill sergeant," would never come from my lips again.

Even the way I marched drew negative attention.

"Who do you think you are, private! Why are you diddy bopping (marching like you are cool) in my formation like you are back home on the block! This isn't the street corner!"

The incident that finally broke me and ripped away from the last shred of civilian in me was during an eight-mile road march around week six. The march was tough, but I was up for the challenge. At some point during the march, I slung my M16 across my back for a moment as opposed to carrying it in the low-ready position as we were ordered. Drill Sergeant O'Neil took notice and immediately moved in to correct the issue.

"Private Pitts! Unsling your weapon and carry it in the low ready position as you were ordered!"

"But drill sergeant," I tried to reply, but Drill Sergeant O'Neil cut me off before I could even finish."

"Do it now, private!"

I unslung my M16 and proceeded to carry it in the low-ready position as instructed.

"Your ass is mine when we get done with this march Pitts!"

In the back of my mind, I thought to myself, surely, he is not going to remember this small incident, and he is not going to smoke me after marching eight miles with a 45 pounds rucksack. Finally, we arrived back at the barracks and started downloading our gear. As I was getting ready to drop my rucksack, Drill Sergeant O'Neil's pulled me to the side of the formation and proceeded to give me the smoking of a lifetime. I was already exhausted from the eight-mile march, but the party was starting for me. As everyone cleaned their gear, Drill Sergeant O'Neil smoked me into oblivion. By the time he was done, I was lying on the concrete in a pool of my own sweat. Every inch of my body ached with pain.

"On your feet, Pitts!" He commanded me.

I picked up my wrecked body off the concrete as fast as I could and stood at attention, but I was wavering back and forward like a flimsy tree being blown by the wind. Drill Sergeant O'Neil walked up to me and got close enough that I could feel him breathing on me. I could feel the brim of his campaign hat on my temple.

"When you disobey direct orders in combat, or you hesitate, you will get yourself and others killed, private! The appropriate response, when given an order, is "yes, drill sergeant," not but! You hesitate; you die! Do you understand me, private?"

"Hooah, Drill Sergeant," I replied.

Drill Sergeant O'Neil finally dismissed me to download and clean my gear. I remember gazing at the sweat-soaked pavement where my body was lying only moments before, and it was almost as if something inside me clicked. The wet spot on the pavement I was looking at was not just sweat; it was the remnant of who I used to be. At that moment, I realized that I was no longer just a 19-year-old kid from Fort Knox. I was not yet the warrior I desired to be, as I was still learning and trying to perfect my craft as a U.S Army infantryman. That smoke session was my great awakening and shook loose the warrior that was deep inside of me that my drill sergeants were trying to bring out of me. From that moment on, I took my oath to my country at heart, and the Infantryman's Creed became my way of life.

"What makes the green grass grow! Blood, blood, bright red blood!"

"What is the spirit of the bayonet! To Kill! Kill with cold, blue steel!"

"Why is the sky blue! Because God loves the infantry!"

I don't know if I was being naive, but it seemed as though some of the drill sergeants might have started taking a liking to me, and they showed their fondness towards me with extra push-ups and other fun activities. Drill Sergeant Thompson was tall, slim, and had dark skin, just like me. He dubbed me with the nickname Baloo, the bear from the Jungle Book.

"Whenever I walk into the room Pitts, you better start singing The Bare Necessities! Did I make myself clear!"

Without hesitation, Drill Sergeant Thompson would walk in, and I would stand at attention and sing the song as ordered.

Drill Sergeant O'Neil could see me starting to improve physically overall. If he saw me do something spectacular, he would have me do it twice for his enjoyment.

"That is impressive for a fat body, Pitts! We might make an infantryman out of you yet!"

My confidence continued to grow as my waistline continued to shrink. I looked like a soldier, and I felt like a soldier. I was not the same kid who walked across the graduation stage only a few months back. I was in the best shape of my life, and I felt unstoppable.

Despite the progress I was making, I was still struggling with my running. Our time in Bootcamp was coming to an end, and graduation was drawing near, and I had yet to pass a PT test run. Drill Sergeant O'Neil informed me that if I did not pass my last PT Test that I would not graduate with my class and that I would be rolled into the next class of recruits. I was riddled with fear at the thought of failing and not graduating with my class. Even more so, the thought of having to stay in Sand Hill longer was unbearable.

Every night before lights out, I would sit on the edge of my bunk, reading my Bible and praying. I had written a letter to my mom weeks before telling her that I was concerned about falling out because I kept failing the run. She responded in her next letter by telling me to read Isaiah 40:31: "But those who hope in the Lord will renew their strength. They will soar on wings like eagles; they will run and not grow weary; they will walk and not be faint."

The day of our final PT test had come. I was so nervous because I had come all this way and put in all of this effort into becoming a soldier, and everything was weighing on this two-mile run. For my age group, 17-21, the minimum amount of time allowed for me to complete my two-mile run was 15:30. I had missed the mark every time by 45 seconds to one minute. As we were moving to the starting line for our two-mile run, Cody Wilson, my battle buddy from Washington, Indiana, walked over to me, put his hand on my shoulder, and said to me, "No worries, Pitts. You got this."

The whistle sounded, and I took off. As I was running, I recited Isaiah 40:31 as I ran. I pushed myself so hard that I thought I was going to pass out as I was approaching the finish line. Out of nowhere, Cody came running towards me. Cody was a runner and completed his two-mile run with ease, and he came back to push me and encourage me.

"Pick up the pace, Pitts! Dig deep! You got this!" He yelled at me.

As I crossed the line, I heard my time yelled out,

"Pitts, 14:15."

By the grace and power of God and the boost from Cody, I made it. I would be able to graduate with my class. About a week before graduation, Drill Sergeant O'Neil came in to talk to us about a rare offer being made to all infantry recruits at OSUT. With the army fighting the war in Iraq and Afghanistan, the army had a critical need for Rangers. Drill Sergeant O'Neil informed us that all we had to do was volunteer and that after we graduated, we would automatically be sent to Airborne School, and once we graduated from Airborne School, we would go straight to the RIP (Ranger Indoctrination Program).

This was the opportunity I wanted. This was my motivation to join the army. It was an amazing opportunity, except I had one major problem. Dede and I were so madly in love and had planned on getting married as soon as I graduated.

"Drill Sergeant I am supposed to be going home and getting married."

"Get married later, private. This is your chance. Either you want to be a ranger, or you don't. It's that simple."

At that moment, I made a choice that I would live to regret the rest of my life. I choose love over my dream of becoming a U.S. Army Ranger. Graduation day had finally come. We stood before our families in our Army Dress Green Uniforms with our blue infantry cords on our right shoulders, signaling that we were your run-of-the-mill soldiers. We were infantry soldiers—the tip of the spear.

The excitement of graduation was short-lived. After being released to our families, I was frantically looking for my mom, dad, and Dede. I saw my dad and Dede, but my mom was nowhere to be found. My dad told me that my mom fell ill and had to be admitted to the hospital. At that moment, I could think of nothing else but getting out of Sand Hill and getting home to my mom.

As my dad's car drove north to Radcliff, a strange feeling came upon me. I felt like I was doing something wrong. I had spent the last 14 weeks in a strict training environment, and now I was free. I felt like I was an escaped slave who had made it north to freedom.

As soon as we made it home, I got in my truck and drove to Ireland Army Hospital where my mom had been admitted. She appeared as though she was doing fine. She hugged me and smiled. She was so proud of me, and she was in absolute shock at how much weight I had lost. I went to boot camp weighing 250 pounds. I was now a lean 214 pounds. My mom gave the best hugs. It felt so good to be in her embrace as she lay in her hospital bed. Thankfully, her condition had stabilized, and she would be released from the hospital a day later.

As we promised to each other through our letters, Dede and I tied the knot in a small ceremony in my parent's living room on November 28, 2003. I bought a cheap ring from Wal-Mart because I was an E-3 with very little money, but that did not matter to either of us at the time. All we knew was that we loved each other and that we wanted to stay together for the rest of our lives. And just like that, I was a married man at age 19 and had no clue what I was getting myself into with marriage or army life. The next six months of my life were about to be turbulent.

[6]

THE NOT SO GOLDEN DRAGON

At the ripe ages of 18 and 19, my new bride and I arrived at our new home in Fort Drum, New York, in early December 2003. The cold cut right through your clothes, all the layers of your skin, and chilled you to your bones. I had been cold before, but I had never experienced a cold of this caliber. Not to mention the waist-high snow that made life in Fort Drum miserable.

Upon in-processing into Fort Drum, I was informed that I was being assigned to the 2nd Brigade Combat Team (BCT) as part of Alpha Company of the 2nd Battalion 14th Infantry Regiment: The Golden Dragons. When I heard where I was being assigned, a jolt of excitement shot through me.

The Golden Dragons were the battalion that led the rescue mission into Mogadishu, Somalia, to help get the Rangers and Delta Force operators to safety. I joined the army to become an Airborne Ranger; however, being a Gold Dragon was a close second place win. To be a part of the legacy of the Gold Dragons and the same men who I was inspired by watching the Black Hawk Down movie was an amazing opportunity.

I had no clue what to expect going to my first unit, but there was one thing that I knew for sure going forward: expectations were going to be high. You do not earn the title of the most deployed unit in the military being mediocre. The 10th Mountain Division was known for its deployment tempo. As a 19-year-old Private First Class fresh out of army boot camp going to my new unit, I was even more nervous reporting to my unit on day one than I was going to boot camp. All I wanted was to live up to what was expected of me and be accepted. But acceptance in the infantry is not just given out for showing up in your uniform. It is earned through sweat and hard work. I was willing to do both to be accepted.

I awoke early the following day and dawned my heavily starched BDUs and my freshly shined black boots and drove onto post. I had printed out the directions from MapQuest directing me to my company. As I drove through the base, I could see soldiers in PT formation running alongside the roads. According to the directions that I was following, I was just around the corner from where I was supposed to be going and had to make a left turn. As I made the turn and headed towards the 2-14 INF barracks, a group of soldiers ran in PT formation just ahead of me. A short, black soldier broke away from the formation, approached my slow-moving vehicle, and knocked on my window.

I rolled down my window, and I was greeted with a thunderous voice,

"Why in the hell are you driving on my PT route during PT hours?"

Fear swept over me, and I had no idea what to say. I had no clue who was yelling at me, but he wanted an answer.

"Get off my PT route, Soldier! Right Now!

I snapped back to reality, hit the gas, and drove the short distance up the street to the parking lot of the Alpha Company barracks, where I sat for a moment trying to figure out what the heck had just happened. It was my first day, and I had already messed up big time. I was off to a rough start, and I had not even stepped foot inside of my company.

Upon walking into the Alpha Company bay amongst a sea of BDU uniforms, the first thing I noticed was that most of the soldiers I was looking at had SF (Special Forces) tabs and insignia combat patches on their right shoulders. The battalion had just recently returned from Iraq. They worked with SF units conducting combat operations in Northern Iraq alongside the Kurds during the initial invasion of Iraq earlier in the year. The second thing I noticed was that there were very few black faces like mine. Once again, I was one of eight black guys in the company. Color did not matter to me, but I couldn't help but notice the lack of melanin.

Shortly after my arrival, I was informed that I was being assigned to the 2nd platoon weapons squad as the AG (Assistant Gunner) of the 240 Bravo machine gunner Corporal Fields, who was also my new team leader. Corporal Fields, who everyone referred to by his nickname "Yuck," because of the overpowering smell his feet produced, hailed from Iowa.

As the AG, you are pretty much an ox. They load you up with all the 7.6 2mm ammo for the 240 Bravo machine gun and the tripod. Not only was I expected to carry that gear, but I was also expected to keep up and perform at maximum capacity. Being an AG was a job that no one wanted, and somehow, I was the one who drew the short straw and landed one of the worst jobs in the company.

I do not remember a lot from my first day in Alpha Company, but I remember what the floor looked like because I spent most of the day in the push-up position and doing bear crawls throughout the building. I was being properly welcomed into my new life as the new guy by Corporal Fields. My uniform was drenched with sweat, and my legs and arms were shaking uncountably by the time the end of the day. Our entire company had gathered at the battalion parade deck for the final formation of the day. As I stood in formation soaking wet, I saw a familiar face that I had seen earlier in the morning while driving to the battalion. It was the same short, black mystery man who had yelled at me for driving on the PT route during PT hours. What was different now was that he was wearing

BDUs with a sharp crease that could cut steel. The sun scowled off of his impeccably shined boots and his black beret with our battalion insignia donned on his head. I saw his last name on his uniform that read, "Epps." I glanced at his collar and saw his rank, and my soul immediately evacuated my body.

"Oh crap! It's Sergeant Major!" I thought to myself. His uniform boasted his impressive military resume: Airborne Wings, Air Assault Wings, EIB (Expert Infantry Badge), CIB (Combat Infantry Badge), and a PathFinder Badge. He had the coveted Ranger Tab seated just about the 10th Mountain Division patch on his left shoulder.

"Please do not notice me. Please do not look at me," I said to myself repeatedly as the Sergeant Major walked up to the formation. He walked back and forward in front of our formation examining us. Then, just as he was nearing my position, he stopped and stared at me. I could feel his eyes dissecting me. I then heard the same thunderous voice in my ears that had caused my heart to skip a few beats and speak in a low and slow tone.

"You're the soldier who was driving on my PT route this morning."

I was unaware if he was asking me a question or making a statement. Either way, I did not respond, but I knew that I had better reply and sound off loud and proud.

"Roger that, Sergeant Major!" I sounded off.

"Don't you ever let me catch you driving on Sergeant Major's PT route during PT hours ever again! Do you copy that Dragon!"

Being that our battalion was the Golden Dragons, Sergeant Major affectionately referred to all the soldiers under his command as Dragon(s).

"Roger that, Sergeant Major!" I replied.

I wish that I could say that this was my only up close and overly personal encounter with our super high-speed Sergeant Major, but I would find myself in his office standing before him again, answering to yet another bad judgment call.

Staff Sergeant (Staff Sergeant) Sampson, one of our platoon's squad leaders, was going through a divorce and was moving out of his house and into the barracks. I was informed that he needed help moving, and due to me having a pickup truck, I was "volun-told" that I would be helping him move his stuff into the barracks the coming weekend. I went to Staff Sergeant Sampson's place in Watertown, New York, loaded his stuff into the back of my truck, and drove to the barracks. Instead of parking in the parking lot and carrying his stuff in from there, I was told to drive my truck to the back of the barracks over the grass to the rear door of the barracks.

If you ask anyone who has ever been in the military about grass, the first thing they will tell you is that you never walk on the grass, especially if there is a sidewalk available. The grass is sacred in the military. More so, the grass around your battalion area. Stepping onto the grass is a death sentence, and I had just driven straight onto death row!

Fort Drum, New York, is very cold and very wet during the early parts of the year because of all the snow. My rear-wheel-drive Chevy s-10 was not built to be driven in such conditions and had become stuck in the grass behind the barracks. I tried like hell with the help of guys from the barracks to get my truck out, but it only continued to get stuck further in the grass and mud. Specialist (Spec) Johnny Born, who I often referred to as Johnny Blaze, was also a Kentucky boy like myself but hailed from Hazzard County. He was able to get his good friend, Specialist Ryan Cataline in HHC (Headquarters and Headquarters Company), to pull me out of the mud with his 1988 Chevrolet K5 with 33-inch mud tires. The trail of destruction left by my truck and the 33inch mud tires on the Chevrolet that rescued me was an ugly sight. We had decimated the grass; however, I did not even think twice about it. Nor did Staff Sergeant Sampson or any of the other guys who were present that helped. We left it as it was, and we all went about our weekends.

After our Monday morning formation, Staff Sergeant Sampson approached me and told me in his deep Trinidad accent, "Sergeant Major wants to see you and me in his office right now!"

My chest tightened up, and my heart started racing as I was trying to think of why the man who previously scared my soul out of my body was summoning me along with Staff Sergeant Sampson to his office.

"Oh crap! The grass!"

I walked with Staff Sergeant Sampson up to battalion Headquarters (HQ), and I was riddled with the same fear I had the day I drove on Sergeant Major's PT route. I did have a bit more of a sense of comfort because I was going in with a Staff Sergeant, but I was still dreading the impending doom about to overtake both of us.

Staff Sergeant Sampson and I stood before Sergeant Major as he sat at his desk. Once again, I could feel his eyes burning into the depths of my soul. His face was stone cold and showed no emotion like a seasoned serial killer. In the same, low, slow creepy tone, Sergeant Major spoke,

"Are you the two dragons who destroyed Sergeant Major's grass?"

Being the lowest man of rank in the room, I was terrified to answer because I did not want to speak out of turn, but I was also confused because I was not sure if I was supposed to step up, take responsibility, and confess to the murder of Sergeant Major's beloved grass. I could feel my blood pressure increase and my pulse beating in my neck at a furious pace. From where Sergeant Major was sitting, I am sure he could see the pulse in my neck beating out of control. In my mind, I was on the verge of having a stroke because I was so terrified. I was waiting for Sergeant Major to decapitate Staff Sergeant Sampson and me with his knife hand and step over our headless bodies without remorse or human emotion.

"You two go and fix Sergeant Major's grass right now! I do not care what you all have going on right now! I want my grass back! Do you copy?"

"Roger that, Sergeant Major!" Staff Sergeant Sampson and I responded simultaneously.

We left the office in a hurry. As we moved quickly back to our barracks building, I thought,

"How in the hell do you fix grass?" I thought to myself.

The grooves and divots left by the trucks were long and deep. There was no way to truly repair the damage we had done, but I knew that we had better come up with a quick solution.

"Pitts, grab your e-tool (entrenching shovel) and meet me out back now!"

I ran to my car, grabbed my e-tool, and met Staff Sergeant Sampson at the homicide scene of the sacred grass that we had unjustly murdered that caused Sergeant Major so much grief and anguish.

Staff Sergeant Sampson and I spent the next few hours in the mud, on our knees, trying to piece back together fragments of what was left in the grooves with pieces of mud and grass that had been removed from its rightful place due to the spinning of the tires and trying to fold the sides back into the grooves and divots. I became so desperate at one point that I ran to the woods next to the barracks and started digging up the ground from there and transferring it to the damaged lawn. By the time we were done, we were wet, filthy, and covered in mud. The lawn looked like it had undergone botched plastic surgery. Patches of grass were scattered, and there were smooth spots of fresh wet mud. I was worried that what we had done to repair the lawn was not enough and that we were going to be standing before Sergeant Major again, but we never heard anything else about the grass incident afterward.

When I arrived at Alpha Company, I was the only new person there for about a week, so I was getting all of the negative attention that I could stand until Private Josh Cox, an 18-year-old of mixed race (white and Hispanic) with jet black hair from Kerrville, Texas arrived at our platoon. The first thing I said to Cox when we first met was, "You better hope and pray that they do not make you an AG."

And with those magic words, Cox was my newly assigned battle buddy in 2nd platoon weapons squad and was assigned the position of AG for the other 240 bravo machine gun team. I was happy to have Josh on board because I was tired of suffering alone. Misery really does love company.

With the possibility of us seeing combat soon, our training tempo and intensity were cranked up to max capacity. With a body like Barney the dinosaur, a face like Shrek, and a voice like Mickey Mouse, our squad leader, Staff Sergeant Linder, put us to work. From the moment he and I met, we were instantly at odds. He despised me, and the feeling was neutral. He treated me differently than the other soldiers in the squad, and I loathed him for it.

"You two better hurry up and get the tri-pods set up and get out of the way for the gunner! Do it again!" Staff Sergeant Linder screamed at us.

Cox and I sprinted up the hill again, carrying the tripods on our shoulders, and we were loaded down with all the 7.62mm machine gun ammo that we could carry. We would reach the top of the hill exhausted and out of breath, slam the tripod into the ground, and roll out of the way so that the gunner could place the machine gun into the tripod.

Life at the bottom of the military food chain of command was awful. Nothing you do is ever good enough. You are constantly ridiculed, berated, and reminded of how worthless you are as a person and as a soldier. I took the insults and harsh criticism from those who outranked me extremely hard. I was beat down mentally and physically every day, and I was never built back up. I was a Golden Dragon, but I did not feel so golden.

As tough of a time I was having adapting to my new life, I was putting in the max effort to become a master of my craft. I had become proficient in the knowledge of my tools of war. I knew my weapons systems intimately. I was not the best shot with my M4 rifle, but I was a stone-cold killer with the 240-bravo. I could eradicate multiple targets with extreme prejudice and pinpoint accuracy at ranges up to 3000 meters using the MGO (machine gun optic). I was so deadly with the 240 Bravo that I outshot my team leader Corporal

Fields at one of our training ranges; it was one of my proudest moments.

My dreams of going to Ranger School and wearing the Ranger Tab were just that, dreams. My motivation and desire to wear the black and gold tab faded as I faced the true reality of my current situation. As much as I wanted to be, I was not ranger material.

In mid-April of 2004, the rumor mill started buzzing, and the word was that our brigade was going to be deployed to Iraq soon. The thought of deploying to Iraq was exciting because I had signed up to go fight. As excited as Cox and I were about deploying, we knew not to get our hopes up. Our company commander, Captain Shaw, put an end to the rumors of us deploying fast.

On May 4, 2004, four days before my 20th birthday, I was at home when my phone rang. I noticed the voice on the other end as a sergeant from my company.

"Private First Class Pitts. This call is your warning order."

Warning orders are used to convey to soldiers details about upcoming deployments or missions in order to give them advanced notice. All the rumors had been true, and with that call, everything was officially confirmed. On June 4, 2004, I would be deploying to the Middle East as part of the 10th Mountain Division's 2nd Bridge "Commands" in support of Operation Iraqi Freedom II. The following morning at formation, you could feel a wave of excitement flowing throughout the company. In 30 days, we would be joining our fellow servicemen already in the fight.

We were issued our new uniforms and equipment days later. I loved the look of our DCUs (Desert Combat Uniforms) and our tan boots. The first time I put on my DCUs and looked in the mirror, the first thing that came to my mind was, "this is real!

The war in Iraq was starting to take a heavy toll on the troops, with a new strategy being implemented by insurgents using IEDs (Improvised Explosive Devices). The word from the frontlines was that they were hiding these devices in piles of trash, dead animals, and burying them in the ground, and when troops would approach, they would remotely detonate the device, causing mass carnage and death to troops near its blast radius. With the knowledge of this emerging threat, we adjusted our tactics and training from the standard 7-8 Field Manual to adapt to the changing face of the battlefield, which now incorporated us using Humvees (High Mobility Multipurpose Wheeled Vehicle). This was not going to be a traditional ground war with tanks and infantry battling for landmass.

Our training cycle kicked into overdrive as we drilled and trained daily in all aspects of our jobs. We practiced our battle drills, first-aid and conducted live night-fire exercises using our NVGs (Night Vision Goggles) and our AN/PAQ-4C infrared aiming lasers as we practiced conducting military operations under cover of darkness. After our live night-fire exercise concluded, we road marched 12 miles back to our barracks using our NVGs. My body ached from carrying the 80 pounds of gear that was stacked on me.

It was the last weekend before our deployment. I was in the barracks partying and drinking with my brothers for the last time stateside before we were scheduled to fly out. Beer cans, bottles of liquor, red solo cups, and the pale shirtless bodies of freshly shaved bald-headed underage privates were scattered throughout the entire barracks. The pungent aroma of alcohol-infused vomit lingered in the hallways as heavy metal blared from speakers. Yelling, screaming, and fights were not uncommon on this final weekend. Cox and I were partying with some of the other new guys from the mortar section, and they were putting on a clinic on how to properly drink and get wasted.

Having recently turned 20 and not being of the legal drinking age, I disregarded the law and guzzled down the contents inside the red solo cup, and before I knew it, the entire room was spinning, and I passed out on the floor. I awoke the next morning extremely hungover.

On my final night at home, I laid in bed with my wife of only seven months snuggled in my arms. The feeling of her soft skin and long black hair against my skin was a reminder of what I was leaving behind to travel across the world and kill the evil people who had dragged me and my generation into this war. I did not want to go to sleep because I wanted to savor every last moment that we had together. The truth was this might be our last time together in this lifetime. We did not say it to each other, but we were both aware of this unpleasant truth. We had gotten married, believing that we would be together forever and that nothing, not even war, would be able to tear us apart.

The morning of June 4, 2004, the entire company, dressed in DCUs, in front of our company barracks, kissed our family goodbye. Rivers of tears flowed from the eyes of wives and children as daddy, and his army buddies said their final goodbyes. I hugged and kissed my Dede one final time before we filed onto an awaiting bus, ready to deliver us to the RDF (Rapid Deployment Facility). I called my mom early that morning to tell her that I was leaving in a few hours. I could hear the stress and worry in her voice. It was almost as though I could hear her tears traveling down her face on the phone.

"Baby, I am praying for you. Please remember to pray every day and read your Bible. God will protect you. I love you so much. Please take care of yourself and don't be a fool!"

We sat at the RDF for what seemed like hours waiting for our plane to arrive to take us to our new home in hot and sunny Iraq. I was expecting to see a large military-style aircraft, but that was not the case. There was a large white charter airplane on the runway that read Omni Air International on the side. We grabbed our assault packs and were directed to start heading towards the aircraft. As I was moving towards the aircraft, the entire 10th Mountain Division command staff formed a line to shake our hands and wished us good luck as we embarked upon this great journey. I made my way up the stairs onto the plane and found myself a seat next to my fellow Kentucky brother, Johnny Blaze. Many thoughts rushed through my head as the plane took off towards the other side of the world. One thought kept coming to my mind, and it haunted me the entire flight; "I hope I don't mess up."

[7]

PAPER TARGETS DON'T SHOOT BACK

TWENTY-PLUS HOURS LATER, on the other side of the world, the door to our aircraft opened up. The cramped, frustrated, and anxious soldiers of Alpha Company 2-14 Infantry rose to their feet, grabbed their assault packs, and started making their way to the plane's exit. Before I could even see the door, I could feel the harsh heat of the Middle East breach the cabin of our aircraft and attach itself to my skin. Every time I inhaled, I could feel the burn of the desert heat flowing into my lungs. As I stepped off the plane into the night, I thought we were walking into a giant oven that had been set to broil. I stared into the dark of night and could see small fires flicking and wavering from oil fields in the distance. We grabbed the rest of our gear from the bottom of the plane and rushed onto buses with black curtains to conceal us.

When the buses finally came to a halt, we offloaded in our temporary domicile for the next 30 days: Camp Buehring in Udairi, Kuwait, where we would train and acclimate before crossing the border into Iraq. Those of us in 2nd platoon found ourselves inside of a large general-purpose tent with plywood floors covered in fine sand, along with guys from 3rd platoon. We scattered to find one of the many olive-green cots coated with a light dusting of sand that we would call our bed for the remainder of our time here. But first, you had to pick up your cot, flip it upside down and discard the grains of sand that had been resting and holding your spot for you. Since we had arrived in the middle of the night, I could not take in the landscape, and I enthusiastically waited for the sun to make its entrance the following morning.

I awakened a few hours later, drenched in sweat. My grey PT shirt that I had worn to sleep looked like I had gotten up in the middle of the night and decided to go and take a swim. The creature comforts of things we take for granted, such as air conditioning and running water ready for our consumption at any time, did not exist in this chapter of my life. I stepped outside of the tent into the brightness of the Kuwaiti sun. It felt like the sun was sitting on my shoulder as its luminous rays blinded me, and my eyes slowly adjusted to its overpowering brightness. Once I could fully open my eyes, beyond the row of tents, all I saw was an endless stretch of sky and sand; It was breathtaking. I would have never thought that the vastness of nothingness could be so beautiful.

Although we were on the other side of the world, the United States Military did its best to give the soldiers deployed a taste of home. Unfortunately, I can only describe it as low-quality, knockoff, fast-food eateries that tried to mimic some of our favorite places back home. For example, there was a coffee shop named "Green Beans Coffee Company." My eyes lit up, and my mouth watered when I saw the familiar Subway sandwich sign. I bit into the sweet onion chicken teriyaki sandwich I ordered, and it tasted like a heap of confusion in my mouth. I was expecting the taste of my favorite sandwich to transport me back home in a sense of euphoria down memory lane, but all I tasted was dissatisfaction. It was the same with other fast food places as well.

"What the heck is a whopper royale with cheese?" I asked myself as I stared at the Burger King menu.

I wanted to complain, but I had no right when I thought about the Soldiers and Marines who dashed across Iraq during the initial invasion and only had two options: MRE (Meals Ready to Eat) or starve to death.

Once the rest of the 2nd BCT finally arrived at Camp Buehring in the coming days, we were briefed and informed that on July 19, 2004 that we would depart from Camp Navistar in northern Kuwait. Our next orders were to cross the border into Iraq and drive two days across the hostile and insurgent besieged country to our home for the next year: Camp Victory Iraq. We were briefed that we would be attached to the 1st Cavalry Division, who had been in the country since January of 2004 and had encountered some heavy fighting and had taken a lot of casualties in the Baghdad suburb known as Sadr City in April. The 1st Cav's battle in Sadr City had become known as Black Sunday. Learning that we would be conducting combat operations in Iraq was a grim reminder that we were going into the heart of the fight. But before we went storming into the heart of the battle, we had a lot of training to do and boredom to endure between our July 19th departure.

We conducted live-fire ranges in the middle of the Kuwaiti desert as our date of departure got closer. The only thing that was missing was actual enemy combatants at the business end of our barrels. We arrived back at camp, and we were riled up and filled with enthusiasm, ready to carry out violence and demolish any insurgent force that would dare challenge us to fight. We boasted of how courageous we would be in the face of combat. We felt invincible with our gear, high-powered weapons, and the training we were receiving. However, we were young, naive and our lack of life experience, specifically combat experience, showed. 3rd platoon's squad leader, Staff Sergeant Bryant, heard all the bragging we were doing as he sat on his cot cleaning his M4 rifle. He lifted his head and crushed our overinflated sense of self with a straightforward statement.

"Y'all are some real badasses shooting at paper targets that don't shoot back. Just wait until the bullets are flying towards you," He said as he lowered his head down and continued to clean his rifle.

No one spoke a word after his comment. All that we could hear was the scrubbing of brushes against the medal as we removed the carbon build-up from our weapons. Little did I know that I would be awakened to the realities of war before I even journeyed across the border into Iraq.

"Hey, Pitts! You are famous! You made it into the Blizzard!" Specialist Petterson said to me.

While at one of our live-fire training, I was pulled aside by a writer from the Fort Drum Blizzard and interviewed. They snapped a picture of me nestled behind the 240 Bravo as I stared off into the distance. It was exciting to see myself in the paper, but that was not my concern. Instead, my mind was preoccupied with my first combat experience on the horizon.

June 26, 2004. I awoke that day to great news from our squad leader. We were informed that we were being given the day off to rest and relax. I rushed to the MWR (Morale Welfare and Recreation) tent with Cox to beat the endless lines for the phone. I dialed my wife's phone number and waited anxiously as the phone rang. She picked up the phone, and the sound of her voice put my heart at ease for a moment, but I could sense that there was something wrong.

"What's wrong?" I inquired.

"It's Ronald's brother, Deshon. He was killed in Iraq a few days ago."

The excitement and joy that I had to hear my wife's voice was replaced with rage, sorrow, and fear. The realities of war had seized what little joy I could find in a simple phone call home.

"I'm so sorry, Dexter. I didn't want to tell you because I know that you guys are heading into Iraq soon, but I just had to tell you."

Marine Lance Corporal Deshon E. Otey, 24, of Radcliff, Kentucky, was KIA (Killed In Action) on June 21, 2004 in Ramadi, Iraq. He was a Marine sniper assigned to the 2nd Battalion, 4th Marine Regiment of the 1st Marine Division. He, along with three of his fellow Marine snipers, were ambushed and killed in the most savage fashion by insurgents. Since I am not aware of the facts surrounding Deshon and his fellow Marine's deaths, I will not go into detail or speculate out of respect for him, his family, and the Marines he served with. Deshon was the oldest brother of one of my best friends in high school, Ronald Otey, who was currently in the Marines himself and gearing up to be deployed to Iraq as well. Not only was Ronald getting ready to deploy, their little brother, Domenique, was at Parris Island training to become a Marine just like his older brothers.

My mind immediately flashed back to Deshon strutting the halls of our high school in his Marine Corps Dress Blues as he gleamed with pride. I thought of his mom, Robin Mays, whose home I had spent a lot of time hanging out with Ronald and Domenique. The amount of hurt, disbelief, and grief that Ms. Mays, Ronald, and Domenique were experiencing at the loss of their courageous and beloved Marine was inconceivable to me at the age of 20. I had experienced the death of loved ones and friends before, but the death of Deshon was different as it exposed me to my mortality. I was going to be crossing the border into Iraq in two weeks. I would be going into the same country and fighting the same war that had cut my best friend's brother's life short at 24 years. The sense of invincibility and being untouchable had faded, and all I was left with was the raw reality of war and the fact that I might not make it back home. Everything that Staff Sergeant Bryant had said to us days prior about being tough guys until the bullets started flying back towards us echoed in my mind.

I spent the remainder of our rare day off in a trance. I did not shed a single tear, but my heart ached for my friends and all those back homes that would be impacted by the death of Deshon back home in Radcliff. I would be lying if I said that I was not scared or fearful going forward. I was very much afraid of the unknown inching its way into my life as every second faded and pushed us closer to our departure date. But instead of focusing on my fear, I focused on the rage, anger, and hate aspects of my emotions that I had become accustomed to as an infantryman. I wanted to drink the blood of the insurgents who lay in wait for our arrival in Iraq. I wanted to rip their beating hearts out of their chest and deliver it to their grieving families.

Before Deshon's death, I wanted to fight in this war out of love for my country. After Deshon's death, this was no longer a war about just fighting for the honor of my country. The war in Iraq had become a personal vendetta to me. I was out for blood and revenge. I wanted nothing more than to repay the bastards who robbed my friends of their son/brother.

We were days away from crossing the border north into Iraq. Our journey north to our new home at Camp Victory in Baghdad would be a three-day trip on MSR (Main Supply Route) Tampa. IEDs, VBIEDs (Vehicle Borne Improvised Explosive Devices), RPGs (Rocket Propelled Grenades), and hand grenades tossed from insurgents lurking on the overpasses were all possible. I was confident in the training that I had received, but I was not confident in the vehicles we would use to make the dangerous journey.

The Humvees assigned to us in Alpha company looked as though they were dug up from the boneyard of the first Gulf War in 1991, and someone had put brand new tires on them. Not even a used car salesman would dare try and sell these things. I knew our Humvees were terrible, and I could only imagine what the boys in HHC, Bravo Company, and Charlie Company were being issued. These Humvees were not equipped to withstand a blast from an IED. Some of them had non-armored doors that shrapnel and bullets would be able to slice through without any resistance. A few of them had no actual roof, but a canvas top that would not protect the occupants if insurgents started shooting us from the overpass. One of the canvas tops Humvees I saw had holes in the floorboard so big that you could see the road below you and touch it with your hand.

"I feel sorry for the suckers who have to ride in this piece of garbage," I thought to myself.

We found ourselves in a scrap yard taking hunks of metal and welding them onto the Humvees. We filled up sandbags and placed them in the floorboards of our unfit for war vehicles hoping that they would give us some protection against an IED blast. I looked over at Private First Class Randy Guerra, our squad's FO (Forward Observer), as we placed the sandbags on the floorboard.

Well, if we get hit by this thing, we will probably die instantly. We won't even know it. So that's a good thing, right?" Randy said with a smile on his face.

Our dark and inappropriate humor was the only coping mechanism to help us deal with the stress. Randy and I decided to have a competition to see who would get WIA (Wounded in Action) first and make it back home.

"No way you are winning this one! I am definitely going to win this!" I joked to Randy.

Despite our less than desirable vehicles, we were blessed with a few of the new up-armored Humvees. These vehicles were brand new and fresh off the assembly line. I felt a lot safer behind the thick armored doors and bulletproof glass protecting my flanks. Even more impressive with the up-armored Humvee was the fact that it came with air conditioning.

I stood up in the turret and was encircled by the blast shield that would protect me from shrapnel and bullets. Although I felt slightly safer in the up-armored Humvee, I was not under the illusion that I would be protected from the unpredictability of war, especially manning the machine gun and being in the turret. The blast shields could only do so much to protect us because the battlefield we would be fighting on was 360 degrees, and attacks could come from any direction.

On July 18, 2004, we gathered for our final formation at Camp Behring before we started the first part of our journey to Camp Navistar Kuwait. Camp Navistar Kuwait is the most northern US Military base in Kuwait. We would stage there for the night and arise early in the morning and make our first push into Iraq.

"Gentlemen! Remember to listen to your Spidey senses! If something doesn't feel right or look right, say something," 1st Lieutenant Michaels reminded us as we stood in formation.

1st Lieutenant Michaels had come to 2nd platoon a few months before we deployed. He was a highly intelligent and thoughtful leader. He, just like many of the younger leaders in our company, did not have any real-world combat experience, but we would all get the chance to obtain that real-world experience together.

Soldiers scurried about gathering the last of their gear, checking their equipment to ensure that it was functioning properly. We were lined up by our leaders and given one last check to make sure that we were all accounted for and all our equipment was accounted for as well. We walked to the row of Humvees loaded down with all our gear, MREs, and water.

Olive green cans of 7.62mm and .50 Cal ammunition were stacked inside of the vehicles. The smell of the diesel engines accompanied by its rumble let us know that it was time to say goodbye to Camp Buehring. I donned my IBA (Interceptor Body Armor) and crowned myself with my ACH (Advanced Combat Helmet), and headed to my assigned vehicle. I was pleasantly surprised to learn that I was riding in one of the new Humvees. I sat in the cramped backseat with my knees almost to my chest because of the ammo cans stacked beneath my feet. I was more comfortable sitting in the Humvee the other day before we tossed all of our instruments of war inside with us. I was cramped and uncomfortable, but at least I was safe. Four other soldiers had drawn the short straw and were riding in the Humvee with holes in the floorboard.

As the sun broke through the darkness on the morning of July 19, 2004, I awoke from my slumber with a heaviness upon my soul. I put on my DCUs, grabbed my M4 rifle and my baby wipes, and walked to the porta-potty for my last moment of privacy and peace and quiet away from everyone before we loaded up and started our journey north to Iraq. I sat in the porta-potty, which felt more like a sauna, sweating profusely and staring at the graffiti etched on the walls.

Typically, I would go into the porta-potty and laugh at the twisted and demented jokes and drawings put there by the creative, immature minds of soldiers, but I paid them no attention that morning. I spent that moment with God in prayer, asking for his protection of not only me but also my brothers as we prepared to roll into battle.

We mounted our four-wheeled fortresses and drove down the black, asphalt road of Highway 80 to the Safwan Border Crossing that separated Abdali, Kuwait, and Safwan, Iraq. I stared at the wall of dirt that ran off into the distance beyond what my eyes could see. I knew that on the other side of that dirt wall, warfare awaited us.

"We are officially in Iraq," Staff Sergeant Virnig yelled from the front passenger seat.

I peered out of my bulletproof window at the Iraq landscape.

"I'm really here," I thought to myself.

The first day of our trip was uneventful. Day two of our trip brought about a large amount of anxiety. I am not sure what I did to anger someone, or maybe God was playing a trick on me, but our seating arrangements had changed prior to the start of our second day on the road. I was now the sucker who drew the short straw and ended up sitting in the rear of the Humvee with the canvas top and holes in the floorboard covered with sandbags. I watched the road pass by under my feet at 55 miles per hour as I gazed through one of the holes in the floorboard not covered by a sandbag.

"Pitts! You are the .50 Cal gunner on my truck today," Staff Sergeant Virnig notified me.

On the third day of the trip, I took my place behind the .50 Cal, adjusted the strap, and rotated the turret to cover the right flank of the convoy. I pulled the charging handle of the .50 Cal, making it ready to fire at a moment's notice. I had to be extra alert and pay attention to even the slightest details for the last part of our trip because we were traveling the most dangerous stretch of highway leading to Camp Victory, known as Route Irish, also referred to as IED alley.

"Expect enemy contact," We were told at our last briefing.

I bounced around in the turret like a ping pong ball due to the unkept roads we were traveling on. The radio inside of the Humvee crackled, and I could hear someone's voice on the other end.

"Someone has eyes on a possible suicide vehicle heading straight towards us!"

I stood erect behind the .50 Cal and gripped its wooden handles. I scanned my field of fire to see if I could spot the suicide vehicle. My eyes located the white four-door car with orange doors driving down a frontage road straight towards our convoy with a trail of dust behind it.

"This is it!" I thought to myself as I stood ready and eager for my first official kill.

I placed my thumbs on the butterfly trigger, ready to sling lead and destroy whoever was driving the vehicle. The taxi slammed on its brakes and performed a U-turn, and sped off in the opposite direction. I let out a sigh of relief that was also laced with a hint of disappointment as I loosened my grip of the 50.

The Baghdad skyline was now in view. The open desert slowly transitioned into a densely populated neighborhoods with people wandering about. Every grunt inside of the Humvee was alert. Their rifles no longer sat in their laps. The buttstocks of their rifles rested in the pit of their shoulders, their hands wrapped around the pistol grip and their trigger fingers resting on the side of their lower receiver, and their thumbs on the selector switch ready to take their rifle from safe to semi-fire or full auto if needed.

The convoy was now in the sprawling urban landscape of Baghdad. Iraqi civilians and vehicles were everywhere. The convoy started to slow down due to the flow of traffic.

"Don't stop! Keep driving," Staff Sergeant Virnig hollered.

Stopping a convoy in the middle of traffic surrounded by buildings was a potentially fatal mistake that we could not afford. If we stopped, we would have been even more susceptible to attack than we already were. Just before the sun was getting ready to set, we entered the safe embrace of the fortified walls of Camp Victory. Our three-day odyssey to our new lives finally came to its end, and we had all survived the initial days of our yearlong combat deployment. The politics and personal opinions as to why we were in Iraq at this point did not matter. The only thing that mattered was surviving the next 11 months and getting back home to our families. It was a soothing feeling being behind the walls of Camp Victory and being enveloped by thousands of Soldiers, Marines, and Airmen. For the moment, I felt safe, but I knew that feeling would eventually subside because my job was not on camp. I was a grunt. My duties would take me away from the safety of Camp Victory to the IED laden streets of Baghdad, where scores of American soldiers and Marines were losing their lives.

[8]

THIS IS WHAT YOU WANTED

AUGUST 1, 2004: My stomach rumbled, alerting me that it was time to replenish myself. Cox and I grabbed our rifles and started to walk towards the Camp Victory DFAC (Dining Facility) for evening chow. As we strolled to the DFAC, we saw an ominous plume of black smoke billowing far off in the distance deep in Baghdad.

Cox and I kept walking and could only wonder what had occurred to cause the giant plum of black smoke to hover over the city. Finally, we walked into the DFAC, and soldiers were eating their dinner and staring at the rear projection big-screen TVs that were broadcasting the CNN news. I looked at the screen and saw the same black cloud of smoke that I had just witnessed outside with my own eyes. The title on the screen read, "Car Bombs Target Churches in Iraq."

Insurgents had launched multiple attacks on Christian churches during their evening services throughout Baghdad and a separate attack in Mosul, killing 11 people and injuring more than fifty. The largest explosions occurred in central Baghdad in the Karada district, which produced the cloud of smoke visible from Camp Victory.

As I watched the news story of the attack, I realized that I was taking part in something special that was bigger than myself. I had a front-row seat to a current event that was holding the entire world captive. Down in my heart, I knew that I was supposed to be here and that this was where I belonged.

Being at Camp Victory was a luxury itself and was a true upgrade from Camp Buehring Kuwait. We had all of the amenities on camp that we head back home to make our stay in this war zone bearable. We lived in air condition trailers, had hot and cold showers, real toilets, laundry services, internet, and a dining facility that produced three delicious meals a day for the troops. The meals we consumed were not some low-budget meals either. Instead, these were gourmet meals of steak and lobster. The troops coveted the DFAC meals so much that the army had to put soldiers on guard in the DFAC, who we dubbed the Chow Hall Nazis, to control the consumption of food and condiments. The chow hall Nazis would stand at the entrance of the DFAC and make sure that our uniforms were decent before we could enter. If your uniform was not up to their standard, they would deny you entry.

Once inside the DFAC, the chow hall Nazis would watch us and make sure we did not take more than our fair share of nutrition. We grew weary of drinking unflavored water and looked forward to going to the DFAC so that we could load up on Gatorade packets. We would stuff our cargo pockets full of Gatorade packets as we would leave the DFAC; however, once the chow hall Nazis noticed, they would force us to return most of the packets, leaving us with two to three packets each which angered us greatly.

"There are thousands of Gatorade packets, and you want to give me grief about how many I am taking?" Soldiers would argue.

Some of the military personnel on Camp Victory seemed to be oblivious that a war was raging outside the walls of Camp Victory. I'm sure they felt at home on Camp Victory until the air-raid alarm would sound, forcing them to seek shelter in the nearest bunker as insurgents launched mortars and rockets that landed indiscriminately inside the camp and would discharge shrapnel with no consideration of your MOS.

Cox and I grew restless as we waited to go on our first patrol. The leaders of Alpha Company were already in our AO (Area of Operation) doing right-seat-rides with a unit from the 39th Infantry Brigade of the Arkansas NG (National Guard) in the area of southwest Baghdad, learning the lay of the land before we took over all combat operations. As we waited for our first patrol, we were stuck doing the typical duties of soldiers in a war zone, such as guard duty and cleaning weapons and equipment.

There was a loud knock on my door. I answered to see Corporal Fields before.

"Grab your gear. You are going to be escorting the Iraqi septic truck driver around camp for the day."

I was not thrilled about the septic truck duty assignment, but I grabbed my gear and did as told. I sat inside the truck with my protective gear and my rifle firmly secured in my hands at the low ready. I sat with my back firmly against the door as opposed to the back of the seat. I had never met an Iraqi up close and in person before. In my mind, I was sitting next to the enemy. I was afraid that if I even blinked too long that he would take the opportunity to kill me.

"It's ok, mister. You can relax. I no bad guy." He said to me in broken English.

I did not say anything and just sat and stared at him, watching his every move. I wanted to let him know with my facial expressions and the positioning of my body and rifle that I did not trust him and that I had zero qualms killing him if need be. My orders were to go everywhere he went and to not let him out of my sight, and I was hell-bent on making sure that was what I did. The Iraqi exited his vehicle and proceeded to do his job of removing all the septic waste from the porta-johns and septic systems on the camp.

I was only one hour into my eight-hour assignment as I stood next to him outside of the truck when I heard a loud hissing sound coming from the truck. Pop! One of the hoses he was using to suck the waste out of the port-a-john had ruptured. A wave of blue port-a- john juice laced with the urine and feces of hundreds of soldiers doused me.

"It's ok, mister. It's ok. I fix."

Without hesitation, as though he was immune to the smell and bacteria that flowed from his truck, he reattached the hose without even gagging. I was about to lose my mind as I sat covered in the excrement of my fellow service members, as the Iraq sun baked it into my DUCs and IBA. I sat in the cab of the truck in disgust with no way to rid myself of the stench that had affixed to me. I would have to endure the smell for the next seven hours.

"Mister, my friend. Why so angry?" the Iraqi questioned me.

Once again, I said nothing. There was nothing for us to talk about. I wanted nothing to do with this stranger. He reached up into his visor and pulled out a photo.

"Mister. This is my family."

I looked at the photo of him and his family, and I saw a fellow human being for a brief second. Maybe I was being too aggressive, and a bit of a jerk, but my training since boot camp had embedded in my head that he was the enemy and that he was going to kill me. At age 20, with zero life experience outside of high school, I was unable to think critically for myself. I had been trained on what to think and how to think and follow orders. The human side of me wanted to open up and talk to him, but the soldier in me struggled to let my guard down.

"What is your name, mister? Do you have a family?"

Something inside of me decided to give him a chance.

"My name is Dexter. I have a wife back home."

"My name is Fockly. It is nice to meet you, Dexter."

Slowly, little by little, I started to open up more, and the next thing you know, we were laughing and talking about our families. He told me what it was like growing up under Saddam's reign of control and how he was able to learn English. It turned out that we had a lot more in common than I realized. He explained to me that working on the base was the best job that he could find to take care of his family and that it was so dangerous because the insurgents did not want Iraqis working for the Americans. He was putting his life in danger to take care of his young family.

Even though I smelled of human waste, I enjoyed the remainder of my duty. I can even say that I felt like I had made a friend. Before the end of my detail riding with Fockly, I pulled out my Kodak disposable camera and snapped a picture of him. Many years have passed since my ride with Fockly. Whenever I pull out my photo album and take a trip down memory, I always look at his photo and wonder what became of him. I can only hope that he survived the chaos of war in his homeland and that he, his wife, and his kids are alive and well and enjoying life.

I walked back into my room after I was done watching over Fockly and Cox's nose immediately turned up in the air.

"You smell like crap, Pitts!"

I gave him a brief explanation as to how I came to smell like a walking porta-john. I stripped myself of my disgusting uniform and walked to the showers, and spent an hour scrubbing my skin and letting the warm water cascade over me, washing away the DNA of the soldiers and marines that had sat upon my skin for the last seven hours. To be able to take a nice warm shower and wash away the day's filth was an absolute blessing that I did not want to take for granted.

After waiting for what seemed like never-ending weeks, I finally received word that I was going to be going on my first patrol outside of the wire. I would be riding with Lieutenant Michaels in his assigned Humvee Alpha 26. Knowing that I was getting ready to go outside the wire for the first time, you could easily assume that I would have been a nervous wreck considering that less than two months ago, Deshon had met his untimely death in Ramadi, but that was not the case. I was fired up and ready to be an infantryman at war. I was ready to put all of my infantry skills to use. I sat in the rear of Alpha 26 as our convoy of four Humvees left the Camp Victory ECP (Entry Control Point).

What I was expecting going on my first patrol was an intense trial of combat where I would be able to show myself worthy of the 10th Mountain Division tab on my uniform like the bold 10th Mountain soldiers who had come before me. What I got was the exact opposite of what I was expecting, which was mind-numbing boredom. We rolled around the Iraq countryside in what seemed like a circle. I was positive that we had rolled past the same mud hut more times than I could count. I remember seeing an Iraqi lady hanging up her laundry outside as her kids played.

This did not feel nor look like the brutal battlefield that I saw on the news. For weeks we rolled around in the same area with no sign of danger to our lives or the sound of gunfire or explosions in the distance.

"A vehicle just rolled over in the canal! We need help here, fast!" A panicked voice yelled over the radio.

The canals in Iraq, which we referred to as "turd ditches," were dangerous and always filled with water. They had claimed the lives of many soldiers. As we pulled up, the dust was starting to settle, and my buddy, Private First Class Paul Orgler, or as we all called him, OG, was standing at the top of the canal. His DCU's were drenched, and his IBA was sitting on the ground. He was nervously smoking a cigarette. He had been in the machine gun turret when the vehicle rolled into the canal. OG, along with everyone, narrowly escaped with their lives.

"Pitts. Download your gear. We are going in to recover the sensitive items," Lieutenant Michaels ordered me.

Lieutenant Michaels, myself, and others from the platoon waded into the filthy muck and attempted to salvage anything we could from the vehicle. We pulled out boxes of ammunition and all of our radio equipment. It was not uncommon for the insurgents to go into the canals after a rollover and try to recover items such as ammo or explosives that they could use it against us. The insurgents were crafty and innovative. So much so that we had to be careful in how we disposed of our own trash because they would use that against us as well. We were not even allowed to discard our dead batteries because the insurgents were known to use those as shrapnel in their explosive devices to wound and maim us.

Alpha Company commander Captain Shaw took it upon himself to have us set up a combat outpost in one of Uday Hussain's palaces that had been bombed during the initial invasion of Iraq. It was not long until our new outpost was nicknamed OP (Out Post) Shaw. We would spend the majority of our time at this location and conduct our operations from there. There were no creature comforts here like those of Camp Victory. We relieved ourselves in MRE boxes and tossed them into the trench that surrounded the former party palace. We were constantly exposed to the 110 plus degree temperatures of the Iraqi summer. White streaks of salt marked our uniforms from the excessive amount of sweat and electrolytes flowing from our pores.

Not too long after our turd ditch recovery, I started to feel ill. I sat on an empty MRE box as my body expelled everything from the inside of me. I violently dry heaved to the point that I thought I was going to pass out. The blood vessels in my eyes had ruptured from dry heaving leaving my eyes bloodshot. The last thing I wanted was to leave my brothers out here without me. I was combat ineffective in my current state and was sent back to camp.

"You seem to have a stomach viral infection of some sort." Our company doctor informed me.

I spent the next four days in my room on lockdown, recovering from viral gastroenteritis (stomach flu). The soldiers referred to it as Saddam's revenge or the Iraqi ass fire. I was unable to eat and keep any of my food down. I would drink water and it ran straight through me. If the insurgents did not kill me first, the foreign bacteria that had invaded my body felt like it would. If I had to guess, wading around in the canals was where I contracted the virus.

Once I recovered, I was ecstatic to be back with my brothers at OP Shaw. I did not miss anything significant in the time I was gone, but things were starting to pick up in our AO. We started erecting checkpoints and conducting cordon and search operations looking for suspected terrorists, bomb makers, and weapon caches. I was often stuck manning the 240 during the cordon and search operations, which I did not mind at first, but I soon grew frustrated watching all the other soldiers patrolling on foot through the neighborhoods and fields. As much as I loved the 240, I wanted to be on foot and in the stack of soldiers storming the building, not outside pulling security.

When we were not conducting combat operations, we were back at the OP Shaw, pulling guard and waiting for our next set of orders. Even though life at OP Shaw could be miserable, the local Iraqi kids would come around and hang out.

"Mister, mister, give me food." Mister, mister, give me water." They constantly begged. You could not help but feel bad for them. Many of them looked malnourished and wore clothes that were either way too big or way too small for them. One young Iraqi boy, probably no more than four years old, looked as though he was wearing his little sisters' pink shirt that was way too small for him.

We would give the kids all the less than desirable, uneaten MREs. Most of us did not trust the kids because we had heard the horror stories of kids being strapped with bombs and walking up to troops and detonating themselves and kids picking up rifles and firing shots at American troops as well. For our entertainment, we would have the kids fight each other, and we would give the winner the candy from our MREs. There were a few kids who had become some of our favorites and that we slightly trusted. The Ali brothers, whose parents thought it would be a good idea to name both of their sons Ali, were two of our favorites. We could give them money, and they would go and retrieve any items that we wanted from Iraqi sodas, DVDs, and food. A lot of the soldiers became accustomed to buying the "freaky, freaky" DVDs that we were forbidden from having in the country.

After one of our long stints at OP Shaw, we went back to Camp Victory for a break. August 19, 2004, Staff Sergeant Linder ordered Cox and me to put on our PT clothes and to meet him in front of his room for PT. We ran up the road to commo hill to run sprints. Commo hill was the largest hill on Camp Victory and housed all the major communication equipment for the camp. Once at the top, you could see the entire camp. We ran wind sprints up to the top of the hill until our lungs were about to pop. As Cox and I were crouched over with our hands on our knees trying to recover, Staff Sergeant Linder spoke.

"Do either of you know Titus and Risner from Bravo Company?"

I took one hand from my knee and placed it in the air in response to his question. I was not a real friend of either, but I remembered having run into each of them back at Fort Drum during our pre-deployment training.

With his hands on his head, trying to catch his breath and in a cold and callous manner, Staff Sergeant Linder spoke, "Well, they are dead."

Specialist Brandon T. Titus of Boise, Idaho, was KIA on August 17, 2004, in Baghdad, Iraq, by an IED that had exploded while he was manning a checkpoint. He was only 20 years old. Private First Class. Henry C. Risner of Golden, Colorado, was KIA on August 18, 2004, in Baghdad, Iraq. He was shot by an insurgent at a checkpoint as he and his fellow soldiers passed out candy to Iraqi children. He was 26. Bravo Company had been tasked with overseeing combat operations in the Baghdad suburb of Sadr City that was controlled by the Mahdi Militia led by Muqtada Al-Sadr. Sadr City had a reputation for its strong resistance to the US Military and undying loyalty to Muqtada Al-Sadr. Many brave and courageous American soldiers would breathe their last breaths in the sprawling streets of Sadr City; Specialist Titus and Private First Class Risner were the most recent to meet their fate in the Sadr City Slums.

What I can only describe as a feeling of disbelief and shock gripped me at my core. I was shocked at the news of their death, but I was also shocked at how Staff Sergeant Linder had relayed the news to us in such a careless way. I expected the news of their deaths, or any soldier's death for that matter, to be delivered in a more compassionate manner. It was no secret that Staff Sergeant Linder and I did not get along. What little respect I had for Staff Sergeant Linder was no more. I would do as ordered by him out of respect for his rank, not him as a person.

After having returned back to our rooms after PT, I showered up and put on a fresh uniform. As I was stepping out of my trailer, I saw Bravo Company lined up in a formation in front of their trailers. I could hear Taps being played as the warriors of Bravo company paid their final respects to their fallen brothers. I stopped at the top of the stairs of my trailer and watched as they mourned and paid them their proper respect.

I was sad and angered by the loss of Risner and Titus, but I felt more frustrated and useless by what I had done with my time in the country thus far. While Bravo Company was in Sadr City taking the fight to the enemy, we were rolling around in the country doing what seemed like a whole lot of nothing from my viewpoint as a Private First Class, not looking at the big picture. I had hoped that things would change. I did not want myself or my brothers to die in this foreign land, but I came here to fight, and I had yet to get the opportunity to do so, but I remained hopeful that I would get the chance.

"Pack enough stuff for seven days. We are going on an operation." Corporal Fields ordered Cox and me.

Insurgents had been using a palm tree groove in our AO to launch mortar and rockets at BIAP. Our mission was to go to that palm tree grove and deny them a safe and secure place to launch their rockets. We drove to the palm grove and searched and secured the area before we set up our temporary outpost. For seven days, we lived and operated from the palm tree grove, exposed to the unrelenting environment of Baghdad. The palm tree leaves provided very little to no shade from the sun. My already dark skin got even darker, making me look like a walking shadow draped in combat apparel. I always believed the myth that black people could not get sunburned. I proved that myth to be false. The skin on my face and my neck burned and peeled from its overexposure.

I would lay on my back at night and stare at the stars through the palm trees. The stars seemed to shine extra bright in the Middle East sky. The gentle breeze cooled down my overheated body. It was a beautiful and peaceful moment, although I was in a war zone where people wanted to kill me. Small drops of rain started to fall from the sky, landing on my face. In the wink of an eye, the heavens opened and rain-soaked us as we sat in our patrol base. My uniform was soaked. Thick clumps of mud started to cling onto my boots and uniform.

The thought of taking part in a seven-day operation sounded thrilling on the front end; however, in actuality, it was boring beyond belief. We continued our bizarre conversations, rotated in and out of guard duty, and did whatever we could to occupy our minds. At the end of our seven-day stint in the palm grove, we broke down our patrol base and prepared to return back to camp.

Upon returning to base, I went to the communications tent to check my email. I saw that my mom had emailed, and I was overjoyed to read her message. What I expected to read was a heartfelt email of her telling me how much she missed me, but what I read was another reminder of the cost of war.

My mother's email informed me that a member of our church, Gary Vaillant, had been killed in Iraq. The pit in my stomach had returned once again and was becoming all too familiar to me. The feelings of sadness and anger were starting to become the norm in my world. Army Staff Sergeant Gary A. Vaillant of Trujillo, Puerto Rico (41) was KIA September 5, 2004, in Khalidiya, Iraq, when an anti-tank mine exploded beside his M1A1 Abrams tank that he was commanding. He was assigned to the 2nd Battalion 72nd Armor

Regiment. Brother Gary Vaillant was loved and adored by all. He was the Spanish interpreter at our church and a true man of God and preached the Holy Bible with a fire in his soul. He and my father were great friends, and I had the opportunity to spend a lot of time with him and his family in my teenage years before the war.

My last time seeing Brother Gary Vaillant was when I was working at the PX (Postal Exchange) on Fort Knox. He had come in to buy a new refrigerator before he deployed to the Middle East for the invasion of Iraq. I disclosed to him my decision to join the army infantry and how excited I was to serve my country. Instead of trying to talk me out of joining, he prayed over me and embraced me with a big hug, and told me how much he loved me. Not only was he a great soldier, but he was also a true believer and follower of Jesus Christ. There was nothing on this earth that could shake his faith, not even war.

I was pained reading about his death, but I also felt comforted knowing that Brother Gary Vaillant was no longer on this war-torn earth and that he was now resting in the arms of his savior in heavenly bliss. Not only would I miss him, but his church family and his wife and kids would miss him, and they would have given anything to have him back in their lives.

Thus far, Alpha company had been spared by the gods of war. We had a few close calls here and there, but we were all still accounted for. Death had not come to Alpha Company, but it seemed to be hovering over us and sweeping up all those around us. October 1, 2004, a convoy of soldiers from the 1st of the 509th Infantry Battalion were attacked with an IED near our AO. The IED had engulfed the Humvee in flames. We were tasked with going to the site of the attack to help secure the area and extract one of the soldiers who was trapped inside.

Just prior to arriving, we were told to disregard as they were able to get their brother out of the Humvee. Specialist Andrew Brown of Pleasant Mount, Pennsylvania, had been wounded in the IED attack and suffered severe wounds and burns to his entire body. He was

MEDEVAC (Medical Evacuation) by helicopter from the site of the attack to the CSH (Combat Support Hospital) in BIAP. I had hoped that he would recover from his injuries and continue to live his life. Seven days later, on October 8, 2004, he succumbed to his injuries at the age of 22.

Bravo Company continued to suffer casualties in their AO. We were stunned when we learned that another Bravo Company Barbarian, Private David L. Waters of Auburn, California, was KIA on October 14, 2004, in Baghdad. During one of their patrols, his vehicle was struck by an IED. He had only lived for 19 years. Our hearts cried for our Bravo Company brothers because they had lost another one of their brave brothers.

The night of October 16, 2004, a platoon from Alpha Company had been called to secure an OH-58D (Kiowa Warrior) crash site not too far from OP Shaw. Pilots of the 1st Battalion of the 25th Aviation Regiment were flying a recon mission in our AO when the two Kiowa Warriors unexpectedly collided in mid-air. I listened to the chaos on our radios as I lay prone on the balcony behind the 240-machine providing security to OP Shaw.

Killed in the crash were Army Captain Christopher B. Johnson (29) of Excelsior Springs, Missouri and Army CW3 (Chief Warrant Officer 3) William L. Brennan (36) of Bethlehem, Connecticut. As I stared off into the darkness of the night and watched green tracers fly in the distance, I thought about the soldiers who had just died in service to their country not too far from my location. I had only been in Iraq for four months, and I felt very fortunate to have made it this far, knowing that many others had not.

A stream of death seemed to be flowing, and it was constant with no end in sight. It felt as though we would soon be forced to drink from it and taste its bitterness at any moment. Thoughts of my own impending death or someone from Alpha Company started to creep into my mind, but I could not let those thoughts take hold over me, or else I would become ineffective in my duties. I learned to suppress and lock away my feelings in the deepest part of my mind so that I could continue to function. I felt numb due to the constant exposure to death and bad news that was now the norm in my life. I had no right to complain about anything that I was experiencing because I volunteered for this. After all, this was what I wanted. And I would soon get what I wanted in a place called Abu Ghraib.

[9]

THE REAL IEDS OF ABU GHRAIB

Abu Ghraib's name had become infamous worldwide just seven months prior due to the media releasing photos depicting US troops abusing and degrading Iraqi prisoners of war in the Abu Ghraib Prison. We knew that we were going into hostile territory. The insurgents wanted nothing more than to maim, kill, capture, and torture any Americans in the area to avenge what had happened to their brothers in Abu Ghraib Prison.

Shortly after the media released the details of the Abu Ghraib prison scandal, insurgents released a video portraying Nicholas Berg, an American contractor, being decapitated by Al Qaeda leader Abu Musab Al-Zarqawi. They discarded his headless body on an overpass in Baghdad not too far from ECP 4. We sat and watched the video of Nicholas Burg being savagely beheaded, and it stoked the flames of the American fighting spirit within us all. It was officially terrorist hunting season, and Abu Ghraib would be our hunting ground. We were ready to execute our next mission, but we were fully aware that the insurgents would also be hunting us as well.

The smothering Iraq heat that had greeted me five months prior had retreated and given way to a bone-chilling November cold. Not only had the weather changed, but the scenery of our AO had changed with the seasons. I stood in the turret behind the 240 Bravo as our convoy slowly crept down the street of one of the many slums of Abu Ghraib. My gloves, beanie, and neck gator gave my skin refuge from the cold. The sun was starting to rise, casting light into the shadowy positions around me in which I could not see. A light fog lay over the neighborhood, and my breath could be seen leaving my body every time I exhaled. My nose detected the scent of fresh sewage haunting the air, accompanied by the visual of solid and liquid waste polluting the unpaved, muddy street. My head, eyes, and neck worked in unison to cover my sector of fire, but there were too many dangerous areas for me to cover, and I had to make peace with that. The two-story Iraqi homes were draped with laundry and rugs hanging off of the balconies. The houses were secured behind eight-foot-tall mud walls that all looked suspicious to me.

"This is a great place to launch an ambush," I said to myself. I envisioned the legendary and mythical insurgent sniper Juba prowling on one of the many rooftops that surrounded us as he patiently waited to take his shot and make one of us famous with his sniper video.

From the first moment we stepped foot on the streets of Abu Ghraib I could sense the enemy around us. The disparity between Abu Ghraib and our previous AO was unequivocal. Peaceful days and nights had been replaced with the echoes of explosions and gunfire in the distance. The beautiful rural countryside we viewed daily was now a Middle Eastern slum. Even the atmosphere had shifted, the sinister ambiance of Abu Ghraib gave me insight as to why this place was known as Abu Nam, Abu Grave, or simply the Grave amongst those who patrolled here. The way the populace would stop and stare at us as we drove and walked past them communicated to us that we were infidels and we were not welcomed in their country or community.

"That guy has a cell phone! Stop him!" someone yelled.

Everyone in our dismounted patrol looked to the right in sync. I looked at the person in question through the optic on my rifle. I saw an older Iraqi man wearing a black suit with a cellphone in one hand and plastic bags in the other as he strolled towards the nearby homes. The red dot from my AimPoint optic stood out against his black suit. Insurgents frequently used cell phones to detonate IEDs, so there was a legit reason to be alarmed. We moved towards the suspicious Iraqi man, but there was a small creek between him and us. I looked at the water, and the first thing that stuck out to me was the thick green froth resting on top of the still water. The pungent smell that radiated from the creek was offensive, but we could not let that creek and its filth stop us from possibly preventing an attack. We plunged into the syrup-like water that came up to our waist, careful not to let our weapons get wet and keeping our muzzles aimed at the Iraqi and the cluster of homes that he was approaching.

We accosted the Iraqi and had our interpreter question him. Someone took his cell phone and examined it. My adrenaline pumped, and I could hear my heartbeat in my ears. I scanned the row of buildings with my trigger finger ready to spring into action, but just as fast as things escalated, they deescalated. We released the Iraqi after we determined that he was not a threat to us at that time.

Abu Gharib was an intense area to patrol. But what we were experiencing in Abu Ghraib was not uncommon at that time in Iraq; the entire country was a menace to any troops or Americans that were there during this time. The Marines and various Army units were preparing to launch Operation Phantom Fury, a major assault on the city of Fallujah, to reclaim the city from insurgents. We were only 30 miles from Fallujah, and we were ready for spill-over violence to trickle down to us in our AO.

I had grown weary of riding in the Humvee and manning the 240 Bravo. I had yet to unleash the full power of the 240 Bravo onto the opposing force and grew bored just waiting. Lucky for me, moving to Abu Ghraib allowed me more time out of the turret and on foot in our walking patrols as a rifleman. However, every time we left Camp Victory and drove to our AO in Abu Ghraib, I was uneasy. Whenever

I would open the door of my Humvee to step out into the unknown dangers of Abu Ghraib is one of our roving patrols, I was edgy because every step you took in Abu Ghraib could have been your last. We all had legit reasons to be fearful, but all of us were somehow able to push aside our fear to focus on the mission at hand. I had to work extra hard to stay focused because I would be going home on R&R (Rest and Relaxation) in a few weeks, and I could not afford to let my mind wander from my current assignment.

"IED! Get back!" I shouted. As we were patrolling down the side of a busy road parallel to a densely populated neighborhood, I looked down at my feet and saw black wire partially covered with dirt. Everyone pulled back and took cover, and we set up a security perimeter. My heart was beating at max capacity.

"Where is it again, Pitts?" Corporal Fields asked.

"It's about 25 meters ahead of us and runs into the asphalt," I explained and pointed.

EOD was hours away from us, and we were in a tactically bad spot. We could not afford to sit and wait for hours, so we sent a few guys to investigate. They determined what I found was an old telephone wire buried in the ground and was starting to become uncovered. There was no IED threat.

"Good eye Pitts!" someone acknowledged me.

We found ourselves walking down a crowded city street close to the Abu Ghraib Bizarre during one of our patrols. All eyes were on us as we boldly walked in a place that we were not welcomed. My eyes caught the attention of this young, adorable Iraqi girl. She appeared to be maybe four years old and melted my heart. As I walked past her and who I assumed was her father, I reached into my cargo pocket and pulled out a bag of skittles that I had been carrying with me. I kneeled onto one knee and handed the little girl the bag of skittles. Her eyes lit up, and I could tell that I had just made her extremely happy. I rose to my feet and started walking again. I had only taken maybe three or four steps, and I felt something hit me in the back. I turned around to see what it was. I looked on the ground and saw the bag of skittles that I had just given to the little girl. The man that escorted her looked at me with disgust. His fist was bawled, and his eyes filled with hate and rage. He wanted nothing to do with my attempt to win the hearts and minds of him and his daughter. The only thing he wanted was for all of us to die a violent and painful death. I could feel his wrath penetrating my armor into my soul.

"Pitts, grab the extra 240 from the back of the Humvee. You are carrying it for this patrol," Lieutenant Michaels advised me.

You would have thought someone told me I won the mega millions lottery. I grinned from ear to ear, dashed towards the back of A26, and removed the extra 240. I loaded a belt of 7.62 ammo into the feed tray and closed the cover. I slung the sling over my right shoulder, and I could feel the pressure and weight of the 240 resting upon me. My back muscles tightened from the load. It was so heavy, but it felt so good having the power of the 240 at my fingertips for our patrol down Phase Line Magenta. Phase Line Magenta was in the heart of Abu Ghraib and was crowded. Typically, I would have been nervous going into such a location, but not on this day. On this day, I felt impenetrable. I was more super than Superman. I knew that I was the most intimidating soldier the people of Abu Ghraib had ever seen. I walked with perfect posture: my shoulders back, head raised, and my nose in the air pompously. I was fearless. I walked with an arrogance that dared anyone to challenge my brothers and me to a fight.

I cannot recall how far we walked, but I did not want this patrol to end without a fight. I had the power of the highest casualty-producing weapon in my grasp, and I wanted to use it for the purpose in which it was created. We finished our patrol, and I begrudgingly unloaded the 240 and placed it back into the rear of A26. We were done running patrols for the day, and we all loaded up in our Humvees to return to camp.

On a rare day off, I learned that Bravo Company lost another soldier. Specialist Brian K. Baker (27) of West Seneca, New York, was killed by a car bomb while on patrol on November 7, 2004.

Hearing of another loss for Bravo Company hurt. But what made his death even more painful was learning that his wife was pregnant with twin girls who would only know their father's face from photographs. Yet again, my heart went out to Bravo company.

As the first-ever national Iraqi elections were nearing, we continued our blazing pace of patrols and operations in our AO, trying to secure Abu Ghraib and flush out the insurgents operating in the area. We worked around the clock 24/7. The pace was draining, but I loved every minute of it. Moving under the cover of darkness into an urban setting with no light. Gazing through my NVGs and seeing my brothers moving in tactical formation with their rifles dialed in on the buildings scanning for threats as the streams of light from their PAC4 lasers transitioned covering their sectors of fire. It was a glorious feeling seeing and being a part of the American war machine in action.

November 21, 2004, we were on a routine patrol; it was a relatively calm day. Nothing appeared suspicious or out of the ordinary as our convoy maneuvered down the busy street. I stood in the turret surveying the landscape and droves of people moving about the area when I heard a loud explosion behind me. I whipped my head around, and the Humvee behind me had disappeared in a large black and orange fireball. The world moved in slow motion until time came to a complete stop; the people in the area scattered, trying to flee the violence while the smoke from the explosion wafted away, revealing Private First Class Luke Post lying on the ground. A pool of blood formed around his head.

Private First Class Luke Post, a native of New Jersey and a good friend of mine, laid upon the blacktop, not moving. Soldiers kneeled over him and proceeded to give him first-aid. I could not take my eyes off the carnage.

"Post!" I screamed out, wanting to hear him yell back at me that he was OK.

"Pitts! Pull security! You can't help him from there!" Sergeant Cardenas shouted at me.

My focus was on my friend, who had possibly just died right before my eyes, as opposed to the possible threats right in front of me. My lack of experience in dealing with such traumatic and horrifying experiences was evident. I aimed the 240 at the crowd and looked for additional threats. Anger swelled up inside of me, and all I wanted to do was squeeze the trigger of the 240 and mow down every Iraqi in my sights with a fury of machine gunfire. They were all guilty of killing my friend. Post sat up and was helped to his feet by those who had rendered first aid to him. He held a bandage to his neck, and I could see his blood leaking through the gauze. His IBA and uniform had been stained by his blood as well. He was escorted to another Humvee and placed in the back. I was elated that he had not been KIA as I first thought.

After the explosion, a squad of our guys exited their Humvees and went on a hunting expedition to find those guilty of detonating the IED. They returned with two young Iraqi men who they had handcuffed. They placed sandbags over their heads and put them in separate Humvees. I looked at him with unfiltered hatred and contempt. I wanted to kick him square in the face with my boot and knock all of his teeth out, but I had to maintain my composure and professionalism. It took everything within me not to give in to the temptation to do so.

We took Private First Class Post to the 31st CSH (combat support hospital) in the Green Zone. We learned that one of the pieces of shrapnel narrowly missed a major artery in his neck. He was lucky to be alive.

I had survived my first encounter with the insurgent force, and I was grateful. Even more grateful were the guys in the Humvee who took a direct hit. We had a platoon AAR (After Action Review) to discuss what we did well and the areas we could have performed better during the attack. Sergeant Cardenas took it upon himself to point out the critical error I made during the incident.

"Pitts, I know you were concerned for Post. We all were. But you cannot lose focus of your job in the heat of the moment. Instead of watching the crowd for threats, you were focusing on Post. This is a first for many of you in this environment, but we cannot afford to lose focus on the task at hand. Do better next time."

I have never been an egomaniac, and I always resolved to be a humble person, but at that moment, what little ego I might have had was annihilated. I was embarrassed by my actions. I felt I had failed my brothers in the heat of the moment, and I was being called out for it. My heart was in the right place, but my mind should not have been where my heart was. I wanted to try and refute Sergeant Cardenas and explain to him and the platoon my actions, but I knew that there was nothing that I could say that could justify my actions. I had to swallow my pride and accept that I was not up to par in my responsibilities at that moment. I knew it was not a personal attack on me. Sergeant Cardenas was trying to help me be a better soldier. Days later, I would be presented with another moment to show that I had learned from my mistake.

Alpha Company had been tasked with going into an uncharted and dangerous section of Abu Ghraib. Our job was to clear the insurgents and their IEDs from the area along Route Forest Green. Route Forest Green ran parallel to the Abu Ghraib Dairy Factory, a hotbed for insurgent activity. Our convoy sat in a line on Route Forest Green, getting ready to push forward to the end of the route. I stood in my Humvee and noticed a family of ducks swimming about in the small creek that ran along the right side of the road. Greenery was abundant in this area ranging from grass to bushes that ran alongside the road, hence the name Route Forest Green. An Iraqi man and his young daughters were in their front yard playing but soon retreated inside their residence. From the look of where we were, you could almost assume this was not that bad of an area, but looks can be misleading.

A large explosion erupted from the ground and consumed the Humvee driven by my best friend, Randy Guerra. I was two vehicles behind where the blast occurred, and the shock waves rattled my insides, followed by a deafening boom.

After yelling some obscenities, I placed the buttstock of the 240 into my shoulders, pulled the charging handle sending a round into the chamber, and was ready to launch rounds downrange. My initial instinct was to check on the status of my best friend and all those riding ahead of me. Still, I had to fight my compassionate nature and fixate on my soldiering responsibilities and scanning my sector of fire for any threats.

The dust slowly started to settle. My ears rang and ached from the percussion of the blast. I could hear faint yelling and screaming through the buzzing in my ears. I could see my brothers scurrying about with their rifles at the ready in my peripheral. The seconds and minutes passed, but they felt like hours. I then saw Randy stumbling around the outside of the severely damaged Humvee. I could tell that he was shaken up, but I was happy to see him standing upright.

"Randy! You good?" I shouted to him.

He shot me a thumbs up and let me know he was OK, and that was more than enough for me.

"You are not going to win, Randy," I said to him referring to competition.

Randy shot a smile my way and laughed. The rest of the guys in the Humvee were OK as well. They all had their bells rung, but they were alive and did not have a single scratch, and we could not ask for anything more. I can only attribute their surviving the IED to the prayers of our friends and family back home.

This was our second contact with the enemy. However, it is more accurate to describe this as our second contact with the enemies' weapon of choice because we did not see the enemy, but they saw us. They hid from us like cowards and launched their attacks on us. This was the second time we had been targeted, yet we could not return fire because no one had fired at us yet. This only entrenched our distrust and hatred for Abu Ghraib, Iraq, and its citizens even more. We could not clearly see the enemy; everyone we saw in our AO was complicit. Not only does fighting an unseen enemy play with you psychologically, but it was also frustrating and stressful. And with things started getting very stressful, we started taking our stress out on each other.

Being away from home, operating at such a high tempo, and being under the constant threat from IED attacks or mortar rounds started to take a toll on all of us. Aside from the gym or running, there was no true outlet to release your anger and frustration. You can only suppress your anger, fear, and irritation so much before it naturally starts to release itself.

Cox and I were not only battle buddies, but we were also best friends. We depended on each other daily, but we also lived together and learned to annoy the hell out of each other. We would argue over the dumbest things, but all those small arguments and the frustrations started to build up in a major way as tensions began to build between us.

Tensions between us had been bubbling for quite some time. I cannot recall what sparked the argument, probably something so unimportant, but we were in a full-blown yelling constant, and then the stupidity escalated.

"I will knock you out!" I yelled to Cox.

"If you touch me, I will lock and load and shoot you!" Cox replied.

Had this happened back stateside, I would have ignored all of this nonsense and just gone about my business. But here in Iraq, it was different. I could not resist my primal instincts or my violent urges anymore. My bullcrap meter had finally filled up and was overflowing. Not even the threat of being shot point blank in the chest registered to me. Common sense was nowhere to be found between us, and we had both gone over the edge.

I walked over to Cox as he sat on his bed, and I slammed my fist into his face. I wanted to say it felt good, but I did not feel anything. Cox looked at me with a rage in his eyes that I had never seen. He was always cool, calm, and collected, but his eyes and face expressed to me that the Cox I knew before was not in the room with me. He reached over, grabbed his rifle, put in a 30-round magazine, and pulled the charging handle, putting a round into the chamber. He lifted his rifle and pointed it directly at me. I walked up to the muzzle of the rifle, grabbed it with my right hand, and pushed it into my chest.

"Do it then! Do it!" I shouted.

Cox looked at me, and I heard the selector switch on his rifle go from safe to semi-fire, and I waited. We stared into each other's eyes without blinking, not thinking of the consequences of our actions in that intense moment for what seemed like hours. In an unexplainable moment, the tension between us magically vanished, and we were back to normal. I looked at Cox, and I was not mad anymore. He lowered his weapon and sat on his bed, and I walked over to my bed and sat down.

"I'm sorry, man. I shouldn't have hit you." I said regretfully.

"Yeah, I'm sorry too, man. I should not have done that either." He replied.

"What is wrong with us?" I asked.

We looked up at each other with confusion, trying to sort out what had just happened, unable to logically explain the potentially deadly event that had just transpired between us.

"Man, I'm super stressed out," Cox relayed to me.

"Yeah, me too." I coincided.

In a bizarre twist of events, we laughed at the incident simultaneously, and we never had another issue between the two of us for the remainder of the time we spent together.

My aggression had started to grow out of my control, and it would soon lead me to step out of line and call out Staff Sergeant Linder. It was no secret that Staff Sergeant Linder and I did not get along. I obeyed any order I was given from him out of respect for the rank. Regardless of my obeying orders and trying to be a good soldier, nothing I did was ever good enough for Staff Sergeant Linder, and the way he looked at me let me know that I was on his black list. A part of me wondered if he even really cared if I came home alive or not.

While conducting checkpoint operations, I witnessed him point his rifle at another Staff Sergeant and pull the trigger, which was followed by a loud click. Staff Sergeant Linder laughed, but the other Staff Sergeant did not think it was so funny; however, they were good friends, so it was a joke between them. Had I done something like that, he would have ended my world. I was appalled at the hypocrisy that I had just witnessed. He was supposed to be my leader, but the only thing I learned from him was how not to lead and the type of leader I did not want to be. I viewed him as a bully and a coward who hid behind the rank on his collar.

The final straw was drawn during a routine patrol. The higher-ups wanted us to wear our ESS ballistic goggles anytime we stepped out of the wire due to troops taking shrapnel to their eyes from IEDs. As I stood in the turret, I briefly pulled up my goggles as I was scanning my area so that I could see better.

"Pitts! Put your goggles back on!" Staff Sergeant Linder yelled at me.

He was not wearing his goggles either, as he corrected me.

"Come see me when we get back to base Pitts," he demanded.

The rage inside of me started to build up and slowly started to overflow at the double standards and his lack of leading by example.

"From now on, you will wear your helmet and goggles anytime you step out of your room!" He berated me then disappeared to his room.

I had spent the last 11 months of my life in fear of Staff Sergeant Linder. The fear of him, his rank, and UCMJ (Uniform Code of Military Justice) action against me no longer mattered. I had once again journeyed to that place in my mind where common sense, decency, and respect were void, and violence, anger, and rage were the only things I could comprehend.

I ran up to Staff Sergeant Linder's room and violently slammed my ACH into his door multiple times while telling him to step outside.

"Come out here now! I am tired of your crap! Take your rank off, and let us handle this like men!"

I had heard the stories of how problems used to be solved in the army back in the day. If two guys had a problem with each other, they would "take it to the wood line" and solve their problems one on one, and rank could not be used as a weapon. I wanted to take Staff Sergeant Linder to the wood line and see what kind of a man he was without his rank, which was where he drew all of his power from.

As I kicked and pounded away at his door and jiggled the handle to try and open it so that I could see him face to face, my entire squad ran up behind me and pulled me down from his door.

"Calm down, Pitts! You are going to get yourself in trouble. It's not worth it!" one of them said.

It was absolutely worth it to me. Anger and adrenaline swished through my veins. I was no longer in control of myself. My emotions had taken full control of me, and I was being driven by pure fury.

Once my rage faded, I was able to start thinking clearly. I was not a problem child. I never got in trouble, nor did I do anything to discredit the army or bring shame upon my unit, so I couldn't understand why I was always being treated as though I was. And because of that, I was ready and willing to face UCMJ action just to make a point, but my squad stepped in to spare me having to go that route.

"Pitts. If it makes you feel any better, we will all wear our ACHs and goggles with you. We will not let you do it by yourself."

We all donned our ACHs and goggles and marched to the DFAC for dinner. As we sat and ate, wearing our combat gear looking like complete morons, we all shared a laugh at my uncontrolled outburst.

"Pitts, I didn't know that you had that in you."

Not too long after this incident, I learned that I was going to be reassigned to another platoon as a SAW (Squad Automatic Weapon) gunner. The changes would not happen right away, but I was happy knowing that I would no longer be under Staff Sergeant Linder's toxic leadership.

November 25, 2004, Thanksgiving Day- I knew we had a long day ahead of us. We were heading back to Route Forest Green to continue our clearance mission. Despite the nerve-wrecking mission ahead of us, we had one thing to look forward to at the end of the day, and that was a delicious Thanksgiving meal. Being away from home during the holidays was tough. I thought about everyone back home gathered around the table enjoying each other's company.

Captain Shaw tagged along with us for our Thanksgiving Day patrol. He walked up to my Humvee and casually chatted with me.

"Are you ready for some turkey, Pitts?" He questioned me.

"You know it, sir!!"

"Me too! We are going to get ready to call it for today and head back to camp."

As he walked away towards the front of the convoy, Randy emerged from the Humvee in front of me. He stood with his rifle in hand and chatted with me. As I chatted and joked away with Randy, I saw the members of 1st squad walking back to our convey. They were about 50 yards from the front of the convoy. I was mid-laugh when the ground beneath 1st squad opened up and spewed out flames, dirt, smoke, and shrapnel. Time once again moved in slow motion as the 1st squad were swallowed up in the explosion. I could see the shock waves from the blast ripple through the ground. Boom! The delayed and deafening sound of the explosion rumbled in my eardrums.

I watched my sector of fire vigilantly and stood behind the 240, ready for a fight. I knew that the bullets were about to start flying because of our location. The Milk Factory was just ahead of us on the left and was about 75 yards off of the road; it had been used before by the insurgents to ambush troops in the AO. I had no clue as to the status of the members of 1st squad. I prayed over them as I manned the 240.

I briefly glanced over at the chaos at the site of the blast and saw Corporal Tolleson being carried to a Humvee, followed by Sergeant Pedro. I could see blood on the ground where they had been.

Corporal Tolleson, the tall, skinny, and outrageously funny Texan, had taken a large piece of shrapnel to his ankle, almost severing it from his leg. Sergeant Pedro had taken a decent-sized piece of shrapnel to his forearm. Private First Class Domenique Misuraca was caught in the middle of the blast as well, but he miraculously did not suffer any major injuries and was able to walk away. The power of the blast blew Specialist Piant across the street and into the canal. He suffered from small shards of shrapnel in his face and was concussed.

As we loaded the wounded and started to get our convoy turned around, I heard a loud whistling sound followed by a loud boom. A puff of smoke rose from the field to the right of us, about 50 yards away from our convoy.

"Mortars!" Someone yelled.

The insurgents had been watching and anticipated us being in this exact spot and had the location dialed in and started dropping mortars on us. Another mortar impacted the field, and this one was even closer. They were starting to walk the mortars into our exact position. The longer we sat in this position, the more likely we were to have mortar land directly in the middle of our security perimeter.

"Let's get the hell out of here!"

My adrenal glands dumped another load of adrenaline into my veins and went straight to my heart, causing it to throb and pound violently inside of my chest. It was flight or fight, and I was ready to fight, but there was no one to fight. We were able to get the convoy turned around. The Humvees engines roared from the accelerator being mashed to the floor as we moved out of the kill zone to Route Huskies and rushed our wounded to the 31st CSH on BIAP. Our convoy came to a screeching halt in the front of the building. I watched from the turret as the medical staff poured out of the building with gurneys in hand. Corporal Tolleson and Sergeant Pedro were placed on the gurneys and rushed inside. Private First Class Misuraca and Specialist Piant walked in just behind them.

After waiting for an update on the wounded, Captain Shaw informed us that they were going to be fine, but they had a long road to recovery ahead of them. Tolleson and Pedro would soon be on their way to Landstuhl Regional Medical Center in Germany to have their damaged limbs repaired. We were happy that they were going to be OK.

We left the 31st CSH and headed to a nearby DFAC for Thanksgiving Dinner. We were dirty and sweaty from our day's mission. As we paraded into the DFAC, we were stopped by a chow hall Nazi who informed us that we were not permitted to enter the DFAC because of our appearance. If looks could kill, this young soldier would have died an instant and violent death. We started to gripe and complain. The tone of our voices comminuted our displeasure at what he just told us. Who was he to tell us that we were not fit to eat in this DFAC? He had no clue as to what we had just experienced outside the safety of the camp walls. He had no inkling that two of our brothers had been severely wounded. We felt insulted and disrespected.

As we started to voice our opinions about the situation, Captain Shaw stepped forward and told all of us two go outside. He knew that if he did not step in and pull us back that we were going to traumatize the young troop in front of us. We hastily went outside and waited.

Even though we were all offended, having been denied entry into the DFAC, our true wrath had originated from what happened to Tolleson and Pedro. The young soldier was unfortunately caught in the wave of our anger, and we were taking out our frustration on him for simply trying to follow the orders he was given. It was no fault of his own, and he did not know what we had just gone through.

Captain Shaw came out of the DFAC a few minutes later and waved for us to come back in. One by one, we went down the line and received our fair share of turkey, mashed potatoes and gravy, and vegetables. It was later in the evening, and the DFAC was mostly empty. We all sat in the dimly lit DFACE in silence, looking down at our food. It was the quietest I had ever heard our platoon. Typically, you would hear laughter, vulgar language, and trash-talking amongst us, but not on this Thanksgiving Day. We collectively sat in the heaviness and stillness of the moment.

My appetite perished with the sight of my brothers being blown up and the chilling sound of mortars falling and impacting close to me. I shoveled a heaping spoon of mashed potatoes and gravy into my mouth, but my mind was still too busy trying to process what I had just witnessed and would not let my taste buds experience the taste of Thanksgiving.

[10]

NO REST NO RELAXATION

"Welcome home, baby." My mother gently whispered to me with tears in her eyes.

"I missed you so much, baby," Dede said as she greeted me with a big kiss.

"Thank you for your service, sir. And welcome home." Strangers said to me as they passed by.

My heart overflowed with joy and happiness, which were exotic emotions to my hardened heart. I had become so detached and emotionally numb that I had forgotten what happiness felt like. Despite the confusing concoction of emotions that swept over me, I was home from the battlefield, but I was never made aware that the battlefield comes home with you.

My family and my wife's family all cried uncontrollably as they sat in the front row of the church pew dressed in black. With tears streaming down her face, my wife stands up and walks towards the flag-draped casket that held my remains. Lifelessly, I lay in the casket dressed in my green Class A uniform. My CIB, awards, and ribbons covered the left side of my uniform, and my blue infantry cord wrapped around my right shoulder. The 10th Mountain Division patch rested upon the left and right shoulders of my uniform. My 20-year-old wife was inconsolable as she laid across my casket and the tears from her face fell onto the American flag. As her family ran up to the casket and tried to pull her away, someone walked up to the casket and closed the lid, and trapped me inside the darkness, and I was unable to escape. I start to scream.

"Please let me out! I'm not dead!"

I was immediately awakened from my slumber covered in sweat and yelling as Dede shook me.

"Wake up, Dexter! You are having a nightmare! You are home. Calm down." Dede reassured me.

It took me a few moments to realize that I was home and sleeping in my bed and room.

Dede and I spent the first three days together in a hotel, getting reacquainted and celebrating our first wedding anniversary. Then, after spending three days of bliss together, we spent the remainder of our time together at my parents' home. It felt great to be home and be surrounded by the people I had missed so much in the last five months. However, as good as it felt to be home with my family, I had a deep sense of guilt for being comfortable at home and not being with my brothers on the other side of the world still engaging with enemy force.

While Dede and I were out driving one day down Dixie Highway, we approached the Wilson Road overpass. Upon seeing the overpass, my brain instantly associated it with danger. My adrenaline instantly spiked, and my muscle memory kicked in. I flattened the gas pedal to the floor and gripped the steering wheel tight. As soon as we passed under the overpass and were a good distance from it, I eased off the gas and let the car coast. I looked over at Dede and looked at me with a grave look of concern and worry as she gripped the door handle. I had another incident while driving through my parent's neighborhood.

As Dede and I returned to my parents' house one night, we cruised down Hill street. I saw a random and strangely placed pile of trash on the side of the road. As I took notice of the trash, I violently yanked the steering and throttled the engine, and crossed the centerline to avoid the pile of trash. Thankfully, there was no oncoming traffic. I looked over at Dede, and she was terrified as she gripped the door handle again, and her eyes were wide open.

"I'm sorry. I thought I saw something." I said to her as I tried to justify my actions.

"Dexter, please let me drive." She asked.

Without saying another word, I exited the car and sat in the passenger seat, and let her drive us the rest of the way home. When I was at home, I felt safe and secure, but whenever I left my parents' house, I had an overwhelming feeling of danger that I could not shake. I hated the way it felt. And since I did not have a weapon or anyone to truly watch my back, I hunkered down in the house as much as I could for the remainder of my time home.

I would go out to the store if I had to and, I would go and visit with friends when asked, but I stayed home as much as possible. Grand Theft Auto San Andreas had just come out, and I was eager to play it, so I used that as a distraction to take my mind off everything. I could tell that Dede was worried about me, but I could also tell that she was frustrated. She wanted to spend every moment that she could with me and wanted us to go out more and enjoy each other, but she could not pull me away from my PlayStation.

Taking full advantage of my time at home, my mother constantly hugged and kissed me and reminded me of how happy she was that I was home. It warmed my heart to see her smile so much, and it felt so comforting every time she hugged me. I always felt safe and secure whenever I rested in her arms; nothing could harm me while I was in her embrace.

When I was not playing PlayStation, I watched the news trying to keep up with everything happening back in Iraq. I would see news stories and newspaper articles about soldiers being killed in action in Baghdad, and worry would grip my heart as I thought about all my brothers over there. As much as I loved seeing my friends and family and being home, I could not enjoy my time because my mind was still in Abu Ghraib with all the Alpha Company Terminators.

The time slipped by, and it was time for me to bid my friends and family farewell. I sat in the living room with my mom the night before heading back to Iraq, and I could hear her soul crying through her eyes. I could see the worry resting upon her face as her only son was going back into harm's way. I did my best to enjoy my time home and cherish every moment, but I was ready to get back into the fight and finish this deployment. My mom let Dede and I have our last moments together as husband and wife by letting her escort me to the airport while she stayed behind. As I walked out the door, my mother hugged me and held me tighter than she had ever held me. The way she held me made me feel as though she knew something that I did not know. Her arms made me feel as though this might be the last time that we get to share such a moment. What she did not know was that I had a feeling that I was not going to make it back from the last half of this deployment.

Ever since I had the dream of lying in my casket and Dede crying over me, I viewed it as a dark omen of what was to come for me. And because of that dream, I wanted nothing more than to get my wife pregnant during my two weeks of leave, so she and my mom would both be comforted every time they looked into my child's eyes and find comfort knowing that a piece of me was still here.

Dede and I shared one final kiss in the middle of the airport. I did not care who was watching. This could be our last kiss, and I was not going to let anyone stop me from enjoying it. Tears slowly slid down her face, and I knew that it was time to go and that it would only be harder the longer I stayed. We separated, and I made my way to the awaiting plane, keeping my eyes on her as I boarded until I could no longer see her. R&R was officially over, and it was time for me to get back to work.

[11]

I CAN FEEL THEIR EYES WATCHING ME

To MY SURPRISE, nothing significant had occurred during my two-week hiatus. I was elated to know that I did not miss anything historical or of key value. As much as I enjoyed being back in the states, I was happy to be back with my brothers in Iraq.

The Abu Ghraib Expressway (Highway 97), known to the U.S. Military as Route Huskies, ran west from Camp Victory straight through the heart of Abu Ghraib. Most news stories emitting out of Iraq referenced Route Irish (Airport Road) as the world's most dangerous road. However, Route Huskies was not to be unnoticed. Route Huskies had its own sinister reputation, and we soon started to get firsthand experience into why it had developed its own deadly reputation.

We had finished up a long day of patrolling and were driving back to base via Route Huskies just before sunset. The two Kentucky boys, myself and Johnny Borne, were sitting in the back of Humvee as we made our way back. We were just outside the base when I heard a loud "pop!" The Humvee jolted from the blast.

Everyone yelled the commonly known "mother of curse words" in harmony.

The convoy continued forward to get out of the kill zone and came to a halt. I flung open the rear driver side door, exited the Humvee and took up a security position on the rear driver side, and started to scan to the south of Route Huskies. There was a small palm tree grove about 200 meters off in the distance. I then spotted a small, white vehicle driving away from the palm tree grove, leaving a trail of dust. I switched my weapon to full-auto, and I was ready to pull the trigger in anger. I waited to hear the 240 open up and start firing as well. As I placed my finger on the trigger, I thought about our ROEs (Rules of Engagement).

I could hear the voice of one of the brigade commanders explaining to us the difference between hostile action and hostile intent before we departed from Kuwait into Iraq.

"Hostile action vs. hostile intent Commandos. If you see a guy walking down the street with an RPG or AK-47, you cannot just simply shoot him. That is hostile action. But if he points that RPG or AK-47 at you, that is hostile intent, and you are cleared to fire."

"These bastards, man!" a frustrated voice called out. Lucky for us, the IED missed our Humvee. I was starting to feel as though my luck was eventually going to run out, and I was going to have to meet my fate sooner than later.

Route Huskies was filled with craters and scorch marks from IEDs and served as a ghastly reminder of where we were. The sound of gunfire and explosions constantly hung in the atmosphere. Instead of us driving up and down Route Huskies so frequently, we started setting up a static OP (observation post) on the side of Route Huskies to watch over the area.

With the backdrop of a palm tree grove behind me, I stood in the gunner's hatch of the Humvee facing east while Private First Class Millet stood watch in the west-facing Humvee. We were just west of the Abu Ghraib slums, and there was not much for us to observe south of Route Huskies. The only thing that I could see way off in the distance was a single two-story home. As I stood vigilant watching over my sector, the sound of a single gunshot and the supersonic zip of a bullet passing nearby shattered the silence of the day.

I dropped down behind the shield of my turret for cover. My heart fluttered and thumbed furiously inside my chest.

"Holy Crap," I yelled. "Millet! Did you hear that!"

I peered through a small opening in the side of the ballistic side shields to see if I could get eyes on Millet. I could see Millet's hands draped over the left and right ballistic shields as he was crouched down behind the front ballistic shield.

"Yeah, I heard it too! That was close!"

"Where the hell did that shot come from?" I thought to myself.

The only thing that I could think of was the single, two-story house far off in the distance, but the shot sounded too close for it to be that house. It was clearly a pop shot intended for me. It felt personal. The worst part was that I could not shoot back because I could not identify a target, and that agitated me—yet another close call.

January 1, 2005, New Year's Day: I awoke and stepped out of my trailer into the chilly Iraq weather. 2004 was officially behind us, and 2005 did not seem as appealing considering we still had six months left in the wastelands of Abu Ghraib. We were at the halfway point in our deployment, but home still felt so far away. It was a new year fighting the same war. The only thing that felt new on this New Year's Day was this dreadful, gloomy, and dark heaviness that seemed to linger in the atmosphere. Deep down in my spirit, I could sense that something was not right about this day. Something felt off, but I could not point out exactly what it was.

It was not unusual for me or anyone deployed to a war zone to have a sense of doom and uneasiness because of the nature of war. But this uneasiness was different. I could feel the uneasiness deep in my bones. The atmosphere and energy around me felt tense and thick.

Before I exited my room, I kneeled before God to pray. I asked God for his protection for not only me but for all my brothers on this New Year's Day. I tried to get up off of my knees and head to the waiting convoy, but something in my soul would not let me get up until I asked God to forgive me for all of my sins.

I ended my prayer with an Amen and arose to my feet, grabbed my gear, and made my way to the convoy. I looked at the faces of my brothers, and they all looked as they did as usual. Tired, frustrated, and ready to go home, which was completely normal. It was clear to me that I was the only one catching this mysterious negative vibe that seemed to encircle me. I tried to ignore the feeling and play it off as I took my position behind the 240 in A26. Lieutenant Michaels took his place in the TC seat, Private First Class David Bild sat in the driver's seat. Specialist Piant sat behind Lieutenant Michaels and our Iraqi interpreter, Saul, sat behind Bild.

As our convoy exited the heavily fortified walls of Camp Victory and traveled down Route Huskies, I took a deep breath and tightly grasped the grip of the 240-machine gun with my left hand. The frigid air penetrated through my cold-weather gear and uniform as I stood in the turret, looking for any potential threats coming our way. A chill traveled up my spine, and the hairs on the back of my neck stood at attention. I could not differentiate between the weather giving me cold chills or the feeling that I was not only being watched but targeted specifically by the enemy.

We spent the first part of the day patrolling Route Huskies and the surrounding neighborhoods. The day was turning out to be eerily calm, but my sixth sense would not allow me to let my guard down as the lingering feeling of being watched continued to plague me.

To watch over and secure a larger section of Route Huskies during the night, we would split our four-vehicle convoy in half. We would place two Humvees at one location along Route Huskies, with one truck covering east and another truck covering west. The other two Humvees would drive a quarter-mile to a half-mile down the route and set up their OP just as the other two vehicles.

The past two nights, we established our static OP on the north side of Route Huskies in front of a small compound surrounded by a mud wall that housed an Iraq family. Lieutenant Michaels ordered

Private First Class Bild to park our vehicle facing westbound in the same spot, just as we had done the two previous nights. Before we parked our vehicles, a few of our guys exited their vehicles and did a quick sweep of the area to make sure that it was safe before we parked and settled in for the night. Our vehicles were about 10 yards from the frontage road that ran parallel to Route Huskies. On the south side of Route Huskies, directly in front of our OP, was one of the many sprawling Abu Ghraib neighborhoods. The first row of two-story buildings was roughly 100 to 150 yards from our position. The lights from the neighborhood constantly flickered and provided little to no assistance in illuminating the area. I used my NVGs to help me peer into the darkness to reveal any potential enemy threats from the location.

The Iraqi man who lived in the compound was generous enough to come out and introduce himself. He gifted us with hot chai tea the first and the second night. He smiled and did his best to converse with us despite the fact he did not speak English. As nice as the Iraqi man appeared to be, I had grown hostile and developed a pessimistic view towards the Iraqis who resided in Abu Ghraib. I did not trust him, his family, or his chai tea. I wanted nothing to do with him.

I stood guard in the turret behind the 240 Bravo struggling to keep my eyes open, battling against fatigue. I had spent all day in the turret watching over our convoy. I was exhausted, but the ghastly feeling of an impending catastrophic strike on our position was all the motivation I needed to stay vigilant. We had been parked in our static OP for about two hours when I suddenly realized that the Iraqi man who lived in the compound did not come to greet us.

"Where the heck is he?" I pondered.

When we pulled in front of his compound the first two nights, he did not hesitate to meet us. Before we could even turn off our vehicles and dismount, he was there waiting for us. Now he was nowhere to be found, and that made me extremely uneasy. Regardless of how I was feeling internally, under no circumstances did I ever feel compelled to voice any of my concerns that arose from my sixth sense with anyone, but tonight was different. Tonight, I felt an urgency to let everyone know what I was feeling.

Back in Kuwait, during one of our AAR's following a live-fire exercise, Lieutenant Michaels reminded us that if something did not feel right or if something felt out of place, that we needed to speak up.

"I don't know about you all, but something feels off. I have a bad feeling about sitting here in this spot tonight," I said as I crouched down from the turret to communicate with everyone inside.

No one else seemed to share the same concern or even had the same feeling. Realizing that I was the only one feeling this mystical sense, I started to think that maybe I was overreacting and experiencing some form of combat fatigue.

"Pitts, we are going to be fine. We were in a good position, and we checked the area. If they try to sneak upon us, we will be able to see them long before they could launch an attack on us." Lieutenant Michaels assured me.

"I don't know, Lieutenant, I just can't shake this feeling." I replied.

"Pitts, you have been in the turret all day long. I am sure you are tired. I think you need a break. We are going to start the security rotation. You guys rotate out of the turret every hour. Pitts, get into the driver seat, take your helmet off, and relax. Piant, you pull security." Lieutenant Michaels proposed.

Before getting into the driver's seat to relax, I needed to relieve myself. I spotted a small hedge of shrubs about 10 yards to the right of the vehicle. I grabbed my M4 and jumped down from the turret. As I walked towards the hedge of shrubs, I surveyed the area. Headlights from cars traveling on Route Huskies periodically crept past, and I watched them like a hawk. I stood before the bushes relieving myself with the buttstock of my M4 secured under my left armpit, my left hand firmly clutching the pistol grip, and my thumb on the sector switch ready to go from safe to full auto in a moment's notice.

Just as I was finishing up, the same chill traveled up my spine, and the hairs on the back of my neck stood at attention. In that instant, I knew that someone had me in their sights. I could not see whoever it was, but I could feel their eyes watching me. I had no proof, but my gut instincts were sounding the alarm.

I quickly made my way back over to A26, where Private First Class Bild and Specialist Piant were having a smoke next to the driver's side door. The cherry of the cigarette seemed extra bright, and the scent of burning tobacco made its presence known.

"Guys! We should not be here! Someone is watching us! I can feel it!" I reiterated to them with supreme confidence.

They could hear the seriousness and urgency in my voice, and they soon echoed the same concern.

"Now that you mention, Pitts, this place does seem a bit eerier tonight. And the Iraqi guy who lives here did not come out to greet us," Bild spoke.

"Yeah, that is super odd," Piant conceded.

Maybe I was not crazy after all or overreacting if they were noticing the same things. I climbed into the driver's seat of A26. Bild sat directly behind me, and Piant climbed into the turret to pull security. I looked over at Lieutenant Michaels as he was fiddling around with the radio and our Blue Force Tracker, who told us the locations of other military units in the area.

"Lieutenant, I don't think we should be here," I proclaimed to him once more.

I could see the frustration and annoyance on his face. I do not know if he was frustrated with me or the radio. Possibly both. Either or, I could tell that he did not want to deal with either.

"Pitts! I already told you once before! We are fine. There is nothing to worry about! He responded hastily.

With that last and final response, I unbuttoned my chinstrap and removed my ACH from my head to unburden my neck and relax.

"Wake up, Dexter! Wake up! You have to wake up! You are going to die! Open your eyes and move if you want to live!" I frantically screamed at myself.

In a fleeting and bizarre moment, I was floating outside of my body. I gazed down upon my limp and unresponsive vessel sitting in the driver's seat. In whatever plane of existence I was presently in, it was tranquil. I was oblivious to the carnage unfolding in my presence. Just as swiftly as the inexplicable moment occurred, it ended even faster.

The peacefulness and absence of everything that comforted me wherever I had been was replaced with an obnoxiously loud ringing in my ears. A thick concoction of blood, saliva, and dirt overpowered my taste buds and slushed around in my mouth. My tongue slid back and forward over the jagged and sharp remains of what used to be my top left and bottom left molars. The smell of gasoline and ammonium nitrate dangled in the atmosphere. Insufferable and sinister pain rifted through my body. Every breath I took embedded the pain deeper into my soul. I wanted to move, but my body felt weighed down. I was helpless.

The ringing in my ears slowly started to give way to intense yelling and screaming.

"Pitts! Are you okay? Answer me, Pitts!" someone shrieked at me.

I slowly opened my eyes and looked around. Everything appeared to be moving in slow-motion Hollywood style. It was still dark, but dim traces of light exposed small specs of dirt floating inside our vehicle. A dark and shadowy profile of some unknown person appeared in my peripheral vision. My mind struggled to comprehend the massive amounts of information my senses were trying to process.

"Pitts!" yelled the same voice again.

In the midst of my pain and confusion, the only thing I could muster up and say was, "Oh, God! oh, God!" in a low, pathetic, and pain-filled mumble.

"Pitts! Your door is wrecked! I am going to get you out here! Hold on!"

I looked towards the sound of the voice and saw Lieutenant Michaels's face. I felt his hands grab my IBA by the shoulders as Lieutenant Michaels started to pull on my vest in an attempt to drag me from the mangled mess that was A26. He grunted loudly as he struggled to pull me over the center console and out of his door. As he yanked on my vest and started to pull me from our decimated truck, the pain I was experiencing magnified. Lieutenant Michaels and I screamed in harmony as he gritted and struggled to unhinge me. Lieutenant Michaels was an average size man. He was about 5'11 with an average build. With his gear on, he probably weighed around 220 pounds. Me on the other hand, I was about 245 after R&R and weighed around 275 with my gear. Regardless of the size difference, Lieutenant Michaels tugged and pulled on me until he freed me from the vehicle.

My broken and fragile body fell to the ground with a loud thud. When I hit the ground, my pain spiked to levels that no human being should ever have to experience. I was unaware of what had transpired and placed me in this predicament. The agony reassured me that I was not yet dead, but it also signaled to me that my death was looming.

I lay on the cold Iraqi soil gazing into the star-filled night sky, knowing that I was taking my last breaths on earth before death ushered me away to the great unknown beyond the stars and darkness I was fixated on. The hard, cold ground extracted the warmth from my body. The pain was too much for me to bear. I laid feeble in death's clutch, ready for everything to go black. Even though I was petrified at the thought of dying, I anxiously waited for death because I wanted the grief to subside.

"Not like this. Not in this horrible country. Not in Abu Ghraib. Not without a fight," I thought to myself.

Thoughts of all the things I would never get to do or experience inundated my mind. I envisioned my mother and my wife answering the knock at the door and being greeted by a U.S. Army CNO (Casualty Notification Officer). He would regretfully inform my mother that her baby boy had been killed in combat. He would tell Dede that she was now a Gold Star Wife.

My mind transitioned to the dream I had on R&R of me laying in my casket dressed in my uniform while my wife's tears rolled off my casket and onto the floor. I now realized that it was more than a dream. It was God warning me to be ready, but I was far from ready. I was a Christian, but not a very good one. I knew that I was not ready to face my judgment because of all the things I had done, though, and said the last seven months. The anger and hatred I hoarded in my heart towards the people of Iraq and Abu Ghraib had grown deep roots within me.

At that moment, I knew that God had spared my life for the time being so that I could make things right with him to make sure that I did not die in my sins. I closed my eyes and started to recite the Lord's prayer without ceasing.

"Our Father who art in Heaven. Hallowed be thy name. Thy kingdom comes, thy will be done, on earth as it is in Heaven. Give us this day our daily bread and forgive us our trespasses, as we forgive those who trespass against us. Lead us not into temptation but deliver us from evil. For thine is the kingdom, the power, and the glory forever and ever. Amen."

"What's he saying?" Someone questioned.

"He's praying." Someone replied.

I heard the voices and opened my eyes to see Doc Paasch, our platoon medic, and Lieutenant Michaels kneeling over me.

Doc Paasch sprang into action and started to assess my injuries.

"Pitts, you are going to be fine!" he reassured me.

I wanted to believe that I was going to be fine, but the pain and anxiety made me believe otherwise.

"Lieutenant! Please tell me that my junk is still there," I requested.

Lieutenant Michaels reached down and placed his hands on my genitals. In a strong and reassuring voice, he said, "Pitts! You are good!"

I let out a brief sigh of relief. I could deal with the other injuries no matter how severe they were but having the parts of me that made me a man taken away from me was something I was not prepared to deal with or live with.

"His left arm is shattered! I'm going to put a splint on it," Doc yelled.

I slightly lifted my head off the ground to look at my arm. Doc Paasch had used his medical shears to cut off my DCU top so that he could assess my injuries more accurately. My left arm, still attached to my body, was mutilated and warped. Non-compound fractures and a dislocated left shoulder rendered my left arm useless.

Doc Paasch proceeded to move my arm as gently as possible in order to place a hastily made splint. Despite his gentleness, the damage to my arm was so traumatic that even the slightest touch enthralled me with pain. As Doc Paasch placed the splint on my arm to stabilize it, a scream laced with complete torment and grief poured out of my mouth.

Even though pain dominated my consciousness, my love and concern for my brothers came to the forefront of my thoughts. I knew I was in a bad way, but what about my brothers? Were they severely wounded like me? Even worse, I wondered if they were still alive.

"Piant! Bild! I called out to them.

"They are good!" someone yelled. We need to get out of this spot and get these guys to the CSH!"

"Pitts! We are going to get you out of here, but we need your help. You are a big guy, and we need your help to get you up and into a Humvee," Doc Paasch advised me.

Upon hearing Doc's words, I decided that I was going to fight back. I was not going to check out of this life without a fight. Until death came for me, I was going to do my part and help my brothers in any way I could. The fear of dying was still very real, but the fear no longer oppressed and controlled me. My love for my brothers and my pride was stronger than the fear that tried to paralyze me.

A jolt of adrenaline rushed through my body. Doc Paasch grabbed my right hand and started to pull while Lieutenant Michaels put his arms under my armpits and wrapped them around my torso from behind, and started to lift. I let out a violent war cry of a scream as I engaged my leg and abdomen muscles to assist them with getting me off the ground. I stood to my feet with their help. The world around me spun out of control; I was clearly concussed. Had it not been for Doc Paasch and Lieutenant Michaels, I would have lost my balance and crashed to the ground. Every step I took was packed with overwhelming pain to the point I was sure I was going to pass out.

The other half of our patrol, who was just west of our location down Route Huskies, heard the blast and rushed to our position. When they arrived, they established a 360-degree security perimeter around our position. The rear passenger side door of one of their Humvees' was open and waiting for me to enter. Just before I entered the vehicle, my muscle memory and infantry training kicked in. I was missing something, and I felt exposed without it.

"My rifle! Where is my rifle! Bring me my rifle!" I insisted.

One of the first lessons you learn in Army Infantry OSUT is that you and your rifle are one. Everywhere you go, your rifle goes with you. Your rifle should always be attached to your body and never more than an arm's length away from you. Under no circumstances do you ever leave your rifle unattended. Your rifle is your best friend. Without your rifle, you are not as effective. The price a soldier must pay for forgetting their rifle is a steep price that I never wanted to pay. Even in the fog of war, knowing that my life was hanging in the balance, I was still cognizant enough to know where my rifle was.

"Someone has already secured it, Pitts!" Someone communicated to me.

In the back of the awaiting Humvee was Private First Class Taylor. Taylor, who hailed from Boston, Massachusetts, was the smallest guy in our platoon. He stood at 5'6", weighed 150 pounds. and had a physique that resembled a Greek god. What he lacked in size, he made up for in strength, speed, and being extremely proficient and knowledgeable in all of his soldier tasks and skills. Taylor was manning the 240 in the other Humvee opposite A26 facing east. During the event, he suffered a concussion.

"Watch his arm!" Doc yelled as they placed me into the back of the Humvee.

Since A26 had suffered catastrophic damage and was no longer operable, we had to cram everyone and all of our equipment and sensitive items from A26 in the other vehicles. I leaned on Taylor as he sat in the middle amidst the rucksacks and assault packs. As I leaned on him, I continued to pray the Lord's Prayer. Taylor patted me on the head and said, "we are going to be alright, brother."

"Let's get out of here!" Someone yelled with authority.

Whoever was driving violently mashed the gas pedal, and the Humvee jerked, causing my left arm to shift, causing me to let out a blood-curdling scream. I then used my right arm to hold my left arm close to my body to keep it from bouncing around.

Our now three-vehicle convoy rushed down Route Huskie towards BIAP with our RPMs and speedometer maxed out to get me and all of those who had been injured to the 31st CSH. The roads in Iraq were never known for their smoothness or how well they were kept. The IEDs that repeatedly damaged and destroyed the blacktop we rode on made for a bumpy and painful ride back to BIAP. I felt as though we hit every bump and pothole on the way back, and the nerves in my left arm felt every bit of it and caused me to scream in pain.

Even though we were heading towards the safety of BIAP, I was still awaiting death's embrace as I continued to pray. The allure of dying a warrior's death looks and sounds glorious in movies, but that all fades when you come face to face with your own mortality in a combat zone, and you realize that you much rather live than die. Hollywood does an amazing job capturing and depicting the glitz and glamor of war, but this was not a movie. This was real life. This was my life at stake. There was no director to yell cut. There was no intermission. There was no coming back from this moment in time if I slipped away into the darkness. I would be gone forever from this life like a vapor.

The convoy came to a screeching halt in front of the 31st CSH, where we were greeted by a slew of the Army's top medical professionals. They pulled me out of the Humvee and laid me on an olive-green litter, and wheeled me into the building. I looked up at the bright lights on the ceiling passing overhead as my mind continued to travel at the speed of one thousand thoughts a second.

"Pint! Bild! Lieutenant!" I cried out in concern, wondering where my brothers were.

"We're good, Pitts." I heard Bild yell out from across the room. I let out a sigh of relief, knowing they were OK and that they were with me.

The ER staff started to cut my uniform off me. I could feel the coldness of the AC on my exposed skin. They continued to assess my injuries.

"You are pretty banged up, soldiers, but you are going to be OK."

At that moment, the fear and anxiety started to dwindle, and I knew that I was going to live. But I also knew the road to recovery that was ahead of me was going to be long and arduous.

After I was given an IV, the nurse injected my first dose of morphine into it. My heart rate sped up immediately. A warm and fuzzy feeling fell over my body, followed by an extreme calmness. I felt like I was floating up towards the ceiling. The pain I was feeling was no more. I was fully relaxed and at peace.

The room started to fill with familiar faces from my company. Our battalion chaplain, Chaplin Won, stood by me as I stretched out on the gurney higher than Mount Everest. Chaplin Won was a South Korean native, and he spoke with a strong Korean accent. I had grown very fond of Chaplin Won before we deployed. I spent a lot of time in his office seeking his spiritual guidance in reference to my personal life and the troubles I was having as a new lower enlisted soldier in the Army. If there was one person from my unit who I wanted to be with me at that moment, it was Chaplin Won.

"Pitts, how are you feeling?"

"I'm happy to be alive, sir. And I do not feel anything right now," I said with a grin on my face.

Chaplin Won pulled a cell phone from his pocket and asked if I wanted to call my family back home. Oh, how bad I wanted to talk to my mom at this moment and hear her sweet voice tell me that everything was going to be OK. I wanted to hear her loving and calming voice reassure me that not only was I going to be OK but that God was going to pull me through whatever lay ahead of me. As desperate as I was to talk to my mother, I was also terrified to tell her that I had been injured. Heck, at this point, I was still unaware of what exactly had happened.

Chaplin Won asked me for my number back at home and dialed the number. The phone rang a few times, and I heard my mother's voice pick up on the other end.

"Hello, Mrs. Pitts. This is Chaplin Won from Alpha Company 2-14 Infantry Regiment. I am here with your son Dexter. He was injured in an IED attack. He wanted me to call you and let you know that he was OK, and he wanted to talk to you as well."

"Oh, My Lord! Not my baby!" I heard my mother scream and panic on the other end of the phone.

My heart sank hearing my mother's reaction. Chaplin Won held the phone up to my ear because I did not have the strength to do it myself.

"Hey, Mom." I muttered as I choked back my emotions and tears, trying not to cry from hearing my mother's panic-stricken and tear-filled voice."

"Baby, are you OK!"

"I'm OK, mom. I am in a lot of pain, but they have me on some pretty strong stuff right now. I have no clue what happened, and I do not know what is going to happen to me next, but as soon as I find out, I will be sure to let you know. Please pray for my guy's mom and me. Please pray," I pleaded with her.

"Dexter, I have been praying for you ever since you left, and I have yet to stop. I pray over you night and day around the clock. I never stop praying for you all. I love you, baby. You are going to be OK."

"I love you too, mom. I will talk to you in a little OK."

Chaplin Won hung up the phone and asked if I wanted to call my wife. I knew that Dede would flip out once she heard the news, but I knew I had to tell her before she heard from someone else. Chaplin Won dialed the number, and the phone rang a few times, and I heard Dede pick up on the other end. Chaplin Won introduced himself to Dede and informed her of my current situation just as he had done with my mom. He once again held the phone up to my ear.

"Hey, baby. I am OK. I am hurt pretty bad, but I am going to be OK."

"Oh, my God! Dexter! Baby!" Dede cried back to me.

The morphine continued to do its job, numbing the pain, and soon began to numb my mind. My eyes started to get heavy, and sleep started to fall upon me. As I was starting to doze off, my gurney started to move as the staff started to roll me out of the ER where all of us had been. In my sleepy and foggy haze, I looked up, and I was surrounded by people who I had never seen before. The only thing that I knew for sure about them was they were all high-ranking enlisted soldiers and officers. One of them started to speak.

"On behalf of a grateful nation, I would like to present you with the United States Military's oldest award, The Purple Heart."

As this high-ranking army officer laid the Purple Heart on my chest as I laid on the stretcher, a bright flash of light blinded me and caught me off guard. Someone had snapped a photo, and my mind started spinning from the combination of the bright flash and the morphine. I just laid there, closed my eyes, and hoped for the world to stop spinning.

"You are going to be OK, Pitts. We are going to take care of you and get you home." A voice spoke out to me.

Although the world was still slightly spinning, I knew that voice, and I immediately knew that face. It was Captain Shaw. And as soon as I saw him, I was instantly struck by remorse and became apologetic at the thought of having let him and the rest of my Alpha Company down.

"I'm sorry, sir! I'm sorry!" I apologized to Captain Shaw as the guilt of being injured struck me. "I don't want to go home. I want to stay here with you all. I will be back, sir. I promise I will be back. Save my spot, please!"

"Pitts. You have nothing to be sorry for. It is not your fault. You did not do anything wrong. Your mission now is to rest up and get better. Do not worry about us. You take care of yourself and heal up. We will see you when we get back."

As I was carted off to my room, I was consumed with grief, knowing that I could no longer stand next to my brothers for the remainder of this deployment. I wanted nothing more than to be standing side by side with my brothers on the battlefield. The wheels on the gurney squeaked as it rolled down the hallway to my temporary lodging spot in the CSH. I lay in the darkness of the room staring at the ceiling until the darkness in the room mixed with the heaviness of my eyes, and I slowly drifted into a deep, morphine-assisted sleep.

[12]

ON MY OWN TWO FEET

THE MORPHINE that had once dulled the pain in my body had dissipated, giving way to a fresh round of pain that woke me out of my sleep. I pried open my eyes to see rays from the sun streaking into the room. The pain felt even worse and felt as though it was more magnified than I had remembered from the IED blast originally.

I wanted to yell and scream for the nurse to bring me another dose of morphine, but I hesitated to scream because I knew that scream would only cause my pain to surge. I lay in bed gritting my teeth, trying to brace the waves of pain rolling through my body. I was able to spot the nurse call button on the side of my bed. I pressed the button and anxiously awaited the arrival of a U.S. Army nurse with a dose of morphine.

After waiting for what seemed like an eternity of pain and suffering, a nurse appeared in my room with a new vile of morphine. The nurse took the morphine and injected it into my IV port. That wonderful, warm, fuzzy feeling fell upon my body again, and the pain slowly vanished, and I fell asleep.

I was awakened by a U.S. Army doctor sometime later. He detailed to me a list of my injuries.

"Private. You got banged up pretty good. Your left arm is completely shattered. The ulna, radius, and humerus were destroyed. Your shoulder is separated, you sustained a significant blow to your head which left you with that giant contusion on your head, and your back and hips are completely out of alignment. We need to get you to Landstuhl Army Hospital in Germany to operate on you."

"Why does it hurt for me to talk and breathe?" I questioned the doctor.

The doctor explained to me that the pressure from the shockwave of the blast rattled your insides. I did not have any internal injuries as far as they could tell, but I would be sore and hurting for a while. The doctor then explained that I would be put on the next helicopter flight from the Green Zone to LSA (Logistic Support Area) Anaconda. From there, I would fly to RAB (Ramstein Air Base) and be driven to Landstuhl Regional Medical Center (LRMC) Army Hospital in Landstuhl, Germany, for further treatment. After getting treated at LRMC, I would be flown back to the states to Walter Reed Army Medical Center (WRAMC), where I would finish my treatment. I was told to get comfortable because the next flight to LSA Anaconda did not leave until tomorrow night.

I lay in the dark void of my hospital bed, staring at the ceiling with thoughts running back and forward in my mind. It seemed like every time I closed my eyes, my mind traveled back in time to me waking up in A26 right after the explosion. I could still hear Lieutenant Michaels screaming in my ear, trying to see if I was still alive. Every time I closed my eyes, I was trapped in the prison of my mind, and I could not get out. My only saving grace was the morphine. It dulled my physical pain, but it started to dull my mental anguish and helped me escape the thoughts and sounds in my head and doze off once again.

BOOM! A loud explosion sounded and rippled through the hospital, causing my bed to shake violently, waking me out of my sleep. This hospital was a big target for the insurgents and was constantly under mortars and rocket attacks. I would fall back asleep only to be woken up again by more explosions.

"Wake up, soldier. Your ride to LSA Anaconda is here." A U.S. Army nurse told me.

I was wheeled outside into the cold Iraqi night. The hospital staff turned me over to the awaiting UH-60 Black Hawk crew, ready to take me to my next destination.

"We got him from here," the UH-60Q Crew Chief said to the medical staff.

"We are going to take good care of you. We are here to help you get back home to your family." The crew chief spoke to me.

The Black Hawk crew members lifted my gurney into the aircraft and strapped me down to the floor. The crew was strangers to me, but I felt safe and secure in their charge, and I believed with all of my heart that they were going to help get me back home.

Someone then placed a pair of earplugs in my ears to protect what was left of my hearing from the roar of the dual T700 engines and the chopping sound of the rotor blades. Even though the earplugs muffled the sounds, I could hear and feel the powerful chopping of the rotor blades as the helicopter started to lift off the deck.

Within a matter of moments, we were airborne and en route to LSA Anaconda. I felt the Black Hawk quickly bank to the right, and for a moment, I thought that I was in danger of sliding out of the helicopter. As I stared out of the open black hawk door into the night sky, I was captivated by the thousands of glowing lights radiating from the sprawling Baghdad metropolis. The lights from the Helipad, the 31st CSH, and the Green Zone slowly started to fade into the darkness as we coasted through the night sky. As the lights passed by under us, I started to think that somewhere on the ground below us, lurking in the darkness, there was an insurgent with an RPG or SAM (Surface to Air Missile) aiming at us in the Black Hawk as we flew overhead. I looked out of the door, expecting to see the smoke trail of an RPG or missile streaking towards us from the ground. I trusted and believed in the Black

Hawk crew escorting me to my next destination on my journey home. Still, my experience on the battlefield and what I had always been taught in training reminded me that the enemy always gets a vote.

Thankfully, there were no attempts to shoot us down., The city lights disappeared, and we were flying in complete darkness. It was at that moment I realized that my war was over. Not only was my war over, but I was also angered at the fact that I never had the opportunity to fire a single shot at the enemy. I had been shot at, blown up multiple times, and seen my brothers get severely wounded, yet I never got the chance to do what we do best in the infantry-kill the enemy.

My first and only Black Hawk helicopter ride ended as we touched down on the LSA Anaconda Helipad.

"We are here. This is as far as we go. You take care of yourself and get better. Thank you for what you did for our country," the crew chief thanked me.

"No. Thank you, sir. I appreciate the ride." I yelled back at him over the loud mechanical noise of the Black Hawk.

I was greeted by another crew of medical staff dressed in army DCU's and full battle rattle.

"Welcome to Margaritaville!" one of them yelled over the deafening sound of the Black Hawk rotors.

LSA Anaconda, AKA Balad Air Base, was situated 40 miles north of Baghdad. The nickname "Mortaritaville" had been bestowed upon LSA Anaconda by the troops who called it home due to the never-ending amount of mortar attacks they came under from the local insurgents. Like the Green Zone, it was an easy point of attack, so the insurgents focused much of their firepower and attention on the airbase.

As the medical staff carried me off of the Black Hawk, the overwhelming power of the rotors created a large dust storm and almost ripped the multiple layers of blankets off of me. They rushed me from the tarmac into a large tent that was filled with other

American troops who had been wounded and earned an early ticket back home from the war.

The medical staff informed us that we would only be at our current location for a few hours because a C-17 Globemaster transport aircraft was en route to our current location to take us to RAB in Germany. I looked around the tent and took notice of the assortment of troops around me. I was not in the best physical condition after my encounter with an IED, but I was better off than many of the others I saw. Soldiers and marines laid upon litters and gurneys scattered throughout the tent. Some of them were missing limbs and sported blood-soaked bandages that absorbed the blood from their fresh bullet and shrapnel wounds.

A young Hispanic marine stood next to me dressed in his Marine Corps cammies. I gazed at his name tag on his chest, which read "Martinez."

"It looks like they got you good. What happened?" Martinez questioned me.

"To be honest. I am not 100 percent sure. I know we got hit by an IED, but that is it."

"Is there anything I can do for you?"

"My morphine is starting to wear off. Can you get a nurse for me, please?"

Without hesitation, Martinez took off in search of a nurse to help relieve my pain. He returned a short time later with a nurse who had a fully loaded syringe of morphine. I thanked Martinez for his help with a tremendous amount of gratitude because he did not have to do what he did.

As my pain eased, I conversed with Martinez. I looked at him and tried to figure out why he was amongst those of us who had been wounded. So, I decided to ask.

"We were driving down the road, and an IED went off. I got my bell rung pretty good. I have a concussion, and my ribs are cracked." Martinez responded to my inquiry.

Yet again, a stranger, someone who I had never met, just like the

Black Hawk crew, went above and beyond to help me in my time of need. Not only did Martinez help me that one single time, but he practically became my battle buddy and never left my side. A soldier and a marine. One black, one Hispanic fighting the same war in different parts of the country as part of different fighting forces were joined at the hip. Despite having numerous injuries and excruciating pain, he took it upon himself to help me deal with my pain and my inability to care for myself. If he saw me trying to sit up, he would rush over to me, put his arms behind me, and help lift me up.

It had been a while since I had talked to my family. With the help of Martinez, I walked over to the phones so that I could call home and inform and update my family. I spoke briefly to everyone back home who mattered and let them know that I loved them and was doing OK. As I scrolled through my small, green phone book, I saw Staff Sergeant Linder's number in my book. Staff Sergeant Linder was at home on R&R. Even though he and I were not on good terms and never saw eye to eye, I figured that despite all of the bad blood between us, that he would care enough about me as a person to say I am glad you are OK and that you are still alive considering I had almost been KIA a few days ago. I picked up the phone and dialed the number.

"Hey, Staff Sergeant Linder, it's Pitts."

"Yeah. What do you want?" He said in a stern and grouchy tone.

"I just wanted to fill you in. I got hit by an IED a few days ago on patrol. I was wounded badly. I am on my way to Germany to get treated."

"Yeah. OK."

I was then greeted by the cold sound of silence and Staff Sergeant Linder hanging up the phone on me.

With that simple and single incident, I immediately concluded that all the time I had been under Staff Sergeant Linder's chain of command, all the close calls with IEDs that he did not care about my life or if I made it back home alive to my family.

My anger and internal rage started to swell inside of me again, but I had no one to take it out on or the means to do so. Buried deep below my anger and rage were feelings that I had chosen not to expose myself to and had convinced myself that I was void of and incapable of feeling. And for the first time in a long time, I was feeling those feelings. I could feel the hurt and sting of betrayal. How could this person, who is supposed to be my leader and care about me and my well-being, not care enough about me to say, "get well soon?" I know I was not the greatest soldier to ever put on a uniform. I made plenty of mistakes, but wasn't I deserving enough of at least having a leader who cared about my life? Was I that bad of a soldier?

"Pitts! Our ride is here. It's time to go." Martinez shook me awake.

I looked around, and the room was filled with even more wounded soldiers and a large number of military medical staff. The room was in perfect chaos as the medical staff started screening and preparing us for our medical flight to Landstuhl, Germany.

A team of military medical staff approached me with a gurney.

"We are going to put you on this gurney and wheel you out to the flight line and load you up for your flight."

I was in pain, and I could barely walk, but my pride as a member of the Fort Benning Blue Cord Boys Club started to rear its ugly head.

"I am not getting on that gurney!" I yelled!

"Well, soldier, you don't have much of a choice. You can't walk on your own, so you are not with the walking wounded."

When I crossed the berm from Kuwait into Iraq six months ago, I did it standing on my own two feet under my power. If I was going to be leaving Iraq for good and not on my own terms, there was no way I would exit this war, my war, laid on my back and be helplessly whisked away.

"Hell no! You all are not wheeling me out of here!" I yelled at someone with a lot more rank on their collar than me.

Just as things were about to get heated, Martinez stepped into the situation. Martinez grabbed me by my waist and helped lift me off of my cot. He then put my right arm around his shoulders, looked at the medical staff, and said, "he's walking wounded!"

"Well then, you all need to get in line for the walking wounded headed to the flight line."

With Martinez's assistance, I hobbled out of the tent and onto the flight line where there was a United States Air Force C-17 Globemaster III sitting on the runway with its ramp down, waiting to receive the huddled masses of wounded. It was pitch black outside, but the lights from inside the C-17 ripped through the darkness and illuminated everything around us. The light was so bright and so beautiful. It was like God's own hands shining through the night, waiting for me to walk into His embrace. I knew that when I stepped into that light that I would be another step closer to getting back to my family and friends back home.

A long line of walking wounded soldiers and marines flowed down the ramp to the tarmac. Martinez and I found ourselves at the end of that line waiting for our turn to walk up the ramp and take a seat inside. I peered to my right and saw military medical staff carrying the severely wounded up the right side of the ramp. As they were carried up the ramp, I could see all the high-tech lifesaving equipment attached to their litters. Tubes flowed in and out of the tattered bodies of the young American warriors who had their flesh ripped apart, and their insides rearranged from the violent impact and high velocity of projectiles that had pierced their flesh.

A wave of gratefulness and gratitude swept over me as Martinez grunted and struggled to bear the weight of my battered body upon his cracked ribs and concussed brain. I could have easily been one of those brave warriors laying on a litter wavering in the delicate void between life and death and being carried out on my back. Yet here I was, with the assistance of a random marine who cared enough about me and recognized the pride I had in being a combat infantry soldier leaving Iraq standing on my own two feet.

Martinez gently laid me down on a litter that was affixed to the floor. I could hear him breathing heavily and grunting from the pain.

Martinez made his way to the row of seats that lined the wall of the C-17 from front to back. He took off his USMC desert cammie top, sat it on the back of the seat, leaned his head back, closed his eyes, and drifted off to sleep.

The medical crew ran back and forward in the cargo hold of the C-17 prepping all of the wounded for the five-hour flight from LSA Anaconda to Ramstein Air Base in Germany. One of the inflight medical staff approached me just before takeoff to check on me and see if I needed anything before takeoff. The last dose of morphine had run its course, and I was left dealing with the raw and uncensored pain of my injuries. I asked the inflight doctor for a dose of morphine before our flight. He looked at my charts and returned with another fresh dose of morphine to ease my overworked pain receptors a short time later. The sound of the hydraulic pumps of the ramp of the C-17 signaled that it was time to take off. The ramp reattached itself to the rest of the C-17, and the bright lights inside the cargo area dimmed. I laid on the litter as the massive C-17 took off from LSA Anaconda. I closed my eyes and tried to sleep, but the loud sounds of beeping from the life-sustaining medical equipment and the groans of those severely wounded haunted my eardrums. I stared at one of the soldiers who had been placed in a medically induced coma as he laid on his litter that appeared to be suspended in the air. I watched the rise and fall of his chest as it was being facilitated by a ventilator forcing air into his lungs.

The only thing I wanted was to go to sleep, but no sleep would come to my eyes because I could not simply ignore the chilling sounds of my fellow service members clinging to life. I tried to drown out the noise by focusing on the sound of the jet engine, but there was no relief for my ears. I wanted to put my fingers in my ears, but due to my new war injury, plugging my ears with my fingers was an activity of the past that I could no longer participate in. So, I did what I had been doing the last seven months and dealt with it all. It was the longest but shortest flight of my life.

Our plane touched down at RAB and the C-17 ramp slowly

lowered. All of us inside knew instantly that we were no longer in the Middle East as the bitter German cold overpowered the cabin. It was early in the AM, and the sun was starting to make its presence known.

Martinez awoke from his slumber and dawned his USMC cammie top. He made his way over to me and helped me up to my feet, but I could not physically get up. Together and for the last time, he placed my right arm over his shoulders and escorted me down the C-17 ramp. At the bottom of the ramp, I paused to not only catch my breath but also to take in the beauty of Germany.

It had been 16-years since the last time I had been in Germany. Vivid memories of living in Hamburg and Friedberg when my father was stationed there back in 1989; I was only five years old at the time. The moment was surreal, and my emotions were tugging on my heartstrings. I had made it out of Iraq alive and was grateful, but I was conflicted looking at all the severely wounded being unloaded. Why was I fortunate enough to be able to walk out of Iraq, and these guys were not? I thought about all the soldiers, sailors, marines, and airmen who had lost their lives over the last six months fighting in the same war.

The guilt of surviving started to cut me deep. And the guilt of knowing that my brothers in Alpha company were still in Iraq fighting bothered me. My war was officially over. However, my war was only seven months long, and I never got the chance to fire my weapon at the enemy once, and that did not sit well with me at all.

Martinez and I made our way to a row of awaiting buses ready to chauffeur us on the short commute from RAB to LRMC. Upon arriving at LRMC and unloading from the bus, Martinez and I said our final goodbyes as we prepared to go our separate ways and have our injuries treated.

"I cannot thank you enough for all the help. You didn't have to do that." I said to Martinez.

"I know. But I could tell you were hurting and needed help.

There was no way I was going to let you sit there helplessly. I hope you have a speedy recovery and get to see your family soon."

"Same to you as well. I hope you can get healed up and get back to your buddies in the sandbox." I told Martinez.

With a single fist bump, we went our separate ways.

"Take care of yourself, Pitts."

"You as well."

It has been 15 years since I said goodbye to Martinez, and I still wonder what became of him and his life. I can only hope and pray that God Almighty has been good to him and blessed him and his family because of his willingness to help me, a stranger, a wounded brother-in-arms, in one of my darkest times. So if you are still out there, Martinez, and you are reading this book, I want to say thank you from the bottom of my heart once again. You proved to me on a personal level why marines are the few and the proud by living out the Marine Corps motto: Honor, Courage, and Commitment in helping a wounded U.S. Army soldier.

The medical staff placed me in a wheelchair and wheeled me into the massive medical facility. My first stop on the road to recovery was the dentist to repair the damage to my teeth. The army dentist shot me full of nonvaccine and proceeded to smooth out and fill in the jagged pieces in my mouth that used to be my teeth. Lucky for me, the damage to my teeth did not require extensive dental work or surgery.

I was then wheeled to a hospital room and placed in a hospital bed. It was still early morning, and the light-filled the room. The walls in the room were bright white and stood out. The smell of the freshly cleaned and super soft sheets on my hospital bed put me at ease. Compared to my living conditions the last seven months, I felt like I was in a five-star resort hotel, not an army hospital. I laid my head back on the soft, fluffy, white cloud of a pillow and closed my eyes. For the first time in a long time, I closed my eyes with the absence of fear, and I felt safe. Gone was the anxiety of living every minute in fear of a rocket attack, a sniper attack, or an IED attack. The peace of mind I had at that moment was amazing, but it did not feel real. It felt borrowed like someone could come and take it from me at any moment.

Soon after, my doctor detailed to me that he would place a titanium rod into my radius to stabilize it. Screws and titanium plates would be installed on my ulna and humerus as well. I was scheduled to undergo my first operation in the morning. The way the doctor explained everything to me sounded simple. I figured that I would be back to my normal self in no time. Even possibly rejoin my unit.

With my single functioning arm, I checked my email for the first time. I had received a message from Captain Shaw. He informed me that they were looking for the guys who detonated the IED. He described the IED attack as two 155mm howitzers shells filled with explosives. It detonated directly under the driver's seat where I had been sitting.

As I read Captain Shaw's email, a chill went up my spine as I realized exactly how close I came to not only being KIA but blown into tiny pieces along with Build and Piant. Just before the blast went off, we were all standing outside the driver-side door of A26 chatting. Was the trigger man asleep? Maybe he was distracted? We will never know why. All I know is that we all survived and walked away with our lives.

I spent the rest of the day relaxing in my hospital bed, waiting for my operation the following morning. I was mentally and physically exhausted. The only thing I wanted to do was lay in my bed. I had no desire to converse, watch T.V. or even think. I just wanted to lay in my bed and embrace the peace, the quiet, and the feeling of being safe. The solace soothed my tormented mind and soul, and I soon fell into a deep and heavy sleep.

I was awakened A short time later by medical staff, and I was carted off to the operating room, where they proceeded to poke and stick me with needles as they prepared me for my first major operation. The OR was bone-chilling cold. The bright OR light reflected off of the shiny bluish/greenish title that lined the OR walls.

I looked up from the operating table at the bright light overhead and all the medical staff as they crowded around me as the anesthesia put me to sleep.

Upon waking up, the first thing I saw was my heavily bandaged left arm. The pain was intolerable. The incisions where the doctor cut me open to insert all the hardware was on fire. I attempted to ball my hand in a fist, but I couldn't. I then tried to lift my left arm, and there was no movement.

"My arm! What is wrong with my arm!" I shouted and panicked.

The physician who had done my surgery emerged at the sound of my panicked stricken cry. He said that the operation went well and that what I was experiencing with my left arm was normal. However, he explained that my nerves suffered much damage from the blast and the surgical incision. Fear of nothing being able to use my left arm ever again started to set in.

The doctor further explained that he was unsure how much mobility and function I would regain from my left arm. I would have to give my body time to heal and recover before I knew the full extent of the damage.

Tears started to swell up in the back of my eyes after seeing my arm and hearing the Dr say that I might not regain use of my arm. The thought of being a 20-years-old with a crippled left arm and living the remainder of my life as such petrified me. The dreaded thoughts of the unknown and "what if" started to play out in my mind. I could feel the tears coming, but I refused to give them an early release from their seven-month prison sentence in my tear ducts to sojourn with my face. I choked back the tears, fixed my stern face, and pushed down all my emotions and fear deep down again where no one could detect them.

After being brought back to my room, I instantly picked up the phone and called my mom. I needed to hear her sweet and soothing voice reassure me that God was in control and that she was praying for me.

"The doctor said that I might not regain use of my left arm, mama," I complained to her. I could feel the tears trying to break free again, but once again, I forced them to submit to my iron will.

"Are you OK, baby?" She asked.

I lied to her and said, "I'm fine, mom."

Why I told her I was fine when I knew I was not was beyond me. Maybe I did not want her to worry about me? Maybe I wanted her to see how tough of a soldier her baby boy had become.

"You are resting in the Lord's hands, and you are going to be OK. I promise you that. I have been praying for you, and so many other people have as well. You are covered in more prayers than you even realize. God is on your side, and you are going to come out of this stronger and better." She reassured me.

Talking to my mom slightly put me at ease, but I still had those negative thoughts and doubts that I would have to contend with on my own once we hung up the phone. I remained hospitalized at LRMC for another two days until it was time for the final leg of my journey back to the United States.

The ramp of the C-17 hung open as the staff started to load the wounded onto the plane. I would be back on American soil in 18-hours. I was given a fresh dose of morphine, and I slept the entire flight back. In the twilight of the night, the C-17 made its descent to the Andrews Air Force Base airfield in Maryland. We were gently unloaded from the C-17 and loaded on a military ambulance bus that would take us to WRAMC in Bethesda, Maryland. I stared out the window as the bus made its way down the streets of Washington D.C. The bus crossed over a bridge, and I could see the moon's reflection off the Potomac River. The lights from the monuments of our nation's capital shined bright in the distance. I reminisced of my adolescence, and the brief time our family spent in Washington D.C. I was roughly ten years old then. Ten years later, I was here again but under different circumstances.

The bus came to a halt in front of WRAMC, where there was a long line of people waiting to greet us. As I was taken off of the bus and placed on a stretcher, someone approached me and draped a quilted American flag over me.

"Welcome home, soldier."

A thunderous applause shook the night as I was wheeled down the sidewalk lined with WRAMC medical staff from the rear of the bus to the hospital entrance to welcome me home.

"We love you! Thank you for your sacrifice!"

There are no words that I can find to describe the multitude of feelings I felt at that moment. To this day, I still cherish that moment and hold it close to my heart. I was officially back home in the country that I loved and narrowly died for. It was a blessing to be back in the USA.

[13]

WALTER HUMBLING REED

I stood wearing my DCU's in the middle of an open, empty, misty, white room. Directly across from me stood my mom, wearing a bright blue dress. Her face glowed and beamed as she smiled from ear to ear as she looked at me.

"Mom! I am OK! Look at me! My left arm is fine! I am all healed up!"

I started to bend and flex my left arm with ease and without pain. I took off my DCU top and looked at my left arm, where the lengthy surgical scars and staples were no longer visible. They had vanished entirely.

"Check me out, mom!"

I dropped to the floor in a push-up position and proceeded to do as many push-ups as I could. My heartbeat increased with every repetition. My chest muscles and arms worked together in perfect unison to lower and raise my body up and down. I looked over at my left arm as it was functioning flawlessly.

"Oh, my, Lord!" It's a miracle!" My mother shouted.

I got up off the floor drenched in sweat and ran to my mother and wrapped her in my arms as tight as I could, and I refused to let her go. She hugged me and held me tight in her arms.

"I knew you were going to be OK. I just knew it." She whispered in my ear.

My eyes opened, and my mother was nowhere to be found. The room she and I had been in was now a dull-looking hospital room at WRAMC. The surgical scars on my left arm had returned, along with the horrific pain and the inability to use my left arm. I sat exhausted on my hospital bed, unable to get up and drop to the floor and do push-ups even if I wanted to. It had all been a dream, but it felt so real.

I awoke to the shrapnel wounds in my back leaking. A deep burning sensation accompanied the slow trickle of blood down my back. A nurse sat me up in my bed and changed out my blood-soaked bandages, and sterilized my wounds before she packed them with clean gauze.

Less than three weeks ago, I was home on R&R. I could not have imagined that I would be returning home as abruptly as I was. In the meantime, I had nothing to do but lay in my bed and watch the news. I was glued to the small tv that hovered over my bed. I watched the news around the clock wanting to stay informed of everything going on in Iraq as the country prepared for its first-ever democratic election scheduled for January 20, 2005. Iraq was preparing to make history, and all my friends would be there front and center, providing security and taking part in this historic event. As I watched video footage of the fighting in Iraq on the news, I kept thinking to myself. "I should be there." Yet here I was, knocked out of the fight with a bump on my left arm as the war raged on without me.

As my flight got closer, I started to feel extremely ill. My left arm had swollen three times its normal size and was burning up with fever. The slightest touch or movement of my arm caused me so much pain and grief that I almost passed out. Nausea dominated my stomach, and I was unable to keep down what little food I had eaten. I developed a headache so bad that all I could do was put a pillow over my head to drown out the light and pray to God to make the splitting headache go away. Despite all these medical issues, my bag was packed, and I was ready to get on that plane to fly home.

Hours before my flight was scheduled to take off, I lay in my bed, sick to my stomach and paralyzed with pain. Then, finally, my doctor and his medical team burst into my room. They informed me that I had developed a severe staph infection (MRSA) (Methicillin-Resistant Staphylococcus Aureus) in my wounded arm. Moreover, they believed it was spreading towards my heart and could have leaked into my bloodstream.

I had a temperature of 104 degrees. Now I knew why I was feeling so bad and why I was so hot. I assumed it was from the damage, surgery, and the time change. The last thing that came to my mind was having an MRSA infection that was racing towards my heart, ready to pick up where the insurgents had left off and were unsuccessful. I was stripped of my clothes, placed in a hospital gown, and swiftly wheeled off the OR for my second operation.

After my surgery, the Dr convened with me in the recovery room to explain to me in detail what he did during the procedure. First, he removed all of the staples from the incisions and left the wounds open, where he performed an irrigation and debridement (I&D) of my arm to exterminate the infection and stop it from spreading. He was sure to let me know that this was only the first of many I&D's that I would have and that I had a long fight ahead of me.

Just before my third operation, Dede had arrived. Having her by my side would prove crucial to my time at recovery while at WRAMC. Every time I went into the OR and came out, I lost more of my strength. The fatigue was so bad that I could no longer walk under my own power, and I was reduced to a wheelchair. Feeding myself became a monumental task, and I had to depend on Dede to feed me. Even more humiliating was the fact that I was unable to go to the bathroom and wipe myself; my combat infantryman bravado and pride were crushed.

The MRSA infection was slowly destroying me physically.

Continuous bouts of nausea, headaches, dizzy spells, and vomiting dominated every second of my existence. On top of those symptoms, restful sleep evaded me. I would toss and turn all night from the pain and discomfort. I was so sleep-deprived that I started looking forward to going into surgery because I knew that the anesthesia would aid me in getting some much-needed rest.

In between my surgeries, my nurse, along with Dede, wheeled me down to the WRAMC PT (physical therapy) room. I sat in my wheelchair like a zombie at the PT table as my OC (occupational therapist) Steve went to work cleaning out my wounds. As Steve pulled off the last of the bandages, the structural anatomy inside of my left arm was exposed. Typically, I have an iron stomach, and the sight and smell of gore did not elicit any sort of reaction out of me. However, the sight of my own blood, muscles, tendons, tissue, and bone made the room start to spin. I was on the verge of passing out.

I looked over at Dede, and she had turned her head. She did not have the stomach to see the grotesque and uncensored mess that was my arm. Steve opened up a sterilized pair of tweezers and started to remove the scabby dead tissue from my wounds. With every piece of decayed tissue he removed, nerve pain ricocheted throughout my arm. Steve concluded his personal torture session with me by pouring sterile water into the wound to clean it out.

I glanced around the PT room at all the other soldiers; they were all mostly amputees of a different variety. There were single and double leg amputees working with their physical therapist learning how to walk using their brand-new prosthetic legs. Single amputees were working just as hard trying to figure out how to proficiently use their new prosthetic arms. There were soldiers and marines who had suffered TBI's (traumatic brain injuries) and sported protective helmets because they were prone to falling. I could hear them struggling to form sentences with their words as they tried to work past their TBI. As I looked around the room, the one thing that I took notice of immediately were the smiles upon their faces. They were laughing, smiling, and joking with each other despite their physical condition.

There were soldiers who were not smiling, laughing, or joking. They were not mad or upset, but they were laser-focused. They were focused on healing up, rehabbing, and rejoining their units back in Iraq. I had never seen so much intensity and focus, and it electrified the room. Of all the amputees in the room, there was one who stood out above them all.

Being at WRAMC around the bravest and most courageous of America's fighting men and women was a humbling experience. However, no matter how humbling it was, I was still in the middle of a physical struggle against the infection in my body. Being able to smile was not my focus. I slowly started to regain some of my strength and was able to walk short distances with the assistance of my IV pole. I would often walk down the nurse's desk and back, trying to build my stamina back up. As I was taking a stroll one day, I came across Sergeant Manuel Mendoza Valencia sitting in his wheelchair in the hallway. He was a young, Hispanic, double leg amputee. He lost his legs when his vehicle ran over a stack of landmines while on patrol in Iraq. Despite his injuries, he still presented himself as a proud and honorable soldier. That was evident by his fresh high, and tight haircut. His room was a few doors down from me, and I would often see him in his room doing pull-ups on the metal bar above his bed.

He said, "For a guy who has all of his limbs, you sure do seem miserable."

As much as I wanted to be offended and upset victim continuing on with my personal pity party, I knew he was right. What could I say to him as I stood on my own two legs shuffling through the hospital hallways as he sat leglessly? There was not a valid excuse I could give him. I had to humble myself before him.

"I am tired of being sick. I am tired of the pain. I just want to go home." I responded.

"All of us here are, but this is our reality right now, and this is our current fight. Think about all of our friends who did not make it home. Just smile and be happy because you are alive. That should be enough for any of us here." He said as he wheeled himself away.

He was right. I needed an attitude adjustment.

The days started to turn into weeks. Dede continued to care for me as best as she could. As great of a job, as she was doing, there was nothing she could do to help ease the mental and emotional load I was carrying that was suppressed deep inside of me.

As I was being prepped for my fifth operation, my attitude was sour, and my anger was becoming unchecked. Poor Dede, who was only trying to help, soon found herself on the receiving end of my wrath. Trying to love back to health a wounded combat soldier with a fragile ego was like walking through a minefield. I sat on my bed, extremely frustrated with life, when my room phone rang.

"What!" I disrespectfully yelled into the phone.

"Dexter! That is not how you answer the phone or how you talk to anyone!" My mother snapped back at me.

"I'm sorry, mama! I didn't know it was you!" I said, trying to backtrack.

"It does not matter if you did not know it was me! You were not raised like that. Boy! What has gotten into you? Where is my sweet baby boy that I raised?"

I sat in silence with the phone to my ear, unable to answer her question.

"Do you hear me, boy! You better answer me!"

I had proven myself to be tough as a soldier serving in Iraq and being WIA. But as tough as I thought I was, I was no match for Idella Pitts. There are just some lines in life you do not cross, and I knew where that line stood firm with my mother.

"I'm sorry, mama. I'm just tired."

"I know you are tired, baby. You have been through a lot, but you cannot hurt and push away those who love you. I am sorry you are going through all of this, baby. I love you. We all love you, and we want you to get better and come home."

A single tear broke free from my tear duct and rolled down my face. My mother's words pierced my soul and somehow unlocked every emotion and bad memory I had suppressed over the last seven months. I had reached my breaking point, and my mother's sweet yet stern voice was the single catalyst that broke me. A river of tears jetted down my face and into my lap, soaking my sweatpants. I sobbed uncontrollably as I lay in my bed. I was sure that all of WRAMC could hear me wailing from my room. The mental and emotional burdens that I had been carrying for months exited by way of my tears. Thoughts of all those who had been KIA that I knew started to come to me. The fear and anxiety of death nipping at my heels every day for the last seven months was completely unloaded.

The more I cried, it felt like a heavy invisible weight was lifted off of my shoulders, and I fell into a deep sleep. It was the first time I had fallen asleep unassisted without any sleep aids or general anesthesia. As I slept soundly, a feeling of warmth and safety engulfed me. It was as if I were lying in someone's arms, and I could feel their love surrounding me.

"It's OK, baby. Mama's here."

My mother's voice flooded my ears, and I thought I was dreaming. I opened my eyes, looked up, and I saw my mother's comforting face. She sat in the bed next to me, holding me in her arms as she gently rubbed my left shoulder and gently kissed my forehead.

When my mom heard me crying on the phone, her motherly instincts kicked in, and she knew that she had to get to me. She packed a bag, drove to the airport, and caught the next flight to Washington DC so that she could be with me and comfort me.

Sitting in my room and talking to my mom, she revealed to me an experience she had with me when I walked out of the door to go back to Iraq after my R&R ended. She told me that as I was walking out of the door and getting into the car with Dede that she saw this strange glowing light that surrounded me. As Dede and I pulled out of the driveway, she had a feeling that something bad was going to happen. She believed that the light was an angel watching over me and protecting me, but she also had a feeling that she was seeing me for the last time in this life. She endured many sleepless nights as she tossed and turned with worry. She avoided watching the news. Her heart would skip a beat every time her phone rang, or there was a knock on the door.

Having both my mom and Dede by my side as I was recovering did my heart good; however, it soon started to prove troublesome when tension between Dede and my mom grew.

"He is my husband, and it's my job to take care of him, not yours! I've been here wiping his ass, giving him his medicines, and tending to his every need!" Dede yelled and pointed at my mom.

"You are right! He is your husband, and it is your job to take care of him! But he is my son, and it is my job to love and care for him as well. I am his mother!"

I stepped in between the two ladies that I loved most in this world and tried to calm things down by assuring both of them how much I loved them. They were both equally important to me. I was beyond thankful that I had two people who loved me so much in this world. Thankfully, they were able to smooth things over. My mom's week stay with us was up, and she kissed and hugged me and Dede goodbye as she got into her cab and left for the airport. I hated to see her go, but I felt refreshed and ready to push forward with the remainder of my treatment.

I slowly started to make incremental progress with moving my left arm and my left hand. Steve saw my progress and dialed in his plan to get me back up to full strength. I loved and respected Steve because of what he was doing to help me recover. I looked at him as more of a friend than my OT (Occupational Therapist), but our relationship started to become one I associated with pain and discomfort.

Instead of Steve waiting for me to be wheeled down to the PT room for our daily PT sessions, he started showing up to my room in person to escort me. I would sit in my wheelchair and wait to be pushed to the PT room, but Steve had other plans.

"No need for a wheelchair today. It's a beautiful day for a walk." He said to me in a sly and evil voice.

Steve would then force me to walk around the hospital and outside, trying to strengthen my body. We would then walk to the PT room, where he would work on cleaning my wounds and doing strength and mobility exercises on my left arm. Steve had even more tricks up his sleeve. He convinced me that I needed to go and buy some snacks at the grocery store around the corner from the WRAMC. As we walked up to the store, I grabbed a shopping cart.

"You are not going to need that." He said to me.

As we walked into the store, Steve pointed at a 12 pack of soda and told me to pick it up. Without thinking, I picked up the soda with my left hand. Steve instantly stopped me.

"Nope! Your left arm!" Steve ordered me.

I walked around the store, grunting in pain and sweating profusely as Steve followed behind me.

"When my arm heals up, I am going to use it to kill you, Steve," I said to him jokingly through the pain.

"If I can get you to that point, I will be very happy." He said back with a smile.

Steve was on a mission to get me better, and he had a plan to do it. One of my favorite exercises during our PT sessions was disassembling and reassembling an M4 rifle. I was still a soldier, but I did not feel one due to my injuries. Being able to put my hands on an M4, take it apart, and put it back together made me feel like I was still relevant.

I was slowly getting better as the days and weeks crept by, and the infection started to dissipate. As I started to feel better and become more independent, I smiled more. I found myself in PT smiling, joking, and laughing with the other wounded soldiers. Going to PT and being around my fellow wounded soldiers, and spending time with them soon became the highlight of my day.

As I got my strength back and started to feel better, I was able to take part in more of the activities that WRAMC provided for wounded troops. There was always an activity for us to do or a famous person for us to meet.

With the wars in Iraq and Afghanistan making headlines in the news daily, WRAMC was a high point of focus in 2004. There was no telling what celebrities you might see and get to meet. Famous actors were constantly stopping in and meeting the nation's wounded soldiers. Politicians constantly graced us with their presence on a regular basis.

Without warning, WRAMC was placed on lockdown. Everything came to a stop. No one could come onto the campus, and no one could leave.

"What is going on?" I asked my nurse

"President Bush is here," she responded.

I was escorted from my room to another small room with a handful of other wounded soldiers, where we sat together and waited for the President. The soldier I sat next to was blind. He lost his eyes from the shrapnel of an IED. He leaned over and said to me,

"Meeting the President of the United States. I never saw this day coming," he jokingly said to me." As he and I shared a good laugh together, into the room walked President Bush followed his Secret Service protection detail. He made his way around the room shaking hands, hugging, and thanking each of us for our service. The room was silent, and you could feel the power of the presence of the world's most powerful and influential man.

"Young man, I cannot thank you enough for what you have done for our nation. I hate that this has happened to all of you, but I promise that we are going to win this fight, and we are going to take care of you boys," President Bush said to me as he shook my hand and patted me on the back.

I was not into politics and paid no attention to them, but I was in awe as I looked at him. It was only four years ago I was watching him give his inspiring speech at Ground Zero in New York City, which inspired me to join the fight and serve my country.

In an email, I learned of the death of another soldier from my battalion. U.S. Army Sergeant Lindsey T. James of Urbana, Missouri, was KIA on January 29, 2005 when an IED detonated and killed him while he was on a dismounted patrol. Sergeant James was a sniper in our battalion and was assigned to HHC. I did not know Sergeant James personally, but a lot of those I served with did, and they were devastated by his loss.

By mid-March, the infection in my arm had been defeated with a heavy dose of antibiotics and eleven I&D surgeries, and daily wound cleaning. My doctors grafted skin from my thigh to place over the healing wounds on my arm. I sent Dede home early to catch a break, and I would rejoin her and my family a few days later.

Before I could be discharged to go home, my doctors told me that I had to be off of all my pain killers, more so, my morphine pump for a week. I had developed an addiction to morphine as it had become part of my daily routine for months and helped me function. I was so determined to get home that I quit cold turkey and fought my way through all the symptoms of withdrawal as my body detoxed itself of the highly addictive opioid. As bad as the withdrawal symptoms were, they failed in comparison to what my body had gone through the months prior battling the staph infection.

A few days before I was scheduled to fly home for leave, the doctors informed me of the medical issue they had discovered in my left arm. A condition known as HO (Heterotopic Ossification) started to develop. HO is described as the abnormal growth of bone in the non-skeletal tissues such as muscles, tendons, and other soft tissues. My HO was located in the joint of my elbow and severely limited the range of motion in mine.

Thankfully, the doctors were not in a rush to put me back in the OR to fix the issue and handed me my discharge papers with a return date the first week of April. I flew home a few days later. As the flight made its final descent into Louisville, the pilot's voice came over the intercom.

"Ladies and gentlemen, we have a special passenger on board with us today: Private First Class Dexter Pitts. He was wounded in

Iraq a few months back and was just discharged from Walter Reed, and is about to be reunited with his family. Welcome home, and thank you for your service."

The plane landed and came to a stop, and I sat in my seat and did not move. I loved the gesture of gratitude from the pilot, but I did not feel worthy of that much praise and admiration. I got up from my seat to the sound of clapping and cheering as I made my way to the plane's exit.

"Thank you for your service, young man!" "God bless our troops!" "Welcome home, and God bless you!"

With my bag in hand, a hard limp, and my left arm heavily braced, I slowly made my way down the terminal to the exit, where a crowd of my family and friends were waiting for me with signs and balloons. I cracked a smile as I was embraced by the crowd. It was good to be home.

[14]

FREEDOM PAPERS FOR A FREE MAN

IN A MEMORABLE MOMENT between my father and me shortly after I arrived, he briefly showed a side of him that I had never seen. I was lying down on my bed trying to rest when my door slightly cracked open.

"How are you doing, son?" He asked in his base, heavy voice.

"I'm doing OK, dad," I said sleepily.

"Well, I am glad to hear that, son. I am glad you are OK. I am sorry this happened to you. This should have never happened to you. We should have finished this in 1991." He said to me, referencing the first Gulf War.

His face did not change much, but I could tell by the tone and tremble in his voice that he felt something. What he was feeling in that moment seeing his war-wounded son back home, alive, laying on his bed, did something to him internally. Of course, he never saw combat in his 20 years of service, but as a military man, I am sure he understood what I was going through to some degree.

After I graduated and joined the army, my mother adopted my little cousin Zack, her nephew, from Milwaukee, Wisconsin. Zack was ten years old and had lived a rough life growing up in

Milwaukee. My mother stepped in to help give Zack a better life, but he was a troubled young kid and caused my parents a great deal of stress.

Zack came into my room begging me to play with him as I lay in my bed resting. I was not in the mood to play. Without warning, Zack hit me in my wounded arm. Regardless of whether it was a mistake, my inner rage took hold of me, and I lost control of myself. I looked up at Zack, and I could see the fear in him. He ran out of my room down the hall, and I jumped off of the bed and followed him in hot pursuit. I caught him, slammed him on the ground with my right arm and wrapped my hands around his throat, and proceeded to choke him.

"You little piece of crap," I screamed at him as I tightened my grip around his throat.

"Get off of him! You are going to hurt him!" My mother shouted at me.

Upon hearing my mother's voice, I loosened my grip and stood up. I looked at my mother's face, and it was full of disappointment, frustration, and sadness.

"I don't know who you are, but you are not my son! You need to get some help! This is not acceptable behavior at all," she said.

I shrugged off my mother's advice and returned to my room, where I isolated myself for the remainder of the evening. I felt no remorse for what I had done. If anything, I felt justified.

I spent the majority of my 30 days of convalescence leave in my room. A constant flow of people streamed in and out of the house, wanting to see me and hug me. It was good to see so many familiar faces that were happy to see me, but it soon grew old, and I became annoyed with the constant visitors and having to explain and relive the worst night of my 20-year-old life. A reporter from our hometown newspaper, The News-Enterprise, even stopped by to interview me and take pictures. My story and picture made the front page "North Hardin Student Wounded in Iraq Returns Home."

All the love and attention were great and felt good, but it was hard for me to enjoy it knowing that my friends were still in Iraq fighting, and I had my 12th surgery coming in a few weeks and months of rehabilitation ahead of me. And to add to my stress, my marriage was starting to unravel. I was mentally and emotionally unavailable for Dede. It started to erode at our marriage of 16 months, in which I was absent for seven months due to being deployed.

Dede and I arrived back at WRAMC in early April of 2005 to address the HO issue in my arm. The doctors sawed away at the excess bone growth, hoping that it would help me regain range of motion in my elbow. After the surgery, my left arm was treated with radiation therapy to prevent the HO bone growth from returning. I was then thrown back into the PT torture shack with Steve.

Steve placed me on a CPM (continuous passive motion) machine. The CPM would bend and flex my arm past its limits to regain my range of motion. Unfortunately, after all of the pain, effort, and countless hours I spent in the PT room with Steve, my left arm had suffered too much damage. My arm stuck in a permanent 90-degree angle which caused my arm to hang and swing with an extremely noticeable and awkward motion that people seem to spot from miles away as they see me walking.

As my time in WRAMC was winding down, so was the deployment for our battalion. I had hoped that we were done shedding blood and losing lives, but that would prove to be a pipe dream when I learned that Staff Sergeant Wells, a squad leader in my company, had been shot in the head by a sniper. Although seriously wounded, he miraculously survived. He would go on to endure dozens of brain surgeries and years of therapy so he could live a quality life. I also learned that two soldiers from our battalion had been KIA.

April 29, 2005, Private Charles S. Cooper Jr (19) of Jamestown, New York, and Private First Class. Darren A. DeBlanc (20) of Evansville, Indiana, were killed in an IED attack on their dismounted patrol in their AO of Baghdad. Both were assigned to Charlie

Company. Just before our battalion was getting ready to redeploy, tragedy struck once more. A Charlie Company soldier, Corporal. Kurt D. Schamberg (26) of Euclid was KIA on May 20, 2005 when an IED struck his vehicle.

I had also received word that members of Alpha Company were wounded badly when a suicide driver drove into one of our Humvees as they sat in an OP in Abu Ghraib by a mosque just down the street from the dreaded Abu Ghraib milk factory. The soldiers who were hurt were sent to Germany for treatment but could rejoin the unit back in Iraq a week later.

I was fully discharged from WRAMC in mid-June with a permanent upper body profile meaning that I could not perform any exercises involving my upper body. I was now what they called a profile ranger. I was ready to return to Fort Drum, but I would be going back to Fort Drum in a different fashion: as a single soldier.

The war in Iraq is estimated to have killed over 4,000 U.S. Troops. But one number the DOD (Department of Defense) does not keep track of is the number of marriage casualties caused by war. Dede and I contributed to whatever that unknown astronomical number is. The stress of war, being wounded, confined to the hospital, and cut off from friends and family taxed our young marriage. Our 18-month union fractured under pressure and came to an end.

It would be so easy for me to drag Dede's name through the dirt, put all the blame on her, and air all of our dirty laundry, but that is not who I am or the caliber of person I aspire to be. Dede did an exceptional job of being an army wife of an infantry soldier at war. Not only that but her care and compassion helped nurse me back to health. Without her, I might not be the man I am today. I will always be thankful to her for all she did for me during those dark and depressing months in WRAMC. And not just her, but her family as well and the love and support they gave me. If you are reading this, Dede, thank you, and God bless you. I can only hope and pray that you have learned and grown from our experiences together as I have. I wish you and your family nothing but the best and many blessings.

As I walked up to the rear of the Alpha Company barracks, I could see a sea of DCU uniforms and so many familiar faces. My brothers were finally home. It was a joy and relief to see all the guys back on U.S. soil. And now that everyone was back, it was officially time to party. Being in the barracks was a non-stop party with plenty of alcohol and ladies. Even though I was sad and depressed going through my divorce, I numbed all the pain by drinking and raging with my brothers.

The partying continued, but after everyone had returned from their leave, it was time for us to get back to what we did best to start training for the next deployment. The rumors were already circulating that the battalion would be heading back to Iraq for a third time by next summer. Of course, this was no surprise to any of us because we were the 10th Mountain Division, the most deployed unit in the military, and that was what we expected.

"Pitts, your new orders just came through. You are being transferred to MH (Medical Hold) to be medically discharged from the army." My First Sergeant informed me.

Before the term wounded warrior came around and things such as the WTU (Warrior Transition Units) were the cool and sexy terms, we "wounded warriors," we were sent to MH unit without any fancy names attached. Plain and simple, we were a company of "broke dicks" as the army called us, who were no longer fit for duty. There was nothing glorious or prideful about being in MH. It was the land of forgotten soldiers.

Since I was unable to continue operating in the capacity of my original MOS as an 11 Bravo, the army had no use for me, and I was sent to work at the Physical Fitness Center where I would wash and fold towels. I had gone from an infantry badass carrying M4 carbines and machine guns to being a POG carrying a broom and disinfect. I was moved out of the Alpha Company barracks, which were rather nice, compared to the old-World War II barracks I was moved into on the other side of the base, which everyone referred to as Fort Drum Section 8.

While sitting at the front desk of the gym folding towels, into walked Lieutenant Michaels. I had not seen him since the night he pulled me from the Humvee after the IED exploded. I was so happy to see him. More than anything, I had always told myself that when I saw him, I would greet him with a loud and playful "I told you so!" which is exactly what I did.

"Lieutenant Michaels!" I screamed at him.

He looked at me and smiled, and moved in quickly for a handshake. Before he could say anything and got to my hand, I pointed my index finger at him, turned my head sideways, and had a big grin on my face.

"I told you!" I said sarcastically as we shared a quick laugh.

Lieutenant Michaels leaned on the front desk and chatted with me for well over an hour. I caught him up to speed on my journey home and my recovery. It was nice to see him after all that we had endured that night. A lot of people were upset and held a lot of resentment toward him for that night. I have never held an ounce of anger towards him, nor do I harvest any recement towards him. He and I are still in contact today and periodically chat. I now hold Lieutenant Col. Michaels in high regard and maintained a lot of respect for him because I knew that he cared about my wellbeing as one of his soldiers under his command. He always encouraged me to do better and be better. He would never let me settle for being just a mediocre soldier. I choose to focus on the positives of his leadership and overall character, not his shortcomings or flaws as a leader, which all leaders have.

In MH, I learned the difference between serving in a line unit and serving in a POG unit. Soldiers would come to formation looking like what we called "a bag of ass" or "ate up like a soup sandwich." Even though I was getting ready to be medically discharged from the army, I still carried myself with a sense of pride. My boots were always shined, and my uniform was always pressed. I proudly wore my 10th Mountain Division combat patch on my right shoulder, signifying that I had deployed with them, and my CIB (Combat Infantry Badge) rested upon my chest.

The way I carried myself caught the attention of the Medical Hold enlisted man in charge, First Sergeant Hall. He took a liking to me and made me a squad leader, which was a position for an E6, not an E4. I soon became First Sergeant Hall's right-hand man and assisted him in keeping track of soldiers' appointments and where they were in the process of being medically discharged from the service.

The one thing the United States Army did better in our current war than in past wars was the focus on troops and their mental health, more so, PTSD (Post Traumatic Stress Disorder). From the time I was carried off the battlefield wounded to arriving in Medical Hold, the army placed me in various PTSD counseling sessions and shoved pills down my throat such as Zoloft and Cymbalta to help deal with my anxiety and depression.

In the summer of 2006, my army counselor enrolled me in a recovery program for wounded soldiers in Belfast, Maine, that was run through an organization called the NTWH (National Theatre Workshop for the Handicap). The organization focused on helping wounded soldiers heal from their traumatic experiences through the performing arts. Me, being the manly, dirty, war-fighting grunt that I was, wrote off the program altogether and wanted nothing to do with it.

As an 11 Bravo, there are just some activities that we did not partake in to keep our tough guy appearance up. Acting, singing, and dancing were at the top of the list. Especially at a place called National Theater Workshop for the Handicapped. Plus, what would all my fellow grunts say to me if they found out I went to such a place? The hazing and harassment would be never-ending. In the end, my counselor convinced me to take the seven-day, all-expense-paid trip just to catch a break and relax.

A slew of other wounded service members was in attendance

with me whose injuries made my arm look like a tiny paper cut. Also in attendance at NTWH were HBO (Home Box Office) producers and a camera team. They were in the process of doing a documentary about the NTWH.

The staff at NTWH were masters of Psychology and were able to tap into my mind and start pulling stories and emotions out of me. The next thing you know, I was on stage singing and dancing with the other wounded service members. At the end of the week, NTWH put on a show that sold out the theater. I performed a monologue that I wrote about my time spent at WRAMC and all the struggles I had endured. When I finished, the crowd stood to their feet and clapped and cheered as I took a bow and exited the stage. I had never thought about acting before, but at that moment, the thought crossed my mind.

When I arrived back at Drum and made my way back to my room, I was greeted by a hailstorm smack-talking from all of my buddies.

"I should have your Purple Heart rescinded, Pitts!" "I can't believe you went and did that bullcrap!" My fellow soldiers said as they laughed and pointed at me.

I started to regret attending the workshop as my buddies pestered me without mercy. I regretted the decision until I received a phone call from an HBO producer. The producer told me that famed actor, James Gandolfini, known worldwide for his role as Tony Soprano on the acclaimed HBO show "The Sopranos," was about to start working on his latest project, which was a documentary about troops who had been wounded while serving in Iraq. He wanted me to be a part of his documentary titled "Alive Day Memories: Home from Iraq."

I was at a loss for words and could not believe that HBO wanted to feature me in their document. But there was a small problem. I still belonged to Uncle Sam, and I was not yet a free man, and I had no clue when the army would grant me my medical discharge. I told

HBO about my unknown timeline, and they were more than happy to work with me and wait for my discharge.

When I was in high school, I counted down the days until I left for boot camp. I remember the U.S. Army poster hanging on my wall in my room that I used to count down the days. I was ready to leave Radcliff and my old life behind. I had dreamed and fantasized about wearing the U.S. Army uniform. Now things were the exact opposite. I had more than my fair share of dealing with the army's bull crap. The glory and allure of being a soldier at war had worn off. I had accomplished my goal and lived out my dream of being a soldier, and I was ready to go home and start my life. Now I dreamed of returning to the one place I did not want to be: Radcliff, Kentucky.

Everyone in Medical Hold kept track of the days they had left in the army and would let everyone know.

"Twenty days and a wake-up!" Some would yell as they walked up to formation.

I understood and could identify with their excitement. I wanted to feel that excitement and know that I would be going home in a matter of weeks, but that was not the case for my medical discharge. My case was a bit more complicated due to all my injuries and surgeries, so it took the Medical Evaluation Board longer to review the case.

While I served out my time in MH, 2nd BCT prepared for their third deployment to Iraq, I made my way over to see my brothers in Alpha Company before they departed. Walking into the barracks, I could see and feel the hustle and intensity in the atmosphere. It was the same lingering feeling that I felt walking the same halls over a year ago before I deployed. I made my way around the company talking to the familiar faces and wishing them the best of luck on their upcoming deployments.

In front of the company HQ, I ran into Steven Packer, who was now a Sergeant. He was decked out in his new ACU's. I greeted him with a handshake. He was packed and ready to go. I ran into my Kentucky brother Johnny Blaze in the hallway. He was a little jealous that I was getting ready to go back to the Bluegrass state while he was heading back to Iraq for the third time. But I knew deep down there was no other place he wanted to be; he was made to be a soldier.

I walked up to the Alpha Company CQ desk stationed in the middle of the barracks, and Cox, now Specialist Cox, had a pair of brand-new cherry privates in the front leaning rest.

"Pitts!" He shouted at me in excitement.

"Why are you not doing push-ups? Did I give you permission to be tired? Keep pushing!" Cox yelled at one of the privates. "Pitts! These cherries are idiots! I have to get them trained, so they don't get themselves or someone else killed," He said to me.

I watched Cox ruthlessly thrash the joes and realized how he and I had come full circle. We were the new guys getting smoked just over a year ago. Now we were the experienced combat veterans trying to train up the next batch of Alpha Company Terminators for what they were about to endure in the coming months of their combat deployment.

Just as I was getting ready to leave the barracks, I ran into Specialist Jason Denfrund. He had recently been moved to HHC. I had met Jason when I first got to the battalion. He was a few years older than me and had been in the army a few more years than me. However, he always greeted me with a smile and a fist bump and his cool demeanor.

"Pitts!" He shouted as he put his fist out for a fist bump. "How is the arm? I hear you are getting medically discharged?"

I told Jason about my time at WRAMC and how horrible I felt because I was not deploying with them. Jason quickly cut me off.

"No way, Pitts! You did your time. You have nothing to feel guilty about. Now go home and enjoy the rest of your life."

Jason had recently got married and had a newborn son at home. He loved the army, and he loved deploying, but he seemed less thrilled about this deployment because he did not want to leave his wife, newborn son, and stepdaughter behind. I watched Jason walk away down the HHC barracks hallway, and I exited the 2-14 INF barracks for the last time.

It had been 20 months since I had been wounded. I continued with my PT at Fort Drum, trying to regain the strength in my left arm. The process of recapturing my strength was a long, slow, and painful grind that I had to endure daily, but one day the grind finally paid off when I finally completed a single push-up without assistance. It started with one, and I slowly worked my way up to 25 as my strength continued to improve.

The last 21 months of my military enlistment had been a drag on my life. But with me having regained so much of my strength, my enlistment was ending on a high note. The last week of October 2006, my military discharge came through. The Medical Evaluation Board concluded that my injuries were sufficient for me to be medically retired.

I spent the last week running around Fort Drum, turning in my equipment to the CIF (Central Issuing Facility) and tying up loose ends. On October 30, 2006, I walked out of Fort Drum's Clark Hall with my freedom papers (DD-214) and retired military ID in hand as a free man. I loaded the rest of my belongings into my car and hit the road. I had spent three years, 11 months, and five days of my life as a soldier. Seven of those months were spent in Iraq, where I took part in over 200 combat patrols. I had proudly served my country, and I was now ready for the next phase of my life. I had no clue what I was going to do with my newfound freedom or where life was going to take me, but I knew I was ready to move on.

[15]

LIGHTS. COLLEGE. ACTION.

THREE DAYS; that was how long it took me to find my place after being home. After staying under my parents' roof for those few days, I was reminded why I had left. I did not want to live under my mom's ever-watchful eye and my dad's strict rules. Iraq was now in my past. I was physically gone from the war, but some nights when I would lay down to go to sleep Abu Ghraib would come alive in my dreams.

Our platoon was sitting in convoy on Route Forest Green by the Abu Ghraib milk factory. Everyone was sitting in their seats with their weapons in their labs. Willy X' shades covered the eyes of everyone sitting in the Humvees. No one moved or said a word. A large crowd of angry insurgents brandishing AK 47's and RPGs made their way up Route Forest Green to our location. Shouts of Allah Akbar echoed in the air. Seeing the large crowd of insurgents getting closer, I start panicking and try to get the attention of everyone sitting in the Humvees.

"They are coming! Why are you all just sitting here! Move! They are going to kill us!" I shouted as I physically shook one of our guys by his shoulders.

He did not react. Everyone sat motionless as the crowd of

insurgents started to encircle us. I pointed my M4 at the crowd and pulled the trigger only to hear a click and not a bang from the firing pin striking the primer of the 5.56 mm shell casing. The crowd of ornery insurgents then starts to swarm me. I struggled to fight back by swinging my M4 at them and trying to kick them, but I am outnumbered and overpowered as I am dragged away, screaming at the top of my lungs. My eyes would immediately open, and I would sit up in my bed, breathing heavily and sweating profusely, trying to regain my grip on reality.

My sister had an extra ticket to a comedy show at the Louisville Gardens and wanted me to come with her, and I accepted her offer. As we walked into the crowded arena, I started to feel a sense of danger as we took our seats. My head switched around, scanning everyone and things around me. I felt exposed with no cover or concealment. It felt like the eyes that were watching me in Abu Ghraib had followed me home to America and were watching me. I could feel myself starting to sweat, and my chest tightened.

"I have to go to the bathroom," I said to my sister. I got up from my seat and ran to the bathroom, where I locked myself in a stall for the remainder of the show because that was the only place I felt safe.

My life went from moving 100mph to the emergency brake being pulled and coming to a sudden halt.

"An idle mind is the devil's playground, Dexter. Sitting on your butt every day with nothing to do is not healthy for you." My mom constantly preached to me.

She was right, but I had no clue what to do with my life. I started drinking more, and my mom started to notice and picked up on that as well.

"Boy! God did not save you from Iraq to have you come back home to party and drink your life away!"

She was correct in that aspect as well, but I felt so lost.

Being back in Radcliff, I was also reminded why I left. I would be out and about running errands and see someone from high school.

The first thing they would always point out was how dark my skin had gotten.

"You got dark as hell, Dexter! I didn't think that was possible!" "How did you manage to get blacker!"

Of all the things I had accomplished and done during my time in the army, it seemed like the only thing people who were almost always black in Radcliff ever seemed to notice about me was my skin color. Deep down, I was angry and annoyed, being constantly reminded of how dark my skin was like it was some sort of surprise that I was not aware of. People made me feel like I was born with a birth defect having dark skin. I did my best to avoid the small, minded people of Radcliff. I had no desire to listen to their snide remarks about how dark my skin had gotten. I was not the kid they remembered, and I was ready to start choking people out.

After sitting around and collecting unemployment for months, I took a leap of faith and went to the VA (Veteran Affairs) office in Fort Knox to sign up for the Vocational Rehabilitation Program to start going to college and using the benefits that I earned. In mid-January, I started taking classes at JCC (Jefferson Community College) in Louisville. Unfortunately, just as fast as I started school, I dropped out even faster. I was annoyed at having to listen to the young students fresh out of high school complain about how hard their 18-year-old lives were. Not only that, but I also had no clue what I wanted to study.

Not long after dropping out, I received the call I had been waiting for. HBO called, and they were ready to start filming Alive Day Memoirs: Home from Iraq. For the first time since coming home, I had something to look forward to. I received my itinerary from HBO, and I was ready to make my HBO debut.

HBO flew me to New York City, where they rolled out the red carpet for me. I was put in a fancy Times Square hotel and given the green light on ordering whatever I wanted and needed from room service. The following morning, I was picked up in a limousine and taken to the studio where I met James Gandolfini, known to us as Jim, for the first time. He was a giant of a man, but his heart was even bigger. He was a truly genuine person and made me and the rest of the cast feel like we were his flesh and blood. If anyone truly loved and appreciated the troops and the sacrifices they made, he did.

As I sat down with Jim for my interview, I was anxious and shaking nervously. Jim had such a way with his words and how he presented himself. With a single pat on the back and a few words of encouragement, he put me at ease. As we progressed through the interview, he was able to peel back the layers of my mind and pull out my true feelings and a lot and the emotions that I had learned to suppress during my time in Iraq. When the interview concluded, I was emotionally drained, but I knew I had made a new friend.

Jim invited me to the set of the Sopranos to spend the day with him. Having spent the day with Jim and the cast of the Sopranos was an amazing experience. But it did not end there. Jim had one more surprise up his sleeve. As much as I wanted to stay in New York City with Jim, I had to return to Kentucky to carry on with my life.

Having no purpose, no motivation, and no drive waking up in the morning, waking up in the morning, and not being forced to PT was starting to show. I was starting to gain what I called the ETS2040. After military members ETS from the service, some veterans gained 20 to 40 pounds. With no one forcing me to do anything and no high standards to abide by, my waistline started to expand. Mama Pitts was quick to call me out on it.

My mom always kept herself in decent shape. She was known around Radcliff for the long walks she would take. When I was living at home, I would go with her on her walks, and people constantly honked, waved, and stopped to say hi. If there was one thing my mother took seriously, it was our appearance. Growing up, we were forbidden from stepping out of the house looking a "hot mess," as my mother would say.

"Boy! You need to get up off of that couch and do something. Go to the gym and stop eating so much. You look a hot mess! You are gaining too much weight, and you are putting your health at risk!

Look at your belly, Dexter!" My mom schooled me. I left the army weighing a solid 240 pounds. I was now tipping the scale at 290.

Knowing that some of my best friends were deployed to Iraq, I continuously watched the news. I grew more concerned when I learned that Alpha Company's AO was in the middle of the Triangle of Death, AKA the Sunni Triangle in Yusufiyah, Iraq.

I awoke on Christmas of 2006 and made my way to my parents' house, where I spent the day with my family. As I was flipping through channels later in the evening, I passed a major news station reporting that a military service member had been killed on Christmas Day. Days later, I found out that the soldier KIA in Iraq on Christmas day was Jason Denfrund. December 25, 2006, Sergeant Janson Denfrund (24) of Cattaraugus, New York, was killed when an IED hit his vehicle.

I thought about the last time I saw Jason and the fist bump we shared in the HHC hallway. I could not even begin to understand the implications of Jason's death on Christmas Day and how it would affect his family every year for the rest of their days. Surely, as time passed, the sting of his death would lessen, but it would never go away. Christmas Day for his family would be forever stained with awful memories of his death.

While watching TV, a news bulletin scrolled across the bottom of the screen. "US Troops feared kidnapped south of Baghdad in Iraq's Triangle of Death." I continued watching for updates and logged onto my Myspace and Facebook account hoping to learn more about the incident. I soon discovered that the soldiers were from our sister battalion 4-31 Infantry, known as the Polar Bears.

On the night of May 11, 2007, members of 4-31 INF were manning a checkpoint when they were ambushed. After the attack, four Polar Bear soldiers were KIA: Sergeant First Class James Connell Jr (40) of Lake City, Tennessee. Private First Class Daniel Courneya (19) of Nashville, Michigan. Private First Class Christopher Murphy (21) of Lynchburg, Virginia, and Sergeant Anthony Schober (23) of Reno, Nevada.

Three Polar Bears were listed as MIA (Missing in Action): Private Byron Fouty (19) of Waterford, Michigan. Specialist Alex Jimenez (25) of Lawrence, Massachusetts and Private First Class Joseph Anzack Jr (20) of Torrance, California.

The incident hit way too close to home for me. I knew that my brothers in Alpha Company would be out looking for the missing soldiers. My heart quivered as I continued to watch the news and saw footage of soldiers searching for their missing comrades.

May 19, 2007, I had just wrapped up doing some paperwork at the VA on Fort Knox when my phone rang. I looked at the incoming call and saw it was OG. I had not heard from him since I left the military. So I grew excited seeing his name and number pop up on my phone.

"What's up, OG!" I answered.

"Pitts. I've got some bad news, brother." OG said with a profound heaviness in his voice. "It's Steven. He was killed in Iraq the other day. They were out searching for the missing 4-31 soldiers the other day, and he stepped on a mine." OG's voice grew somber as he explained to me how my brother was KIA.

"I should be there! I should have been there, OG!" I cried into my phone.

"Pitts. There was nothing you could have done. There was nothing anyone could have done. It's war, brother."

I sat in my car, and I cried my eyes out. I thought back to the last few times I saw Steven. He and I stretched under the tree after PT after they redeployed, and him standing there in his ACU's with his signature grin right before redeploying.

"There is no greater love than to lay down one's life for one's friends" (John 15:13).

On May 17, 2007, Sergeant Steven Packer (23) of Clovis, California laid down his life trying to bring home his fellow soldiers while adhering to the Soldier's Creed: I will never leave a fallen comrade.

The remains of the MIA 4-31 soldiers were eventually found and returned to their loved ones to be given the proper burial so that they could be paid the proper respect for their sacrifice to our great nation.

Even though I was rattled at the loss of Steven and the guilt of not being there, I had to continue to move forward and go on with my life, no matter how much it hurt. I started to think about returning to college, but I was not sure what I wanted to study. Nothing seemed to interest me. Going from combat to a cubicle was not an option for me. Plus, I had a small taste of what it was like to be an actor, so the bar had been set high.

I sat glued to my couch, stuffing my mouth with junk food, when a recruiting commercial for the LMPD (Louisville Metropolitan Police Department) came on TV.

"Police officer?" I pondered to myself.

At that time, I was also a big fan of the History Channel show "Gangland." I enjoyed watching the series and seeing how law enforcement operated to take down criminal gangs. I was a big fan of the HBO show "The Wire" as well. I was starting to become intrigued with the idea of getting into law enforcement. When I told my mom I was thinking about going into law enforcement, she rejected that idea just like she rejected me joining the army.

"A cop! No way, Dexter! Are you crazy! I almost lost you to Iraq! I am not going to lose you to some criminal! She yelled at me.

"It's just a thought, mom. I am not saying that I am going to do it. Just thinking about it." I rebutted.

The premier of Alive Day Memoires: Home From Iraq was just around the corner, and it was now time to start doing promotional events and all the activities that came with it. Los Angeles, California, Washington DC, and New York City were the locations where the promotions would occur. Once again, HBO spared no expense and spent top dollar on all of us involved. We were further pampered with first-class flights, five-star hotels, and five-star dining. In LA, I did my first on-stage press conference along with my other co-stars and Jim. Then there were countless news interviews with people like journalist Brian Williams and many others. Our itineraries followed suit in Washington DC and New York City.

I will never forget the feeling of walking through the streets of Times Square in New York City with the entire cast and seeing our pictures posted on the side of a giant billboard advertising the premiere of Alive Day Memoires: Home from Iraq on September 9, 2007. How did I get this lucky? Thousands of US troops had been wounded during OIF. Yet, somehow, HBO chose me to be one of the faces of the wounded and those battling PTSD coming back from the battlefield. Some call it fate, but I did not believe that. Instead, I believed that it was God's grace shining down on me.

After fulfilling all of our promotional duties for the day, Jim would take us to his private room, and he would supply us with the best alcohol and wines. Jim knew how to party and was a man with a taste for the finer things in life, and he made sure he shared those things with us. But just as fast as the fun and excitement of being a mini-celebrity started, it was over even faster, and I was back to my normal life. After giving much thought to my future, I enrolled in the ITT Technical Institute Criminal Justice bachelor's degree program and moved to Louisville to be closer to school. I was focused on becoming a federal agent. Becoming an LMPD officer was my fallback plan.

Although my mom was not happy about my potential career in law enforcement, she supported me and was happy that I had something to focus on. I wanted to start preparing myself for a career in law enforcement. I started focusing on finding a security-based job to help me build a resume outside of my military background. I learned fast that being a security officer was not my calling and set my mind on becoming a federal agent. Anything less would be unacceptable for me.

While sitting in my apartment one day, my phone rang. When I answered it, I was shocked to learn that movie director Spike Lee had called me. Jim had pulled some strings and was able to get me a role as an extra in Spike Lee's newest film "Miracle at St. Anna," a World

Word II movie about the U.S. Army's 92nd Infantry Division (The Buffalo Soldiers) which was an all-black unit who fought in Italy. I would soon be flying to New York City to meet with Spike Lee and his production company, 40 Acres and a Mule Filmworks, in just over a month, then fly to Italy with them from there.

[16]
HELLO BLACKNESS

ONE OF MASLOW's Hierarchy of Needs is belonging and love in the form of intimate relationships and a sense of community and camaraderie. After my unexpected exit from the army, I missed having a sense of community and camaraderie. When people say they miss the military, it is not their branch of service, their job, the money, or the pride of being in the military they miss. They are saying they miss their brothers and sisters they served with and the sense of camaraderie that comes with being so close in a high-stress environment for an extended period. It is in those stressful settings where unbreakable bonds are formed. The bond I formed with the Terminators of Alpha Company was formed in the harshest of conditions known to man and sealed in blood. My military experience had set the bar high. I was in search of and in need of a new tribe to be a part of. I wanted and needed to belong. When I arrived in New York City to meet with Spike Lee and the crew of film extras, I had hoped that I might find something to give me that sense of camaraderie I was looking for.

I was born black, grew up black, and was constantly reminded of how black I was. I spent time in Mississippi with my black country family, and I had spent time in Milwaukee with my big-city black family. I grew up with a black mother, a black father, and a black sister. I had an abundance of black friends. I even had a black girlfriend at the time. Despite my 23-years of experience living in black skin and growing up in a black household, I was caught off guard when I met Spike Lee, his film crew, and the 30 extras I would be filming with.

We were an all-black cast of extras. The only thing I seemed to have in common with the others was our skin color. I instantly felt out of place and awkward. The way I dressed down to the way I walked and talked was dissimilar. Even my thought process and how I reacted were uncommon.

The first thing I noticed about the Tuscany Region of Italy was how beautiful it was. The mountains looked majestic. I was a 10th Mountain Division soldier, but I never set foot on mountains. I have never been near the mountains my entire life; they were breathtaking. When we finally arrived at the filming location where our boot camp was to take place, we were issued our World War II-style uniforms and equipment. We were then ushered to a barbershop where we have given World War II-style haircuts that were popular at the time for African American soldiers. Once we were geared up, we were ready to start our two-week actors boot camp to get us ready to start filming.

Just as we were starting boot camp, we were joined by the main stars of the movie: Laz Alonso, Derek Luke, Omar Benson Miller, and Michael Ealy. Leading the charge and putting us through the paces for our two-week actor boot camp was military advisor Billy Budd. Billy Budd served in the British Royal Marine Commandos for 15 years. Billy recognized my military experience and some of the other veterans in the group. He also reached out to us on a few occasions to see what we thought about certain things and to get a different perspective.

Of all the training we did in the mountains, the weapons training brought the most excitement. As a former army grunt with an appreciation of World War II history, I was ecstatic to be able to carry an M1 Grand and learn how the weapon functioned and get to fire it. Along with the M1 Grand, we also received training on the Thompson submachine gun.

Once we completed our boot camp and Billy gave up the thumbs up, it was time to start filming. What made "Miracle at St. Anna" such a unique movie was that it was filmed in the actual location of the battle between the Buffalo Soldiers of the 92 Infantry Division and the German military along the Gothic Line at the Serchio River.

The special effects explosions popped off, sending dirt and water from the Serchio River into the air. I could feel the percussion from the safely coordinated detonation. Then the ripping sound of a machine gun opening fire. I knew I was on a movie set, but my mind and the physiological response to the sights and sounds told me it was real. Iraq was still relatively fresh in my mind, and I had been silently battling with PTSD. I would have to walk away and get myself together periodically, which some of the guys did not understand.

One day after filming, Spike Lee had us meet and made the cast watch HBO Alive Day Memories: Home from Iraq. After the credits started to roll, things changed for me greatly.

"Brother. I had no clue you were battling with all of that."

One by one, my fellow Buffalo Soldiers came up to me one by one and thanked me for my service, and hugged me.

"You don't have to feel alone here. You are a Buffalo soldier. You are one of us. You are family now."

For the first time since being out of the army, I felt like I was a part of a community. After filming was done for the day, we would all hang out and get to know everyone on a deeper level by engaging in deep conversations about life, movies, and being black. As I stated before, I grew up black, but I never really had a sense of pride in being black. It was just something that I was. Black power or black pride was not a thing in my house, nor was it discussed. My parents did not raise me to be black. They raised me to be a solid Christian man of character and substance. My time in the military taught me a lot of things. It taught me to be able to set aside trivial matters and to work as a team with a diverse group of people to accomplish the mission at hand. Being black was never a thing for me. I was just who I was, but the time I spent with Spike Lee and the buffalo soldiers cast learning about what it meant to be black, I discovered my blackness.

The way the buffalo soldiers carried and represented themselves inspired me. They knew they were black, and they were proud of it. They were proud of what our people had overcome and accomplished. They were almost arrogant about it. The pride and power they derived from the pigment of their skin were electrifying. This was not them going out of their way to be counterculture, this was the culture, and I wanted to be a part of it. I wanted to feel that sense of pride, that sense of power, and have that sense of community.

"As iron sharpens iron, so one man sharpens another." (Proverbs 27:17) I was being sharpened with the confidence and mentality of black excellence and black superiority. The further I dug into my blackness, the more things I started to question things like race in America and some of my experiences in the military. I was unaware of how racist America was and how the white man was keeping his foot on my neck and holding me back.

As the conversations of racism and discrimination continued, my first thought was of Staff Sergeant Linder and his treatment of me. Now it all made sense. It was because he was a racist, and he hated me because of the color of my skin and nothing else. I had no proof that he was racist, but that was the only logical explanation. He saw my blackness as a threat and used his rank to keep my blackness in check. I was not the problem; he was the problem.

Being surrounded by the Buffalo Soldiers was also the first time in my life I was surrounded by black people who taught me not to be ashamed of how dark my skin was. I had been ashamed of and hated my complexion my entire life. The self-hatred was not because of evil white people but because of uneducated black people who teased and attacked me without mercy. My mind traveled back to riding the bus in the 7th grade and all the taunting, threats, and physical attack I suffered.

The Buffalo Soldiers educated me about black people and colorism and how we were brainwashed to discriminate amongst ourselves based on how dark or how light our skin was due to our connection to slavery. During slavery, slave masters would often pit slaves against one another by separating them based on the color of their skin. The light-skinned slaves were often treated better and given better jobs and often worked inside the slave master's house, hence the term "house negro." The dark-skinned slaves were often treated far worse and lived in rougher conditions, and were often referred to as "field negros." This was all a part of the master's master plan to keep the slaves divided so that they could not unite, take over and become a threat to their masters.

The knowledge filtered into my mind, and soon all the confusing puzzle pieces that made up my life started to connect. Things that I never understood started to make sense. Due to colorism, I had been conditioned to hate the excessive amount of melanin in my skin. The endless black jokes and mockery of my complexion made me feel less than a human and traumatized me. Not only that, I came to realize that my mother suffered all her life due to the doctrine of colorism, but on a much deeper and harsher level that left her deeply scarred.

My mom did not talk much about her past, but I would catch wind of some of her conversations with her siblings as she discussed how the darker-skinned girls were treated differently than the lighter-skinned girls in the family. I now had insight as to why mom was adamant about not telling people that she was not from Mississippi. Mississippi haunted my mother's mind. It was a place of torment that she wanted to forget and wanted no connection to it due to the hurt it caused her.

Sayings my mom used to speak to me when I was young started to come back to me.

"You don't need to wear black. You are already black enough as is." "You have been outside in the sun all day. You better come inside before you get darker." "Wear this. It will make you look lighter."

I scrolled through the catalog of memories in my mind, and I recollected back to my trip to Wal-Mart with my mom purchasing me the Black and White Bleaching Cream and teaching me how to apply it. I was now able to connect all the dots and understand why she did what she did.

I know many will read this and stand in judgment of my mother and criticize her for the things she said to me and some of the things she did in reference to my skin. I understand how someone on the outside looking in can assume the worst about her after reading such things, but you all did not know Idella Pitts as I did. She did not do or say those things to hurt me or make me feel ashamed. She said and did those things to me out of her undying love for me and her desire to protect me so that I did not have to endure the pains that having dark skin in this life can bring. She was all too familiar with the pain and did not want me to become accustomed to it.

"Your skin is beautiful. Why would you be ashamed of how dark your skin is." "You have the skin color of an African king. Your skin deeply connects you to our ancestors and the motherland of our people."

In the few weeks I had spent with the Buffalo Soldiers cast, I developed a confidence and positive self-imagine that completely changed me. I had changed the way I walked, talked, presented myself, and how I viewed the world. My 23-year-old mind, although altered by combat in Iraq, was still malleable. And the conversations and opinions I opened myself up to morphed me into a new man.

The longer I sat in the pro-black echo chamber, the systematic oppression I was under became more evident. All the negative things that had manifested in my life were a result of racism and oppression. White people had become my scapegoat, and I took no personal responsibility for all my failures in life. There was nothing wrong with me. I was a victim of systematic racism. My mind had been set free, and I was officially woke.

Before I met the Buffalo Soldiers, I had no identity. I was aimlessly wandering through life. I was proud to be a combat veteran, but I did not want that to be my entire identity. Being a military veteran referenced what I had done in the past. I did not want to dwell in the past. I wanted to move forward and do something meaningful with my life, but before I could do that, I had to answer two critical questions: who am I? And what was the purpose post-military?

When I got off the plane back in Jefferson County, I was a new person. I enjoyed my brief acting experience and time with the Buffalo Soldiers so much that I decided that I was going to move to New York City and pursue a career in acting. My mom hated the thought of me moving to New York City, but she loved the thought of me bypassing a career in law enforcement. She was happy for me and could tell that I had found something healthy and positive that brought me pleasure. But before I started to pursue an acting career in New York City, my mom had one major request from me.

"Promise me that you will finish college first. A good education will give you more options in life. I do not want you to have to depend on anyone for anything. I want you to be independent and self-sufficient. There are a lot of things in life that people will take from you, but no one can ever take away your education." My mother pleaded with me.

To make my mom happy, I promised her that I would delay my dream until I completed college. I transferred out of ITT Tech and into the criminal justice program at American Military University. Along with my new career goals and newly discovered blackness came a desire to learn more about black culture and the struggle of my people from slavery to current day America. I dove headfirst into my African American history classes.

One of the first term papers I wrote in my African American History class was a paper on slave rebellions where I learned about slaves such as Nat Turner, Cinque of the famous Amistad slave ship, and John Brown and the assault he led on Harpers Ferry. I read books from WEB. Du Bois and Marcus Garvey, to name a few. I also engaged myself in reading the autobiography of Fredrick Douglas, Booker T. Washington and studying the teachings of Malcolm X and many others.

I constantly argued with people about the greatness of America, its forefathers, and the US Constitution.

"Your forefathers were enslaving and hanging my forefathers from trees!" "All men are created equal unless they are black!" "Life, liberty, and the pursuit of happiness never applied to black folk! And that still holds true today!" I would exclaim.

Hearing the conversations and debates I participated in, you would have never guessed that I was a proud Purple Heart veteran.

"Dad. The more I read about this country's past and how it has treated us, I get more and more upset. It's bullcrap!" I said to my dad as I helped him do yard work in front of the house.

My dad paused and looked at me. His usual emotionless face changed for once. I was not used to seeing his facial expressions change, so I could not read him well. If I had to guess, it was somewhere between disappointment and annoyance.

"Don't come at me with that bull crap, son. What do you know about real oppression or racism?" My dad questioned me.

I might have been newly woke, but I knew my history, the struggle of black people in America, and the knowledge I gained from the many books I read. That was enough for me. No one could tell me otherwise, even my dad.

I had rejected everything that my parents taught me growing up and had adopted an Afrocentric life. The frustration my father must have felt knowing that he raised his only son to a certain standard and to have him grow up and reject the principles and beliefs.

I soon found employment with the VA as a part-time housekeeper. I would cruise the halls of the VA, pushing my janitor cart with my textbook on top. I would study and clean simultaneously. I was in a good spot in my life, but being a janitor was not my ideal job, but it would have to do until I graduated and could move to New York City.

Life was good, but there was still a void in my life that I could not seem to fill. It was the absence of a loving relationship with a special lady. I had a few girlfriends here and there since I became a civilian, but none that were worth really keeping around. I had failed at marriage at an early age, but I was not ready to give up marriage just yet. As much as I shouted and talked down America, a part of me still wanted the American dream of having my own family with a house and a picket fence.

[17]

A CHANGE OF PLANS

"Are you reading your Bible? Are you praying? Are you paying your tithe? Are you going to church?" My mom would hound me.

My feelings towards church and religion at that time in my life consisted of a lot of confusion and many questions. After all, I had been through, how could I not be a believer? But I still had a lot of questions.

Once again, at my mother's request and my wanting to make her happy, I decided to find a permanent church home to attend. I came across a church located in Louisville's predominantly black neighborhood, the west end. I enjoyed the church so much that I became a member after my first visit. Not only did I find a new church, but I also found a new love interest.

After striking up a conversation with this young, beautiful black woman named Michelle, we exchanged numbers and entered into a whirlwind of romance. I was instantly infatuated. The Hollywood stars that once filled my eyes faded. All I wanted was to be in her presence. I could not do that from New York City. I did not want to miss out on having her in my life. She soon became more important to me than the fame and fortune that I desired.

I had high hopes that Michelle and my mom's new girlfriend would become best friends and that I would be able to have a spot for both of these special ladies in my life. That was the outcome I dreamed of, but it was the extreme opposite.

My mom said to me, "I don't like her. Not one bit. She thinks she is better than everyone."

"You have to get to know her mom. Please give her a chance." I begged my mom.

"You two are not good for each other. You all are from different worlds."

My mom was right. We were from different worlds. Michelle grew up in The West End and belonged to a well-off family that was highly educated. I was the product of a blue-collar southern family from the deep south with military lineage. I was a bourbon drinking, machine-gun-toting, gutter-dwelling grunt turned janitor. Michelle was the princess of Louisville and was accustomed to the finer things in life. My mom could sense trouble coming from miles away. All the warning signs were there, but I was too far gone to notice. Our relationship was toxic, but I was too in love to notice.

"What the heck do you mean you are not sure who you are voting for in this election! You are a Blackman! How could you not vote for another black man" Michelle said to me as we sat in the living room with her family. Everyone's head turned and looked at me in unison with bewilderment.

When Barack Obama was running for president in 2008, I was not automatically sold on his message of hope and change. I was all about the black community and was down with the struggle, but I was not sure who I would be casting my first ever vote for. I was still trying to figure out where I stood politically. I was educated and knew that the Democrats were the party of slavery and the KKK. That did not sit well with me, nor did I buy into their beliefs and ideologies. I was not completely sold on the republican party either. I was a political nomad. After being intelligently ganged up on by Michelle's family and convinced that it was my duty as a black man to vote for Barack Obama, I cast my first ballot for America's first black president.

Eight months later, I proposed to Michelle, and she gladly said yes. Everyone seemed happy for me except the one person whose opinion mattered to me the most, my mom.

"Did you pray and ask God about this, Dexter? I've prayed about this, and God has told me that she is not the right one for you," my mom said to me.

"Here we go again." I thought to myself, listening to my mom's displeasure and disapproval of my engagement. I wanted my mom to be happy for me, but that was not in the cards, so I had to make peace with knowing that she would never approve of my marriage.

Michelle loved her family, and I knew that she was not interested in moving away from them. Unfortunately, that meant I would have to forgo my ambitions of becoming a federal agent. Instead of pursuing a career as a federal agent, my focus was now on my back up plan-becoming an LMPD officer.

Beep! Beep! Beep! The crackle of the police radio sounded. The First Division is responding to a report of a possible homicide at the intersection of 7th and West Chestnut Street, the dispatcher advised. The lights and sirens of the LMPD squad car flashed red and blue as we pulled up to the scene where officers were setting up crime scene tape. I followed closely behind the officer as we stepped cautiously into the crime scene.

An older white male with a beard and old dirty clothes lay on the sidewalk motionless. His skin was faded white. I looked at his body and noticed a leather belt pulled tight around his neck and a black pen lodged into his left eye. There was no rise and fall of his chest. He was deceased. In my first police ride-along, I spent eight hours with the officers of the First Division riding around downtown Louisville responding to calls, breaking up fights, and taking reports.

The LMPD officer's Class A uniforms looked sharp. Their shiny buttons and their badge stood out against the backdrop of their dark navy-blue polyester uniforms. And the shine of their boots matched the shine of their high gloss leather duty belts. They walked, standing upright with pride, and every step they took had a purpose. Listening to the officers laugh and joke before their shift at the roll call table reminded me of my time in the infantry with the terminators. Likewise, the structure and standards of the police department reminded me of the military. I craved that structure.

I was amazed that people got paid to do this for a living. It was the perfect career for me. I envisioned myself in uniform cruising the streets of Louisville fighting crime. The pay, benefits, and the pension were a plus for me but were the farthest thing from my mind. I wanted that pride, glory, and honor of wearing the LMPD uniform and calling myself an LMPD officer.

In March of 2009, I submitted my application and resume to LMPD. I was confident and cocky that I was going to be hired. I was a young, black combat veteran with an honorable discharge, and I had the required college credits needed. I was in a league of my own. And I knew I checked every box.

"Does anyone have any physical disabilities or limitations that we need to make a note of before we start?" An LMPD officer asked before we started our PAT (Physical Agility Test).

The weight room was filled with roughly 40 police recruit hopefuls. I was the only one to raise my hand. The officer pulled me to the side, and I explained the situation with my left arm.

"If you cannot fully extend your arm for the push-ups or interlock your fingers behind your head for the sit-ups, that might be a problem. I don't know if the DOCJT (Department of Criminal Justice Training) will accommodate you for that. I will let you take the test and let the DOCJT decide from there."

My heart instantaneously sank. Frustration and the feeling of failure swept over me as the rug was being pulled out from under my feet. The pride, glory, and honor that I was in pursuit of were being ripped away from me. I was being barred from achieving my dream or anything meaningful. I was being forced to settle for a meager life as a VA janitor for the rest of my existence. I had put in so much hard work to get myself ready for this day.

I had bragged and boasted to so many people that I was going to be an LMPD officer. The thought of having to face them after being rejected soured my stomach. There was no other plan for me. This was my fallback plan. Even worse, what would my new fiancée say or think about me? Would she still want to marry me knowing that I would be pushing a broom and scrubbing toilets for the rest of my life?

I focused intensely as I took the LMPD PAT. I pushed myself to capacity blowing through the push-ups, sit-ups, sprint, and the distance run, and passed every event. A few days later, I was notified that the DOCJT was OK with my arm's physical limitations, which allowed me to continue in the hiring process.

My wedding day was just around the corner. I was ready to start this new chapter of my life, despite how my mom was feeling. While on my lunch break at the VA, I sat talking to my mom on the phone. My wedding was less than a week away. She called me, hoping to convince me to change my mind.

"I know you love her with all your heart. You are a good man, and your heart is pure, but she doesn't love you as you love her. Trust me. I know. I can tell by the way she looks at you and talks to you. You are pouring yourself into her, and she is not giving you anything in return."

"Why can't you just be happy for me, mom?" I argued back at her.

"I want to see you happy. But mark my words, Dexter. That girl will be your downfall. She is going to break your heart and take everything from you. I might not be alive to see it, but it will come to pass," my mom told me, forecasting her dark omen.

On a beautiful fall day in the fall in 2009, I stood in my tuxedo before our church, my bride and God ready to take Michelle's hand in marriage. After sealing our marriage with a kiss, I looked into the crowd and saw my mother's face. It was covered in sadness. After the wedding, the issues between my mom and Michelle got worse. Every time my mom and I would talk, the conversations would end in an argument over my new wife and my new life. I would hang up the phone then have to fight with my new wife about my mom—the back and forth arguing exhausted me mentally and emotionally.

Once again, I was caught in a fiery struggle between two women who fiercely loved me. My heart was torn into two pieces. My mother had been there to support me on my best days and my worst days. She was my biggest supporter and number one fan. After all, she and I had been through over the years; our bond was something special.

On the other hand, my new wife, who I perceived as the best thing to happen to me, was my future. After Iraq, I did not believe that I had much of a future. However, with Michelle in my life, my future looked bright. I wanted to hold onto that future with all my might.

"You have changed, Dexter! She has changed you! Look at how you talk and dress now. You think you are too good to be around your own family now. This is not who I raised you to be." My mom shouted at me through the phone.

My mom was always throwing Bible verses at me. So I threw one back at her.

"For this reason, a man will leave his father and mother and be united to his wife, and the two will become one flesh (Ephesians 5:31)," I said to my mom. "I cannot keep doing this with you. She is my wife. If you cannot love and accept her, you cannot love and accept me."

My mom said to me, "If that is the way you feel, Dexter, then I am sorry. Just know that I love you, and I will continue to pray for you, but I will not stand in your way."

I could hear my mom's heart shattering into a million tiny shards as our conversation came to an end. For the first time in our mother and son relationship, my mom and I would go without talking to each other for almost a year. The 7,000 miles between us and the violence and chaos of war could not separate her and I. But, here we were, only 30 miles between us, and it felt like we were in alternate universes.

All my hard work had paid off when I learned that I had been selected to be part of LMPD's MAC (Metro Academy Class) 18. I was scheduled to start the police academy in November of 2009.

From the outside looking in, my life looked picture-perfect on the surface. I had everything that people chase after all their lives: the beautiful woman, the money, the job, and the dream home. I was truly living the American dream.

[18]

A FAKE SMILE FOR A FAKE LIFE

"WE ARE PROUD OF YOU, but do not forget who you are when you put on that uniform. Never lose sight of that. You are a strong and proud black man. And remember this, because of the color of your skin, you will have to work ten times harder than everyone else."

That seemed to be the consensus I got from most of my new black friends and members of the church. If you would have asked me who I was before my time with the buffalo soldiers, I would have told you that I was simply a Purple Heart veteran. Color was never part of the equation. Now, I was just a proud black man ready to serve the black community. Being black was now my complete identity. I was not going to be just a police officer. I was going to be a black police officer and a proud one at that.

Dressed in suits and standing in two lines, myself and my 23 classmates who made up MAC 18 marched to the academy from the parking lot with me leading the way calling cadence. As we crossed over Taylor Blvd, an old blacker man, who appeared to be in his fifties, started yelling at us, giving us our first official welcome to law enforcement as he walked out of a nearby gas station.

"Do you people realize that you are getting ready to be trained by and work for a racist, terrorist organization! You all need to reconsider your career choices. Especially you three!" He yelled at us. The three that he was talking to specifically were the only three black recruits in the entire class: Myself, Martez Hughes, and a black female recruit. Having been a black guy in the infantry, I was more than prepared to be the token black guy, and it did not bother me one bit. I was confident in my abilities, and I was proud to be representing the black community as an LMPD officer.

My marriage kicked off in epic fashion and was loaded with passion. But as hot as things started, it seemed to fizzle out even quicker, and we were back to arguing, yelling, cursing, and disrespecting each other. We were two type-A personalities, and we would clash and lock horns like two Rocky Mountain rams trying to establish dominance over one another. There was not enough room in our marriage for both of our egos and pride. Eventually, someone would have to fold, and it was usually me.

While in the police academy, my mom and I started talking again. We both realized that we had hurt each other and wanted to try and make things right between us. So I invited her to family day at the academy. To my surprise, my mom accepted my offer and attended. I had not seen her in months. When she walked into my classroom, I noticed her signature smile and her single gold tooth, but I could see that something was different. She had a smile, but behind that smile and behind her eyes, I could see a deep pain and hurt. I know I had hurt her, but had I hurt her that bad?

"I am so proud of you, baby." She spoke to me.

I knew she was not thrilled with my new career choice, but she found a way to smile for me and support me. We ended the family day by posing together for a picture. As she walked away, I still pondered what was wrong with her. I could tell something was off, but she would never let me know if something was bothering her. I could only hope and pray that whatever it was, was not a result of me.

One month before our graduation, our academy class was detailed to work at the Kentucky Derby, one of the most famous horse races in the world. I was assigned to watch gate 2A of Churchill Downs. Assigned to watch over me that day was veteran police officer and homicide detective Sergeant Kevin Trees. Not only was he a veteran LEO (law enforcement officer), but he was also a veteran and served a tour in the Marine Corps in the early 1990s.

Sergeant Tress was a bit of a celebrity. He had been on the A&E Television show "The First 48." What made him and his appearance special to the show was that he was the first-ever amputee police officer on LMPD. In 2003 he was involved in a motorcycle accident that left him in a coma for three weeks and had to have his leg amputated. He and I took an instant liking to each other. I hung on every word he said and picked his brain, learning about my new career and how to become a great officer.

"Officers! I am lost! I can't find my friends!" A drunk white lady said as she stumbled towards us.

I looked over at Sergeant Trees waiting to be told what to do.

"Handle it." That was the only thing he said to me.

I didn't know what I was doing and ran down the gauntlet of questions trying to help her figure out a solution to this problem. Finally, I called EMS (Emergency Medical Services) to take her to the hospital.

"Not too bad, rookie. Not bad at all."

Before Sergeant Trees and I parted after our detail, he provided me with some advice.

"Your reputation starts day one in the academy. The only thing you have in this department is your reputation; it is everything. Once you develop a bad reputation, it will follow you everywhere. Guard your reputation."

Sergeant Trees and I worked side by side for two 16-hour days dealing with drunk and disorderly Kentucky Derby fans. After our Kentucky Derby detail, Sergeant Trees wrote me a letter of commendation and sent it to my academy instructors. He and I grew close after working together, and he became my first police mentor.

On June 10, 2010, at the Salvation Army Auditorium, I stood

proudly during the MAC 18 graduation. I did it. I was officially an LMPD officer. Walking across the parade field at Fort Benning and becoming a soldier was a significant accomplishment. However, I hold my graduation from the LMPD Training Academy even higher because of all the struggles I endured the last five years to call myself an LMPD officer.

I had not seen my mom since family day. I was so happy that she was here to take part in this day with me. She looked as beautiful as always, but she still had that look in her eyes. She tried her best to mask whatever it was that was dealing with behind her smile. It was a fake smile. I quickly recognized it because I had become a master of putting on a fake smile.

In my 26 years of life, I had never seen my mom in such a condition. I could even hear it in her voice.

"Congratulations, baby! I knew you could do it!" She said to me.

Even her voice lacked the confident, vibrant, and reassuring sound it once had. I could no longer stand before her and wonder. Instead, I had to put my new investigative skills to the test.

I used my new police investigative skills to get to the bottom of what was going on with her, and she finally broke.

"Your dad and I got divorced back in February. We are still having some issues, but I am OK."

The news of the divorce swept over me and hit me like a ton of bricks. My parents had been married for 28 years. And because I had minimal contact with my family after my wedding, I had no clue what my parents were going through. My mom and I had talked on a few occasions, but she left out the stressful details of her life to focus on me. How bizarre we were both in mentally and emotionally taxing times in our lives and were trying to hide our hurt from everyone and each other.

"Is your father here?" She questioned me with a look of fear in her eyes..

"I don't believe so, mom. I've not seen him."

We shared one last hug, and she left the building in a hurry as though she was trying to evade seeing my dad.

Before graduation, I learned that I would be assigned to the Sixth Division for my first FTO phase (Field Training Officer) in the Sixth Division for 12 weeks. If I met the standard and passed the first 12 weeks of training, I would be transferred to my permanent spot in the Second Division to finish out my FTO phase, where I would be protecting and serving Louisville's black community in the West End.

[19]

WORKING IN THE GREY

IT WAS FATHER'S DAY, June 20, 2010; I walked into the Sixth Division police station with a freshly pressed uniform, bulletproof vest securely strapped to my chest, my new leather gear around my freshly shined boots. I took a seat, waiting to meet my FTO, who everyone referred to as Paco.

"What the hell do you think you are doing sitting at the roll call table, rookie! Go and stand in the back of the room and wait for your FTO," an older veteran officer barked at me.

Into the roll call room walked a tall, heavyset, and much older Puerto Rician man. His black hair was dusted with grey, and he sported a thick black mustache on his upper lip.

"You Dexter?" He asked me with a thick Puerto Rican accent.

"Yes, Sir!" I replied.

"We are car 621 C (Charlie). Listen to the radio. If they call for us on the radio and you do not answer, we are going to have problems, do you understand?"

"Yes. Sir." I replied.

We made our way outside to his patrol car, where I took my seat in the passenger seat.

"Where are you mentally and emotionally right now?" Paco asked me.

"I'm good, sir. I am ready to go." I responded to him.

"Here is the deal! Before you come to work and get in this car, you better ensure that you are in the right frame of mind! This is a dangerous job, and you can get yourself or someone else killed if you are not here mentally! I am not ready to die because you are not paying attention to what is happening around us! Do I make myself clear!" Paco ruthlessly coached me.

As soon as our patrol car left the division, we were dispatched to a gas station on Bardstown Road, where staff reported a theft.

We pulled into the gas station parking lot and walked inside the store. As we walked into the store, it was as though a celebrity had walked in through the doors. Everyone stopped what they were doing and stared at us. The attention, power, and presence my uniform commanded were astounding. My eyes swooped back and forward-looking for the suspect in question.

"He's right over there." One of the gas station employees said to me as she pointed towards the suspect.

I looked at the suspect and started to size him up, and read his body language. His demeanor, along with his stature, was very non-threatening. He probably looked like a little kid standing between Paco and me. I looked at his waistband to see if I could spot any weapons he might have holstered. His pants pockets were overflowing with stolen gas station snacks. I knew right on the spot that he was guilty of the crime he was being accused of, and I was ready to punish him to the full extent of the law.

"Check him to make sure he does not have any weapons on him. Then get his ID and run him for warrants," Paco ordered.

After getting verbal consent from the suspect, I checked him to make sure he did not have any weapons then got his ID. His warrant check came back negative.

Paco asked, "well, what do you want to do?"

I immediately reached into my handcuff case and popped it open. As I pulled my handcuffs out, you could hear the metal-on-metal clinging in the ever so silent store as everyone stood by watching. I then stepped toward the suspect, and Paco stopped me dead in my tracks with a hand to my chest.

"What the heck do you think you are doing?" Paco asked me.

"Is this a test?" I thought to myself.

"I'm going to arrest him. He broke the law. He is going to jail." I said to Paco.

"Slow your roll, young man. Have you talked to this man? Do you know anything about this man and his current situation and why he is here stealing? Paco questioned me.

As a rookie officer on my first call, I was beyond lost at this point. I thought my job was to enforce the law.

"Right is right, and wrong is wrong." I thought to myself. What was I not getting or understanding? The elements of the crime fit the KRS (Kentucky Revised Statute), and I had a witness and video footage.

"There is black and white in this job, but there is a lot of grey in what we do. So use your discretion and use it wisely." Paco said to.

Paco started talking to the individual to better understand the situation and a look at the bigger picture. The suspect told us that he had kids in the hotel next door and that they were hungry, and they did not have any food, and he came to steal for his family.

Paco took the items from the suspect's pocket and carried them up to the register, where he paid for the stolen items.

"Happy Father's Day. This one is on me. If I catch you next time, your ass is mine. Do you understand me?" Paco said to the now free suspect as he stood there in disbelief.

"Remember. Not everyone needs to go to jail. Just because we can lock someone up does not mean we should."

I thought I knew what being a police officer was all about, but Paco showed me that I had a lot to learn.

"What street did we just pass?" He asked me as we cruised down Six Mile Lane.

"I don't know, sir."

"If something were to have happened to us just now and it was an emergency, how would we be able to get back up here? We cannot because you do not know where we are! Get out of my car and run to that sign, then run back and tell me the name of the street we just passed."

I exited the patrol car and looked towards the street sign. It was not a far distance, but it was far enough when you consider the humidity, all my gear, and my polyester uniform. I started jogging, and the humidity slowly suffocated my lungs, and sweat started to soak through my uniform. Finally, I got to the street sign and memorized the street, and ran back to the patrol car.

"Brookhollow Drive, sir!" I yelled to Paco while trying to catch my breath and cool down.

I started to gain more experience riding with Paco and adding to my very thin police officer repertoire and knowledge. Every call we responded to was a new experience and taught me a new lesson, but I had yet to make my first arrest.

We were dispatched to a domestic violence call in the Newburg neighborhood. As we walked up to the house, we could see a lady screaming for help inside.

"Metro Police!" I yelled at the top of my lungs.

I looked at Paco as we stood at the front door, and he gave me the nod. I reared back and kicked the door off the hinges.

"Please help me, officer!" The victim called out to me in terror from the kitchen floor as her husband stood over her.

"Get on the ground right now!" I yelled with intensity at the suspect.

The suspect complied instantly, and I took him into custody.

The lady said to me, "Thank you, officer! You saved my life."

It felt great knowing that I had helped save this lady's life from her husband. The rush I had worn off quickly when I realized how much paperwork I had to do, but I needed the practice and experience.

Being a police officer was turning out to be everything that I had imagined it would be. I looked forward to getting up and putting on my uniform every day. I could not get enough of it. Even when I was off, I would count down the days until I went back to work. It did not take long for me to realize that policing was my calling.

Policing provided me with everything I was looking for after leaving the army. Policing quickly became the only thing that I had in my life that provided me comfort. By diving into the chaos of everyone else's life, I could escape the chaos of my own.

"I'm calling the police!" Michelle shouted at me.

She and I had gotten into a heated argument. Neither one of us was willing to back down. She knew how much I loved my job, and she knew that if she threatened to call the police, I would back down because I was still on probation and could be fired without cause for any small incident. I knew this well, but I doubled down with my yelling and screaming, not wanting to submit myself to her demands. Finally, she picked up the phone and called 911, and my fellow brothers in blue arrived a short time later. There was no physical violence between us, but I was called into the sergeant's office about the incident. To my surprise, they were very supportive of me, but they also expressed their concern.

"Pitts. We like you, and we think you are a good officer. You have a lot of promise and potential, but you are too early in your career to be having these types of incidents. Women, alcohol, and lying will strip you of your badge faster than anything." My sergeant took time to educate me on a few matters related to life as a cop.

Then it was Paco's turn to educate me.

"Let me tell you something, mister! You are a liability to this department! We all are. Do not think for one second that this place will put you before its own survival. You have to look out for yourself, make good decisions, and cover your ass!"

As always, my wife and I were able to put a band-aid over the shotgun slug wound that was our marriage and continued with our toxic marriage. However, at the end of my 20 weeks of training, all of my FTO's decided that I had performed well enough to continue to my next training phase in the Second Division.

[20]

THE BROWN PAPER BAGS

"IF ANYTHING WERE to ever happen to me, just know that there is more than enough money for you and your sister. Also, promise me that if anything were to ever happen to me and I end up needing to be put on life support just to let me go? My mom said to me as I cruised the frozen foods section of Wal-Mart.

"Mom! Why do you keep talking like this! Please stop!" I said to my mom.

Against Michelle's wishes, I continued to talk to my mom and tried to mend our relationship further. But, unfortunately, I learned that my mom had recently purchased a 9mm Taurus handgun, and I did not feel comfortable with her having it.

"Why do you need a gun? You live in Radcliff-this is a safe town. Who are you trying to protect yourself from?" I questioned her.

On August 28, 2010, I talked to my mom on the phone while buying snacks for my Iron Man detail the next day. I had promised her that on my next day off, I would come down and spend the day with her.

"Hey, baby! How are you doing?" My mom's sweet voice asked me.

"I am good, mom. Just buying some stuff I need for work tomorrow."

"I was just calling to see if you were still coming down on Monday to see me?"

I had not seen my mom since the day of my graduation. I had been so busy with my new career and trying to work on my marriage that I had lost sight of my relationship with her.

"Of course, I am still coming down. I can't wait to see you, mom." I said back to her.

We chatted on the phone, and I told her all about how much I was enjoying my new job. We ended the conversation with a goodbye as I got into my car to drive home.

As I was driving down Leisure Lane and made the turn into my neighborhood on Brook Bend Way, my phone rang again. It was my mom calling me again.

She corrected me. "You forgot to say I love you before you hung up."

"I'm so sorry, mama. I love you."

"I love you too, baby. I will see you on Monday. Okay?"

As I stood at my post with my fellow officers the following morning securing the road for the Ironman participants, my phone rang.

"This is Lieutenant James with the RPD (Radcliff Police Department). I am trying to reach Officer Dexter Pitts."

My mind deliberated about the many reasons as to why RPD was calling me.

"This is him. How can I help you?"

"Officer Pitts. Your mom was involved in an incident here in Radcliff and was shot. She has been airlifted to UofL (University of Louisville) Hospital and is currently being treated there."

I instantly thought it was a joke and hung up the phone. I did not think twice about it until my phone rang again.

"Officer Pitts, this is not a joke! You need to get to the hospital to be with your mother right now! She has been shot!" He said to me with an urgency.

The tone of his voice and the fact that he called me back so promptly removed any doubt from my mind that I was being pranked. My world started to shrink, and confusion set in, and I felt lost. My mind went blank along with my face.

"My mom has been shot, and she is at UofL Hospital!" I yelled to Officer Fredricks and Savage.

"Get in my car, Pitts! Let's go!" Officer Savage yelled at me.

As we sped towards UofL hospital, I prayed to God because I had no idea what I was going into.

"Please take care of my mom, God! Please!" I prayed out loud.

Questions abounded in my mind.

"Who would want to hurt my mom?" "Did someone break into the house and hurt her?" "Was she carjacked?" "Where was she shot?" "Were her injuries life-threatening or superficial?"

The police car tires screeched as we pulled into the UofL ER, and I ran inside to see my mom.

"Where is Idella Pitts! I need to see her now!" I screamed frantically at the ER staff.

I was breathing heavily and started hyperventilating as I waited for her to tell me my mom's location. A nurse then escorted me to where my mother was.

"Your mother was found with a gunshot wound to her head. She was treated at the scene and taken to Hardin Memorial Hospital in Elizabethtown. From there, she was airlifted here. She is alive, but she is not responsive and is being kept alive by a ventilator. She has no brain activity."

My chest tightened, and it felt like someone slammed a Louisville Slugger baseball bat into the sternum. The nurse opened the sliding glass door and slipped back the curtain to reveal my mother lying on a hospital bed.

Giant tears suddenly tumbled down my face, and I wept uncontrollably as I took in the horrific scene before me. I felt trapped in a nightmare that I could not wake up from as my beautiful mother lay still in the hospital bed.

As I got closer to her bedside, I noticed that her beautiful face was covered in white kerlix gauze that was now stained crimson red as it soaked up the blood leaking from the bullet wound that had pierced her right temple. The ventilator tube was strapped to her mouth due to her being intubated to be kept alive. I could see past the blood-stained bandages and medical equipment that her head was swollen.

As I stood next to her bed, I reached down to grab her right hand but was stopped by the brown paper bags that had been tapped to her beautiful hands. I wanted to rip through the brown paper bags and gain access to the hands that had provided me with so much comfort the last twenty-six years. I remembered those hands stroking my head as my mom laid next to me in my hospital bed at WRAMC, reassuring me that I was going to be okay.

Why were these brown paper bags on her hands restraining me from their comfort? I wanted to strip off all my gear and get into the bed next to her and hold her in my arms, and comfort her like she once comforted me.

I asked the nurse, "what are these brown paper bags for?"

"They are there to preserve evidence," She replied.

I could not get to her hands, so I settled for her wrist.

"Wake up, mama. Please wake up. I need you. Do not leave me here by myself." I cried to her.

I sat next to her sobbing and crying to God to perform a miracle to wake her up and bring her back to me as she once was.

"Who did this to you? Who would want to hurt you like this? Why would someone do this to you?" "I am going to find whoever did this, and they are going to pay dearly." I pondered to myself. Someone was responsible for all of this, and they needed to be held accountable.

Time did not stand still in the moment because it felt like time did not exist. She and I were here at this moment with no past, present, or future. The world around me had ceased to exist as I was enthralled with many emotions spanning the entire emotional gauntlet.

Into the room walked a hospital social worker dressed in scrubs and proceeded to ask me questions that were insulting to not only me but my mother, and they seriously offended me.

"Has your mom ever attempted suicide or made mention of suicide?"

"No! She would never do something like that! Ever!" I clamored at the social worker.

An RPD detective walked into the room and updated me on their investigation. He explained that my father showed up at the police station covered in blood with a large laceration to his head and 3rd degree burns to his body. When an RPD officer responded to my mother's home, which she had been awarded during the divorce, the officers found her in the driver seat of her car, parked in the garage, suffering from a 9mm bullet wound to the right side of her head. She was unconscious but still alive and breathing when they found her.

They initially detained my father and held him for questioning but soon let him go shortly after because they did not have enough evidence to charge him for murder. However, they informed me that they would be conducting a murder/suicide investigation and that charges could be brought against my father later if evidence showed that he was the perpetrator.

"Sir. I know my mother. She would not kill herself. That is not possible. She was the strongest and most confident woman I know. She loves God and would never do anything like that. She was the one who kept me from going over the edge and held me together when I got back from Iraq." I explained to him.

"Did my father kill my mother?" I wondered. That was the only logical explanation for this chaotic situation.

I picked up the phone to call Celeste and inform her of everything that had transpired. She was in shock and disbelief, then spoke words to me that still haunt me today.

"Dexter. Mom has been battling with thoughts of suicide for a while now." She spoke.

The rage within me started to surge hearing this shocking information.

"If you were aware of this, why did you not tell me! Why!" I furiously screamed into the phone at my sister.

Celeste and I lost contact and were at odds over my marriage to Michelle as well. Celeste lived in Alabama, and my mom would often make the 4-hour drive to visit with her. During the visits, Celeste learned of my mother's struggle with depression and suicide and kept it from the rest of the family and me. I was enraged because I only lived 45 minutes away and believed that had I known, maybe I could have intervened and gotten our mother the help she needed.

I hung up the phone on Celeste with the feeling of betrayal. How could she keep all of this from me? All my life, people tried to keep things from me, believing they were protecting me because I was the baby of the family. Even after all I had endured in life, they still viewed me as a little kid and never brought me into serious conversations. Now because of that, I was the one sitting with my mother enduring this all alone because of their failure to communicate or set aside their personal feelings.

My mom did not have a living will. And because of that, I was forced to make the difficult decision that was before me. Do I keep her on life support, or do I pull the plug and let her go? The choice was mine alone to make.

"Why me, God?" I thought to myself.

Before this unfathomable situation in my life, Iraq was the most traumatic and unforgettable thing I had encountered in my short existence. Nothing could top what I went through and experienced in the Middle East and WRAMC. I knew that death eventually comes for all of us, but this was not how I pictured losing my mom. I pictured her passing away as an old lady in her bed surrounded by her family.

As the nurse waited for my decision, I remembered my mother's words during one of our last conversations.

"Promise me that if anything were to ever happen to me and I end up needing to be put on life support to just let me go."

I knew what my mom's last wishes were, and I knew what I had to say, but that did not make it any easier. I did not want to be the person making a choice to bring an end to her 50 years of life on the earth.

"Is there any chance that she can come around from this and come back?" I asked the doctor one last time.

"We have done all we can to help her. I wish there were more that we could do, but the damage to her brain is too severe. We have not seen any brain activity in hours. It is almost certain that she will not recover from this." The doctor told me.

I still had hope in my heart. I had seen God do the impossible and believed that God was going to hear my prayers and bring my mom back. As much as I believed that, I also knew I had to do what my mom wanted me to do.

With colossal tears in my eyes and a bereaved heart, I gave the medical staff permission to end my mother's life. I was escorted to a small private room the hospital staff set up for me and my wife's family. I sat and cried as they surrounded me and prayed. A nurse came to the room just shy of an hour later.

"She's gone, sweetie. I'm so sorry."

On August 29, 2010, at 1410 hours, my beautiful, sweet, loving, God-fearing mother took her last breath and crossed the veil from life to death. I did not think it was possible for me to cry anymore or cry harder than I already was. My soul yelped as my entire world collapsed around me. With my mother's last breath on earth and making her exit from this life, so excited my faith and hope with her.

I soon found myself surrounded by my fellow LMPD officers. They came to the hospital to show me support. Our chief at the time, Robert White, came as well.

"We are here for you, Dexter. Anything you need you just let us know. We will be with you every step of the way through this process. I promise you that." Chief White promised me.

Before I left the hospital for the evening, I wanted to see my mom one last time and say goodbye to her. I asked the nurse if it was possible for me to have a few moments with her alone.

"She is in the back room. They just removed all the badges and cleaned her up. I must warn you. You might not want to see her in that condition." The nurse tried to warn me.

I heard the nurse loud and clear, but I had to see her one last time. It was as though I could hear her calling out to me to come and visit her one last time and spend this last one-on-one moment together.

The nurse escorted me down the hallway to where my mother's body was. I stepped into the room, and it was pitch black except for this one light that shined bright. Under that bright light laid my mother's remains. I slowly walked through the darkness and stepped into the bright light next to her empty shell.

I looked down at her, and her entire body was covered in a white sheet, and only her head protruded from under the sheet. The bandages and medical tubes in her mouth were gone. It was my mother's beautiful face. Traces of dried blood laced her jet-black hair. I could see the bullet hole and the damage the projectile did to the right side of her head and to her right eye. I looked away in pain as my heart shuttered at the sight. But I forced myself to look at her and the damage. I had to remember. I wanted to remember. I needed to remember.

"You deserved better than this, mama. I am so sorry. I am sorry about everything. I love you, mama." I cried over her body.

I called Celeste back to tell her that our mother had earned her angel wings and halo and that she was now in heaven with the Lord. I listened to my sister sob on the other end of the phone.

I had hoped that my sister and I would grow closer after losing our mother so tragically, violently, and unexpectedly. I believed that we would be able to set aside our differences and be there for each other in these times, but my mother's death was the catalyst that would destroy our already shaky relationship and start my descent into a dark place no human should ever have to dwell on their own.

I stood on the bank of the Ohio River at my in-law's house the next day, looking up at the sky, trying to imagine where my mom was and what she was seeing and doing in heaven. I tried to picture her with a giant smile on her face and being at peace. The more I thought about her being gone from this life, the more I cried because I knew that I would never see her in the flesh again.

I drove down to the RPD Headquarters to meet with the lead detectives. The investigation was in its early phase, but they provided me with a copy of some letters and notes that they found in the house that my mom wrote. These were not random notes. These appeared to be suicide notes. As I read through the notes, I got a glimpse into the last few months of my mother's life and the pain she was enduring. The notes detailed the mental and physical abuse she had suffered over the years at the hands of my father. She wrote about how he controlled every aspect of her life since they were married and how he would degrade her. She stated that my dad had everyone fooled as to how good of a man he was, especially the church members. She said that he always told her that no one would ever believe her if she ever came forward about the abuse.

Of all the notes I read, there was one that still sticks with me until this day.

"Dexter. I am sorry that you felt like you had to leave your family. You really hurt me, but you will not have to worry about me anymore."

Just when I thought the pain could not get deeper, the pain plunged to a new level. I knew I had hurt her, but I was not aware of how much I had hurt her. My stomach turned and ached as I looked at the words on the paper. I instantly felt ashamed, embarrassed and regretted my actions and the lack of communication I had with her over the last year.

As grieved as I felt, I had a sense of peace that swooped over me and would not let me feel bad or carry this guilt and shame. I thought back to our last conversation and our last words to each other. Our 26-year mother and son relationship, although rocky the last quarter of her life, ended it on a high note leaving no doubt about how much we loved one another. After all the hurt we put each other through, "I love you" Were the last words we spoke to each other. I had no clue as to when she wrote the note, but I knew, without a doubt in my heart, that she wrote that note at the start of our troubles, not at the end of her life. That note was a snapshot of our relationship at the worst time in our lives together, but it did not define our entire 26-years together.

Celeste drove into town from Alabama the same day. When she arrived in town, she brought enough anger and chaos to bring the entire U.S. Military to its knees before her. She had become a dictator. Going to war prepared me for a lot of things in life, but nothing prepared me to deal with Celeste's wrath. Celeste was on the warpath and had no concern about collateral damage.

"Celeste, you are just like your father. You are so controlling," My mom would constantly tell my sister.

My sister never had the reputation of being a nice person. She was rough around the edges and always desired to be in control. We were never very close, but we could tolerate each other for the most part. We visited our mother's lawyer to view her will. Her lawyer explained to us that our mother had a will; however, she died before she had the chance to sign it. The lawyer showed us the will. It stated that all of her property and life insurance was to be split between the two of us into equal shares. The unsigned will told us our mother's wishes, but the will was not valid, and my sister used that to her advantage. As we left the lawyer's office, my sister spoke, and I knew trouble was brewing.

"I know what was said, but I also know what you did. You do not deserve anything." Celeste snickered at me.

At the funeral home in Elizabethtown, she and I argued over my mother's funeral service and what to do. We wanted our mother's last wishes to be respected. She gave me zero input into how our mother's service would be carried out. And to make matters worse, my sister did not have the money to pay for half of the cost of the funeral services. I paid the money upfront, yet I did not get any say in anything.

The funeral home needed pictures of our mother to make a slideshow for the visitation and memorial service. Celeste had taken all of our family pictures from home. When we went to the funeral home to view the slide show before the service, there were only two pictures of my mom in the entire slide show and me. The rest of the pictures were of Celeste and our mother's family. I caught on quickly to what was unfolding. My sister was blaming me for our mother's death, and she was trying to erase me from the picture.

Instead of a funeral, Celeste demanded that we do a viewing and a memorial service. Afterward, my mother's remains would be cremated. Before our mother's service, Celeste and I met at the State Farm Insurance office to learn about my mother's life insurance policy. As we sat talking to the life insurance agent, he informed us about our mother's life insurance policy. The life insurance agent informed us that he had a long talk with our mother about the policy when she took it out some years ago. According to the agent, my mom put Celeste in charge of everything because she was the older and more responsible sibling. Even though our mother put Celeste in charge of everything, it was not to give her possession of everything and cut me out. My mother wanted my sister to do the right thing and split everything evenly, and take care of her little brother.

As we walked out of the insurance office, Celeste let me know her intentions just as she did at the lawyer's office.

"If you want your half of this money, you are going to have to do what I tell you to do first."

She had what she wanted; total control. She wanted to dominate me in every aspect. She assumed holding money over my head would force me to submit myself to her controlling and overbearing desires.

Little did she know, my pride and ego did not have a price tag, and I defended them with my life.

I screamed and cursed her out in a fit of rage. I unleashed all my anger, displeasure, and disapproval of her cutting me out of our mother's belongings with an ungodly verbal assault directed straight towards her heart. I said things to her that no respectful human should say to another. I perceived that my sister did not have a heart. And if she did, it was black and frozen, and there was no love or respect for me in it. We might as well have been two strangers passing on the street who decided to get into a shouting match.

I grew further enraged when I thought about all I had done for my sister over the years out of love. The times I looked out for her and gave her money when she was a struggling college student or when she fell on hard times, and I gave her some cash after I received my TSGLI (Traumatic Injury Insurance money after being wounded in Iraq. I had always tried to look after her and take care of her. But the first chance she got to burn me, she scorched me to my core and abandoned me.

"You do not deserve anything, Dexter." Celeste's words kept repeating in my head.

I never expected my own sister to be so vindictive towards me.

"What did I do wrong? What did I do to deserve to be treated like this by my own flesh and blood?" I pondered.

My mom's family drove in from Milwaukee and Mississippi to say goodbye to their last goodbyes. I had not seen some of my cousins since we were little kids. We all shared hugs and embraced each other in the solemn moment. Not in attendance was my father's family. Due to the circumstances of my mother's death, they opted out of coming. I was upset with them for many years because of this, but as I have matured and grown, I developed more of an understanding as to why they did not come.

LMPD officers drove down from Louisville to show their support for me. It put my heart at ease seeing the amount of support I had from the thin blue line that I was now a part of. It made me proud to be a part of the department. It felt great knowing that so many people I worked with cared about me and what I was going through.

Dressed in my police uniform, I proceeded into the funeral home to start the viewing. I watched my mom's memorial video with Amazing Grace playing in the background. Fury and grief played tug of war in my heart, knowing that my sister only put two pictures of my mom and me in the video. My family members took notice as well. As I was talking to some of my family members, I heard Celeste scream.

"Go! Get out of here right now! You need to leave! You do not belong here!" I heard her yelling at the top of her lungs.

Everyone in the funeral home stopped to look at what was happening. My sister was yelling at an older white lady and chasing her out of the funeral home.

I looked closer at the lady my sister was yelling at and instantly recognized her. It was my fifth-grade teacher from Fort Knox, Mrs. Bivens. Mrs. Bivens was one of the nicest and sweetest teachers I ever had. She loved my mother and would always talk to her when my mom would come to pick me up from school. I had not seen Mrs. Bivens since I was in the 4th grade. I met her outside after my sister cruelly and embarrassingly chased her out of the service.

"Oh, my goodness, Dexter. Look at you. You are all grown up and a police officer, now." She said to me with tears in her eyes."

I was not sure if she was crying from seeing my mom lying in her casket or from my sister shrinking at her. I apologized to her for my sister's actions and gave her a giant hug.

My family pulled me aside to figure out what was going with Celeste, but I had no answer for them as I was still in the dark as well. The only thing I could think of was that my sister was mad at the world, but more specifically me, for some unspecified reason, and she was going to take out her anger on anyone in close proximity, and she did not care who she hurt in the process.

Emotions were running high, but I had to push all of my feelings at the moment aside so I could tell my mom goodbye one last time. As

I walked up to her casket, the first thing I noticed was her hands. They were free from the brown paper bags that kept me from their comfort at the hospital. I gazed at her beautiful hands. They were the hands that prayed for me and provided me with 26-years of comfort, safety, happiness, and discipline. Her hands had been there for the best and worst moments of my life. I was going to miss those hands. I reached down and placed my hands on hers. The warmth and energy that once flowed through her hands were no more. The magic touch that a mother's hands possessed had faded. In the absence of the magic, warmth, and energy, her hands were now icy cold and void of life.

I stared at my mom dressed in her beautiful gown as she slept in eternity. Her head wound was gone, and she looked almost how I remember her in life. I knew it was her laying there, but I did not feel that connection or that vibrant vigor that being in her presence once brought about. It was just her shell.

I walked away from the casket and retreated to the bathroom, and locked myself inside to hide my tears. Being dressed in my police uniform, I had to show everyone how strong and tough I was. I had to personify everything that a law enforcement officer was: mentally and emotionally tough, professional, confident, compassionate, but most importantly, in control. I put on a top-notch performance for the crowd, but I cried a river of tears into the sink.

After the service, my sister gathered all of our family members outside of the funeral home for an announcement. I looked at my sister and noticed that she had papers in her hands. I recognized the writing on the paper. It was our mother's suicide notes. She was prepared to share them with the family. She read through the notes displaying our mother's pain and suffering for all. She saved the note that my mother wrote to me last.

Celeste read that note with passion and antagonism. At the end of every sentence, she would look up at me and communicate her disgust for me through her eyes. I would stare back at her and not blink, not wanting to back down. She wanted me to hurt more than I was already hurting. She wanted there to be nothing left of me after she was done.

"I don't know what is going on with you and your sister, Dexter, but you two need to fix this." My auntie demanded.

Once again, I had no answer.

I told her about everything involving the will, the life insurance policy, and everything my sister had said to me.

"God can fix anything, baby. We just have to pray and believe."

I wanted to believe that God could fix anything, but he did not take care of my mother, one of his most loyal and faithful servants, from the unfortunate circumstances that befell her. God was the last thing I wanted to hear about. He had abandoned not only me but my mom when she needed Him the most.

Before life could continue, there was one last hurdle—my mother's ashes. I wanted my mother's ashes, but so did my sister. I went to the funeral home the next day to try and collect them, but my sister beat me there. She took our mother's ashes and skipped town. I had experienced a lot of hurt in my life, but nothing hurt me more than Celeste leaving me with nothing from our mother's 50 years of life but the memories she and I made and the pictures I took of her myself. The only thing I was left with was questions.

With my mom gone, a strained relationship with Celeste, and being estranged from my father and his family, I was practically alone in this world. All I had going forward was my wife, her family, and my career. You would think that would be enough for me to grasp onto life and help me move on, but the fake life that I had built started to unravel and exposed the most fragile parts of me.

[21]

SAVED BY THE ONE-LEGGED DEVIL DOG

"Pitts! Did you search this guy before you put in the police car!" My new FTO yelled at me in the jail as he held up an ice pick he had removed from our prisoners' pocket.

"This guy could have killed one of us!" He shouted at me.

The two great lessons I had learned from Paco and Sergeant Trees as to how not only survive in this career but thrive were not being applied in my life or my career. I was on a crash course to outright annihilation. I was becoming a disgrace and embarrassment to the badge and the profession. I was not in a good place mentally or emotionally to be patrolling the streets of West Louisville and carrying a loaded firearm.

Not only was I not in a good mental space, but I was also starting to develop a terrible reputation amongst my cohorts for not being a very smart or safe officer. But, of course, none of this was my fault. My reputation was not suffering because of me. My reputation was suffering because of the color of my skin in this white, male-dominated profession. Like so many black people had told me at church, I was at a disadvantage because of the color of my skin.

My personal life mirrored my professional life; it was a dumpster fire. My second marriage was failing. To add to my long list of problems, Celeste sold our mother's home out from under me and kept the profit all to herself as the executor of our mother's estate. I had failed my U.S. Constitution law class, and my weight was increasing. I was now waddling around at 300 pounds, and my diabetes was out of control.

Somehow, I was given the green light from my FTO's and the Second Division command to be cut loose and ride solo as a probationary police officer without supervision. Even though my life was falling further apart and I was spiraling out of control, I managed to do enough right to make it through FTO training.

Despite my life and career being in absolute shambles, I loved being a police officer, and I loved my wife. And I was fighting like hell to hold onto both because they were the only two things I had in my life. Policing was my escape from my marriage when things were not going well, but my marriage was going to end my career. My marriage to Michelle was now filled with distrust, jealousy, daily verbal sparring, and allegations of infidelity directed towards me, which were absolutely false.

I was afraid of her leaving me and being alone, so I took whatever she threw at me. Plus, I did not want to suffer the shame of being a two-time divorcee at the age of 26. I had to fight and hold onto this marriage and do whatever it took to make things work.

As my marriage continued to circle the drain, Michelle took it upon herself to call the police to our home a few more times. I finally reached the point where I thought it was best that I move out and we separate. I found myself residing in the home that Michelle owned in the West End. The home was within walking distance to the Second Division, where I worked. I was always told that officers should not police work where they live for safety reasons, but I had been forced into this situation that I did not want to be in, and I had nowhere else to. I lived out of my duffle bag and slept on an air mattress, and kept my Glock under my pillow as I slept, fearing that someone I had arrested would come to where I was lodging and try to do me harm.

After months of being separated and mulling over things in my mind, I reluctantly contacted a divorce attorney to discuss my options. My attorney could tell that I was struggling with this decision and advised me to sleep on it, and I took his advice. I was going to do whatever I could to make our marriage right and save it, but I soon learned of the news that crushed my will to fight for my marriage.

Due to privacy and legal concerns, I cannot and will not detail the news I received, but upon learning of this discovery, I knew that my marriage was beyond repair. Instead of trying to save my marriage, I needed to focus on trying to save myself. But trying to save myself was a job too big for just me. I was alone in this world, and there was no one in my corner to help me. The one person that I could truly lean on was now deceased. I would lay down at night, and it was as though I could hear my mother's voice from beyond the grave. I could hear the words she spoke to me before I got married and how she foresaw this very moment and tried to warn me, but I did not heed her wisdom.

"Mark my words, Dexter. That girl will be your downfall. She is going to break your heart and break. She is going to take everything from you. You watch and see. I might not be alive to see it, but it will come to pass."

She was right. She was not alive to see it, but her words came to pass. I was slowly starting to lose my grip on reality. I had reached my breaking point. Michelle broke what was left of me. I was now the most dangerous type of man there was—a man with nothing to lose.

"Take all the time you need, Pitts." Second Division Major Kristofeck told me after my mom's death.

I took one week off from work after my mother's untimely passing. I wanted to get back to work and focus on my career so I did not have to deal with or come to terms with all that had transpired. I did not want time to mourn or time to reflect. I just wanted to move on and forget it all. I wanted to do what I had grown familiar doing; burying it all and just pretending like it never happened.

I wanted to pretend like my family never existed, so I could forget the hurt and betrayal my own flesh and blood heaped on me, ruining my life. I had buried a lot of problems and pain from my past, but this amount of pain could not be buried. It was too large of a mess to just throw dirt on and walk away. I tried to run and hide from all the pain, but there was nowhere for me to run. I was cornered. The only way for me to escape was death.

While working the graveyard shift one night, we received a domestic violence call to Narragansett Dr. The caller advised us that a young boy was hiding in his closet because his father had just shot and killed his mother.

I zoomed to the location with my red and blue light flashing and my siren blaring. As I drove to the location of the incident, my mind was not where it should have been. Hearing that this kid's father just shot and killed his mother put my focus on my own similar incident. I started to think about my mom and dad and how their marriage ended so tragically in a similar fashion. I knew this kid's pain and the horror that had unfolded before him all too well.

I was the first officer to arrive on the scene. I retrieved my Remington 870 shotgun loaded with buckshot and exited my vehicle. I racked the forefend of my shotgun, sending a round into the chamber. I used my index finger to take the safety off as I moved towards the home. Thoughts of my dad putting a pistol to my mom's head and pulling the trigger preoccupied my mind. I advanced forward, not thinking about my tactics or safety as my finger rested on the trigger.

Boom!

I negligently discharged my shotgun into the ground as I tripped and fell. My ears rang and my heart beat uncontrollably as I knew I had just made one of the biggest, most unforgivable, and shameful mistakes an officer or military member can make. A negligent discharge is the kiss of death for anyone in my career field. I had just signed my career death warrant.

I picked myself up off the ground and put another round in the chamber, and took up position behind some cover by the house. My platoon members arrived on the scene shortly afterward to back me up. We made entry into the home expecting to find a gruesome murder scene and a traumatized child hiding in the closet. That was what we expected. But what we found was an innocent family who had been the victim of a prank call.

There was no one on the scene when my negligent discharge happened. The thought of just staying silent and not saying anything briefly crossed my mind, but I knew I had to do the right thing and inform my sergeant of the incident. Walking into roll call the next day, I knew what to expect. An onslaught of jokes and hazing.

"What's up, hotshot!" "Is that you, Remington!" "What did the ground ever do to you Pitts to make you shoot it and kill it?" The jokes were never-ending. They were well deserved on my end. I sat and laughed them off with everyone and just went along with it. The truth was, I did not feel anything. I was emotionally numb, and all I wanted to do was escape this horrible life I was in.

Typically, I was always thankful that I came out of Iraq alive when so many did not. That was no longer the case. I found myself wishing that the insurgent would have killed me six years prior. Had he done his job properly, I could have avoided all of this pain and anguish I was experiencing.

If my mother were alive and saw me in my current state, she would have told me to pray, read my Bible and seek God. But I wanted nothing to do with the God she prayed to because I saw what her prayers and years of dedication earned her-an early grave. I was ready to retire to an early grave, and I did not need her God's assistance to get me there. I could do it myself, or so I thought.

The not so glorious impact of war, two failed marriages, and the catastrophic end of the Pitts family saga had snuffed out my will to live. I had nothing to fight for to keep me here. The driving force behind all I did in life had flatlined. I had been abandoned by God and those who were supposed to love and care for me. I had lived more than enough life at 27, and I did not want to continue on.

In my mind, no one was going to miss me. No one was going to notice that I was gone. I drove myself to the FOP (Fraternal Order of Police) parking lot. I had made the decision to bring an end to my pathetic life. I had driven to the FOP lot because I knew that my fellow officers would find me there. I would make my grand exit from this life by way of a bullet through my head, just like my mother.

I sat in the darkness of my truck with my fully loaded Glock 22 in my lap, trying to work up the nerve to carry out the deed. 5.5 pounds of pressure on the trigger, and it would all be over. 5.5 pounds of pressure, and I could be reunited with my mom and my fallen brothers. My torment would be over. I placed the barrel of my Glock to my right temple.

The steel of the barrel was cold against my skin but would soon be heated up by the firing pin striking the primer of the brass .40 caliber shell casing and igniting the gunpowder. I rested my finger on the trigger and slightly squeezed it, taking the slack out of it just before it would fire. I thought about the last moments of my mother's life and wondered what was going through her head before everything went black. I wondered what was waiting for me on the other side. I had hoped that she would be the first face I would be greeted by.

"Do it, Dexter," I screamed to myself as I shook violently from nervousness.

I was ready to end it, but there was one problem. I was a coward and did not possess the courage to finish the job. I wanted to die, but I was too scared to do it myself, and I did not want people to think I was weak.

"You piece of trash, you are a coward," I yelled to myself.

That was when I decided that I wanted to die a hero's death in the line of duty and be buried with my pride, honor, and tough-guy image intact. Even in death, I wanted to be viewed and known as the tough guy. I cared that much about what people thought about me. And in my mind, the tough guys never killed themselves. The tough guys went out in the blaze of glory. My hope was that some low-life criminal would do it for me. And I was in the right career field and patrolled the right place to make it happen.

I have never been the type to go out of my way to break the rules. I have always been an astringent, by the book, rule follower. I was now a reckless renegade with nothing to lose, and the rules meant nothing to me. They were the only thing standing in my way of me dying the glorious and honorable death that I desired. I cast aside the tactics and SOP (stand operating procedures) that I had been taught to follow for my survival and safety. My bulletproof vest now sat at home while I went and patrolled the streets purposely unprotected. I was a loose cannon running amuck in the streets of the West End.

Tombstone courage was my motto as I cleared houses on my own, searching for criminals during active burglary calls and house alarms. My driving became erratic as I sped everywhere, blowing red lights and not wearing my seatbelt. I would conduct traffic stops without notifying dispatch of my location. Every traffic stop I made, I put myself at a disadvantage turning my back to the car as I walked away and ignoring the hand placement actions of the individuals inside the vehicle. Someone was going to rescue me from my suffering. The public would view the person who killed me as an evil monster for having taken the life of an officer, but that person would be my personal hero.

"Meet me down at Thornton's gas station on Cane Run Road so we can chat," Sergeant Trees requested.

I got lucky and ended up being an officer on Sergeant Trees' platoon. He was someone I could look up to and follow his lead. Aside from his time in the Air Unit and The Homicide Unit, he had spent most of his career in the Second Division. If there was anyone who I truly cared what they thought about me, it was him.

"What the hell is your problem! I told you from day one that your reputation is the only thing you have in this department and to protect it! Do you know what people are saying about you! They are saying that Pitts is not safe, and we do not want to work with him! Not only that, but because of your recklessness, you are putting their lives at risk as well! No one trusts you! You were a grunt in the army! You carried a rifle in your hands for three years! How in the hell do you have a negligent discharge with a shotgun! I bragged to people about you and told them that you were going to be a great police officer for this department and the Second Division! And now you are making me look like an idiot because of your actions! This is not the Dexter Pitts I know. What the hell is going on with you!" Sergeant Tree's ripped into me like the angry devil dog that he was.

I sat in my patrol car next to him, and I started to open up to him about my current life struggles. I did not reveal to him that I wanted to die, but I let him know that I was in a bad way mentally and that I was struggling to maintain my sanity. I told him about how heartbroken I was over Michelle and how angry I was at my sister for how she treated me. My mind was twisted over what had happened between my mom and dad. I had no clue what to believe.

I tried to hold back my tears, but the force behind them carried too much weight. The burden I was carrying was far too heavy to hide. I had never cried in front of another man before. I spilled tears all over my Class A uniform. I knew that I had lost his respect and that he would not look at me the same.

My perception of life was so skewed and twisted from the beat-down life had given me that I expected to lose not only his respect but my job as well. But my perception was not reality. The truth was, Sergeant Tree's cared about and respected me more than I was aware of. He was aware of the struggle I was going through because he had endured a lot of the same struggles with his injuries, his recovery, and a prior divorce. He could see that I was slowly drowning and that if he did not reach down and pull me from the strong undercurrent of life that I would be swept away and lost forever.

The next morning, Sergeant Trees and I met with Major. Kristofeck to find a plan of action for me to get better and get back on track.

"Dexter. We know you have been through a lot. We love you. You are family. We want to see you do well and have a long career, but we have to get you better first. We just want you to be OK. We are granting you 30 days of leave to take care of yourself and figure things out. We are here for you." Major Kristofeck reassured me.

After the meeting, I went home, packed a bag, and I drove to Milwaukee to be with my mom's family. I spent the next three weeks with them, mourning, remembering, and celebrating my mother's life. When my 30 days of leave was up, I felt recharged and refreshed. I was ready to get back to work.

My first call for service after my 30 days of leave was a suicide. My partner, Officer Beth Lankford, responded to the scene with me. Beth and I had become great friends during our time working in the Second. Despite our different skin colors, we were brother and sister. We always looked out for each other.

We pulled up to the tiny blue house on Campground Road and could hear a loud commotion of yelling, screaming, and crying as we approached. We noticed that the front door was open as we walked up. We walked into the home, and there was a white father holding his young kids in his arms in the living room. They were all covered in blood and crying hysterically. I looked at the tears on their faces, and I knew those tears. They were the same tears I cried not too long ago.

"She's in the bathroom!" The father yelled at us and pointed towards the hallway to our left.

Beth and I walked down the hallway and saw a pair of legs covered in blue jeans sticking out from the bathroom. The scene inside the bathroom was ghastly. The bathroom was covered in blood and brain matter. In the hands of the deceased, which rested next to her head, was a black handgun. You could see where the bullet entered her head and blew out one of her eyes, causing it to hang out of her eye socket. As I looked at this poor lady lying in her own blood with a bullet hole in her head, I flashed back to me standing next to my mother's body.

"Dexter!" Beth said to me as she shook me to snap me out of my trance.

"Are you OK?" She asked.

"I'm good, Beth," I replied.

"Let's secure this scene and get the family out of here," I suggested.

I escorted the family outside and started to do my job. As much as I was trying to focus on their tragedy and doing my job, my own personal tragedy kept rearing its ugly head.

"Dexter. You need to get out of here." Beth said to me.

Beth could tell that I was troubled by what I saw. She knew that staying on this scene longer was not a good idea for me and told me to leave.

I met with Major Kristofeck at a local coffee shop early on Saturday morning, and he purchased me a hot cup of coffee, and we sat and chatted for hours. Major Kristofeck was prior service and loved that I was a veteran and admired my military service.

"So, you were 10th Mountain? Do you mind telling me about your Purple Heart?" He inquired.

I told him the story of how I earned my Purple Heart. After we were done sipping on our coffee, the major made me yet another offer. He knew I had been through a lot, and he wanted to let me know that he was here for me. Sitting and chatting with the major did my heart good and reassured me that my chain of command was looking out for me.

As good as I was feeling, I would drive back to my place, where I would sit alone in silence and be forced to confront my inner demons and thoughts all alone. My mind would wander, and I would try to unpack my life and find a logical explanation for the age-old question, "Why me?"

My good friend Ryan from church directed me to the Bible verse James 1:2-4

I was still at odds with God and wanted nothing to do with Him, His Word, or "His plan." I had not prayed, gone to church, or opened my Bible in months. The only reason I still had my Bible was that my mom gifted it to me before I left for boot camp, and she put a special message in it for me. Aside from that, God was not a necessity in my life.

As much as I tried to disregard my train wreck of a life, it was too much for me to ignore. It felt like I was trapped in my own personal purgatory dangling between life and death. I felt stuck. Death was no longer an option, but continuing to live my life as it was seemed improbable. I needed answers and understanding, and leaning on my own logic and understanding, but my was fruitless and only left me more confused and further from the truth.

I was desperate to find a motive to explain all my grief. I was out of options and had exhausted all the resources I knew, from books to people. The one place I had not looked was The Bible. I stubbornly stood my ground in protest of bending the knee to God. Ryan's suggestion to read James 1:2-4 kept coming to my mind. I was curious about the verse, but I was too bullheaded to cave in. I was drifting aimlessly and letting the tides of life take me wherever and I did not put up a fight. I did not know who I was, and I hated the person I saw in the mirror. I had nothing to lose at this point, and I retrieved my Bible and turned to James 1:2-4.

"Consider it pure joy, my brothers and sisters, whenever you face trials of many kinds because the testing of your faith produces perseverance. Let perseverance finish its work so that you will be complete, not lacking anything (James 1:2-4).

My heart had become ice cold towards God and life, but the words I read from the verse started to slowly thaw my heart. I was not a complete person, and I was lacking a lot, especially in the faith category. I tried to fight against the feelings that were starting to manifest inside of me. I had been angry and hurt for so long that I did not want to part from those feelings. I held onto those feelings because, in my mind, I was the victim in all of this. I had a right to my rage and a right to my anger towards God.

"Why me! Why my mom! What did I do wrong to deserve any of this!" I hollered to the heavens.

I had gone through more than my fair share of trials, and I

wanted relief. But more than anything, I wanted my mom back. The more I thought about her, the more I started to cry and called out to her through my tears.

"I miss you, mom. I cannot do this without you. I need you so much right now." I spoke into the empty living room as a lake of tears started to puddle at my knees.

I got up from my knees and went to my bedroom to lay down. I curled up in a ball on my bed and continued to cry. My pillow was soaked in my tears as I sobbed without ceasing, wishing to see my mom's beautiful smile, feel her hands pat me on the head as her soothing voice told me that everything was going to be OK.

As I lay in my bed crying, I felt a warm, loving presence flood my bedroom. I then felt the presence surround and embrace me. It was the same feeling I had as I lay in my hospital bed at WRAMC when my mom climbed into bed with me to comfort me. I knew instantly that my mom was with me at this moment to comfort me as she had done before. Her love for me was so strong and undying that not even death could keep her from her baby boy. My heart aching cry pierced through the veil that separated life from death and reached her.

I pictured my mom begging and pleading with God to let her come to my aid.

"Please let me go to him. Please. My baby needs me. Just this one time."

As I rested in my mom's spiritual presence, I soon fell asleep shortly afterward.

The next thing I remember, I was standing in the same foggy, white room that I was in during my dream at WRAMC. I looked to my right, and I saw my mom sitting on a wooden bench. She was wearing the same flowing, bright blue dress. But there was something different about her this time. She had a bright glow to her, and it drew me to her.

"Mom!" I was full of joy as I ran to her and hugged her.

"Hey, baby." She said back to me every so softly.

I looked down at her hands, and they were free from the brown paper bags that separated me from them in the last moments of her life. I touched her hand, and the familiar warmth and energy had returned. I held her hand so tight, and I did not want to let it go.

"I know you are worried about me. I know you miss me. I know you are hurting. But I wanted to let you know that I am OK. You do not have to worry about me, baby. You can let me go. Everything is going to be OK. You are going to be OK." She said to me in her soft, reassuring voice.

I sat on the bench with her, chatting and embracing this beautiful moment between us that I had dreamed of for months. I awoke from my slumber, and it was morning time. I looked around my room, and my mom was gone. The feeling of her presence holding me had vanished with her. Everything felt different, and I felt at peace.

I had not felt peace in so long. To be honest, I had never known true peace my entire life. My life was a tornado of confusion and disorder disguised by a fake persona. I stumbled my way through life as a chameleon changing my beliefs and everything about me to match the environment I was in. Nothing about me was original or true to myself. I had designed myself to be a photocopy of everyone else because all I ever wanted was to fit in. And because of that, I lived my life at the mercy of others' opinions and what they thought about me.

"The most important thing you can do in life is learning to forgive those who hurt you. Remember what The Bible says. God will not forgive you unless you forgive others." My mom constantly preached to me, referencing Matthew 6:14.

With me, I carried the burden of 27 years of victimhood which morphed into self-consciousness and unchecked rage; the teasing and taunting I endured for having dark skin, the loss of my brother's lives and the life altering wounds I bore due to the atrocity of war, the demise of two failed marriages that I emptied myself into, one of which damaged my heart beyond repair, and the resentful and gut-wrenching sting of betrayal executed upon me by Celeste.

The list of people who offended and trespassed against me was a never-ending list. Being a victim for 27 years and holstering all the anger that comes with it made it easy for me to always find someone else to blame. It has become too convenient for me to live a blame-free life. I never had to take responsibility for any of my flaws. After all, it was always someone else's fault, never the guy in the mirror looking back at me.

I wanted to place all the blame upon Michelle for my second botched marriage. As much as I wanted her to be exclusively at fault, I knew that I had to take responsibility for our downfall. When I met Michelle, I was a broken man. Behind me, I dragged all my past baggage and brought all of it into the marriage. And because of that, I thrust all my troubles upon Michelle. I had tasked her with the insurmountable job of loving and repairing a fractured man. The burden that I put on her was far too great, and it forced her away from me. Even though I was willing to take up for my problems that contributed to the end of our marriage, the damage and pain we caused each other was so immense that it was too much to overcome, and I continued with the divorce.

As I continued to read my Bible, pray, and seek God, I soon started to come to the realization that the prison I had lived in for the last 27 years had been constructed by me. I had been carrying burdens that God never intended for me to carry.

The slate of my life was tarnished and stained. And the only way for me to have my slate wiped clean was to forgive everyone. From the kids on the bus, all the way to Michelle and everyone in between, had to be pardoned. For me to have the power to pardon them, I had to turn to God for the strength to do so. The malice and spite my heart knew existed because I was not familiar with mercy or forgiveness. My thirst for retribution had to be satiated, and only the power of God could extinguish the raging inferno of hatred within me.

I humbly got down on my knees and submitted myself before God to ask him to help me forgive all those who aggrieved me. Because of the mental and emotional wounds I suffered at their hands, I carried an insurmountable number of grudges with me. I crammed the grudges into every corner of my heart, making sure that I had room to store up more. My grudges provided me with a hope that one day I would have a front-row, VIP seat to see the people who hurt me eat a heaping scoop of karma as life ripped away from them all that they loved and cherished. I wanted them to drink from the same bitter cup that life forced me to guzzle. Celeste, Staff Sergeant Linder, the insurgents who hurt me and killed my brothers, the kids on the bus, and anyone who said anything negative about me or looked at me awkwardly deserved to suffer.

My desire for retaliation had been replaced by the desire to love. With my newfound peace, I realized that I no longer had to be chained to the pain of the past. I was officially free. The only thing I needed to find going forward was my own identity.

"Do not conform to the pattern of this world but be transformed by the renewing of your mind. Then you will be able to test and approve what God's will is (Romans 12:1).

My identity and belief system had been shaped and influenced by the world and those around me. Not only had I been lugging my own baggage, but I was also carrying other people's baggage. Because of that, I had taken on their biases, perception, attitude, and victim status according to their life experiences. I ignored my own personal life experiences and the many lessons I learned from my unique voyage. God made me be peculiar and extraordinary, but I rejected his will so that I could be ordinary and accepted.

I needed my identity to be based on my own personal beliefs and my own life experiences, not those of others. God had a specific plan and purpose for me. And I would never carry out that plan or live up to God's purpose if I continued traveling down roads He never intended me to trek and carry weight he never wanted me to pick up.

[22]

I AM PITTS: THE PITTS PRINCIPLES

"Ma'am! You need to calm down and listen to us." I tried to reason with the intoxicated, angry, petite, much older Caucasian lady as my partner and I stood in the halfway house's living room at 315 Southwestern Parkway.

"You can't tell me what to do!" She sassed me.

"Ma'am. You are going to go to jail if you do not calm down." I said back to her.

"Screw you! You dirty ass nigger!"

As I stood before her, she unexpectedly spat in my face. I could feel her DNA in my eyes, my face, and my mouth.

The inner rage inside me rose up. Unlike in the past, when the anger would take hold of me and send me spiraling out of control, I could subdue the rage. It felt phenomenal to be in control of not only the situation but myself. I calmly grabbed the lady by her arms, spun her around, and placed her in handcuffs. I wiped the spit from my face and maintained my professional demeanor. I escorted her to my squad car and put a spit mask on her, and sat her in the rear of my vehicle. As I drove her to the jail downtown, she continued yelling and screaming racial profanities at me.

"I'm going to tell them that you raped me, you dirty ape!" She yelled at me from the backseat of my police car.

That incident proved that the peace I had in my life was legit and that I had been fundamentally changed. The angry, offended, sensitive, victimized Dexter Pitts was no more. Instead, the confident, controlled, forgiving, and loving Dexter Pitts was now in charge.

I did a lot of soul searching and started to extract many of the toxic thoughts and beliefs implanted in me by others. More specially, my views on race. My new beliefs contradict everything I was raised to believe, learned in the Army, and did not align with my life experiences.

"It's us versus them." "These white people do not care about us." "This system was designed to hold you back." "This country was not made for us." "We have to look out for each other because they are not going to." These were some of the many opinions that started to take a foothold in my mind and shape my reality. But when I measured those ideas against the memories of those who had been there for me during the most daunting days of my life, they did not match up.

As I was lying on the ground in Iraq, believing that I would die, my white medic was working to save my life. My brothers, who were white, were doing everything they could to protect me and get me to safety. What color they were never crossed my mind. The only thing that mattered to me was they wore the same uniform as me, and they cared enough about me to get me back home alive to my family. My army doctors who put me back together, and Steve, who helped me regain my independence, were all white. And none of them ever mentioned my skin color. I even suspended the belief that Staff Sergeant Linder disliked me because I was black.

I came to that same conclusion about my brothers and sisters in blue on LMPD. When I was ready to end my life and was begging for death, a one-legged sergeant noticed me struggling and stepped in to save me. My chain of command could have easily stepped back, watched me drown, and found a reason to terminate me. But they did the exact opposite and stepped up and intervened to save not only my life but my career. They did not care that I was black. They cared about me because they saw me as a decent person and a young man deserving of mercy and needing help.

I had reduced all these wonderful people who cared about me to nothing more than the color of their skin so that I could continue believing that the color of someone's skin had more weight than their character and their deeds. I had always known that it was never about color but someone's charter. I lost sight of that. My identity became wrapped up in my skin color, and I used my skin to define me. My mind was hijacked because of my desperation for acceptance, and I had to reconcile that. I could not continue in my capacity as an LMPD officer with that type of thinking and attitude towards myself or my fellow officers, or the citizens.

Even though I knew I was a new man, I knew I had lost the respect and trust of my fellow officers. I was going to have to work overtime to gain my good name and the trust of my fellow officers back. I had to rebrand myself so that when people heard my name or saw me coming, they would not backpedal to avoid me. My last name had to have meaning.

I wanted to shed my current reputation and replace it with a respectable one. I wanted an image that exuded authority and confidence, not weakness. Those traits were naturally occurring in me due to my upbringing and my time in the Army, but they had been buried under my struggles and distress. It was time to bring out the shovel and uncover those traits and pull them to the surface.

My desire was for when people heard the name Pitts, they would associate it with the highest quality of character. Traits that not only made someone a great officer but an outstanding person. That was how I came up with the acronym for my last name Pitts: Personal Responsibility, integrity, trustworthy, tenacious, and selfless. I coined these the Pitts Principles. I would infuse those principles into every aspect of my life and use them to lay a solid foundation upon which I could rebuild my reputation.

"How did you dent the rim on your car?" Sergeant Tree's asked me.

"I was going too fast, hit a patch of ice, and slid into a curve. I take full responsibility for this incident," I admitted.

When people asked me about my shotgun ND, I would get offended, embarrassed, take up a defensive posture, and run down a list of excuses.

"I tripped!" "It's not my fault it was a prank call."

Now my response, when confronted about it, was, "I should have left the safety on and not put my finger on the trigger." "I was not mentally focused on what I was doing and made a critical mistake." By taking ownership of my actions and holding myself personally responsible, I was able to take back power over my mistakes and change people's perceptions of me.

The old me would have come up with many excuses and found something or someone to blame to keep me from having to own up to my mistake. But the new me, who was on a mission to solidify my name, wanted to showcase that I was not only willing to be personally responsible, but I also had the integrity to do what was right. I would soon get the chance to prove how much of a changed person I was.

"I'm not going anywhere!" The suspect yelled at me.

I stared at the suspect in his eyes as we stood on the elevated six-foot porch in the 1600 block of Cypress Street. I could see the beads of sweat clinging to his brown skin under the porch light. Without warning, he lunged at me, and we started to tussle on the small porch. We were of equal size, but I had the advantage in the strength department and could break free from him. He took a swing at me and missed. I shoved him so that I could create some distance between us, and he stumbled backward onto the ledge. His feet flew up into the air as he was about to fall backward over the ledge and plummet six feet down, possibly landing on his head and neck.

Realizing that he was about to fall, my integrity forced me to dash forward, grab him by his overalls to keep him from falling. We locked eyes for a moment as he was dangling backward over the ledge.

When I initially saw him, his eyes communicated his anger and displeasure towards my authority. When he was falling, his eyes expressed fear. Now that I had saved him and kept him from falling, his eyes displayed confusion. I slung him forward away from the ledge and down onto the concrete floor of the porch and cuffed his hands behind his back. I picked him up and escorted him to the back of my squad car.

"Why did you save me, officer? You could have just let me fall." He asked genuinely.

"It was the right thing to do," I told him.

"I'm sorry, officer. It was not my intention to put you in that type of spot. I was just angry and upset." He cried to me as I drove him to the jail.

"All is forgiven, sir. It's not personal."

After taking off his handcuffs at the jail, I shared a fist bump with him and wished him the best of luck going forward as the jail staff took custody of him. I got much more satisfaction out of saving him than I did having arrested him.

I wanted to show my platoon that I was trustworthy after losing their trust. I came to work every day ready to be the best beat partner in the world. So instead of just standing around on scenes trying to avoid work, I started to look for work and did more than my fair share. I would do my best to be the first on scene and be the last to leave. If the officers on the adjoining beats were getting slammed with calls, I would slide over to their beat, pick up calls for them, and take reports to try and lighten their loads.

I was determined to gain back their trust by any means necessary. Working in the streets of the West End, trust between each other was all we had. We had to depend on each other to make sure that we all got back home. So I decided to stop talking and started listening to veteran officers and their suggestions on how we would approach certain situations. When we were not busy, I would ask questions and pick their brains and gain more knowledge.

The one thing my mom wanted was for me to finish college. Even after my mom's death, I continued to pursue my bachelor's degree. In the wake of all the madness that had unfolded in my life, I had failed my constitutional law class and was ready to drop out of school. I had promised my mom that I would finish it, and I was going to live up to that promise, and it was going to take a lot of tenacity on my part to do so.

School was a daily grind for me. I was overwhelmed by the homework, term papers, and test as a full-time student and cop working the night shift. I was burning the candle at both ends, but I persisted. I was set to graduate with my bachelor's degree in May of 2012. What made my impending graduation even more special was my 3.5 GPA (grade point average). I never viewed myself as a very smart person. I saw myself as a below-average person who struggled to be average in every aspect. Graduating with a 3.5 GPA, I proved that I could accomplish anything I set my mind on if I pursued it with a tenacious attitude.

I had been dispatched to the 600 block of North 36th street to do a welfare check on an 86-year-old black woman whose family had not heard from her in weeks. Beth and our other partner, Officer Deidre Mengedoht, who we called Dee Dee, pulled up shortly after. I knocked on the door and could hear the slow shuffle of tiny feet dragging on the floor coming to the door.

"Can I help you, officers?" The tiny, sweet, little old black lady said to me.

"Ma'am. Your family is worried about you, and they wanted us to come by and check on you." I told her.

"I am just fine, officers." She told me.

As we were getting ready to leave, she spoke.

"Officer. Ain't you just the chunkiest, most adorable cop I've ever seen. You are a biggin," She said to me in a sweet and most innocent voice.

Beth and Deidre covered their mouths and turned their backs to keep from laughing. I did not find her comments amusing. I never knew that I could have my ego crushed by a sweet, elderly grandmother. I knew that she did not mean to insult me, but she was brutally honest and held no punches.

I had taken back control of my life in many areas, but I was still struggling with my health and weight. I weighed 320 pounds. I had to make a change, or I would suffer serious health consequences and end up dead. I sat in my patrol car frustrated and fed up with myself and what I saw in the mirror. I knew I had to change. No one was going to do it for me. It was going to take a lot of tenacity and resilience to win the battle of the stomach bulge.

At 0400 hours, my alarm would go off in the morning, and I would drag myself out of bed. The warmth and comfort of the sheets would try and hold me hostage, but I had to silence the seductive voice of comfort. No matter the weather conditions, I would drive to Iroquois Park, lace up my Brooks Beast running shoes and run the hilly 3.2-mile loop in the pre-dawn hours. As I ran, I could hear the voice of the sweet little old lady chasing me, "Ain't you just the chunkiest, most adorable cop I've ever seen." Once I finished running the loop, I would drive to the police gym and hit the weights for an hour. My tenaciousness paid off, and I was able to lose 50 pounds.

Selflessness is defined as putting others' needs and well-being before your own. For most of my life, I put others' needs and well-being before my own, but I did it from a place of selfishness. I sought to help and please others so that I could receive praise, recognition, and acceptance. As a result, I was a self-serving person. If I wanted to live up to the S in my last name, I had to learn to forego my selfish wants, desires and truly put others first.

I picked up a weekly moonlighting job as the on-duty officer doing security for a hotel in downtown Louisville to make some extra cash. The hotel staff informed me that there was a vagrant trespassing on the third floor. As I rode the escalator to the third floor, I could see the silhouette of a small individual at the end of the long hallway sitting on the floor. As I walked towards the vagrant, I took notice of the clothes she was wearing. The clothes were clean and neat, which was not common for most vagrants. However, the overpowering smell of alcohol lingered in the hallway. She sat with her back to the wall, and her head hung low.

As I got closer to the subject, the sound of my heavy footsteps and the jingle of my keys and equipment on my gun belt caused her to lift her head. The vagrant's face had dried tracks of tears. Sorrow and exhaustion rested upon her face. Her face looked so familiar. It was a face I had not seen in many years. It was a face I could not forget. It was the face behind all my fear, anxiety, and insecurities riding the school bus in the 7th grade. It was the face of Rhonda Brown.

"Rhonda Brown," I said confidently and strong as I looked down upon her.

She looked up at me, bewildered because this cop knew her name. However, it was clear that she did not recognize me.

"Do you remember me?" I asked with cockiness.

She looked at me, searching through her memories, trying to figure out where she knew me from.

"It's me. Spook. Blackie. Midnight. Crispy. Tar-Baby," I told her, going down a list of the names she and all her friends used to call me.

Her eyes widened, and her jaw dropped. She instantly knew who I was, and she knew that she was at my mercy. Sixteen years later, the tables had turned. I now held all the power and was raining down fear and anxiety upon her. I had envisioned confronting my tormentors while in my police uniform and putting them in handcuffs for years. It was a dream that I never expected to come to fruition. Yet here I was, with a golden opportunity to make this dream a reality and seize her freedom and crush her under my heel.

As I was preparing to remove my handcuffs from the case and place them on her wrist, a feeling of sympathy and compassion invaded my consciousness. I had to choose at this moment. I could do the selfish thing and serve myself by legally arresting her for my pleasure, enjoyment, and vengeance. Or I could set aside my self-serving desires and use this moment to live up to being the selfless person I wanted to personify to others.

I thought about the undeserving mercy and grace that God had showered me with time after time. I thought about the second, third, and so many other chances my chain of command extended to me when I was at my lowest and was a complete liability. I could hear Paco's words telling me about the grey area in policing and explaining to me that not everyone needs to be locked up.

I had her dead to rights, but how would taking her to jail serve her? There would be no benefit to her or me. It might have given me a temporary rush and some personal satisfaction, but what would I be left with once this incident was done? I had nothing to gain from this, and God had already given me peace over my past, so I had no need for retaliation.

I had not seen her in 10 years. And from the looks of it, life had beat her up good enough. So there was no need for me to add to her long list of whatever issues she was battling. Plus, I knew that look on her face from my battles in life.

"Do you have a room here?" I gently asked her.

"No." She simply replied.

"Technically, you are trespassing. I could arrest you, but I am not going to do that. You are free to go. All I ask is that you exit the property."

She picked herself up from the floor and made her way towards the escalator. As she was leaving, she looked back at me, and we made eye contact and paused. I wish I knew what was going through her mind at that moment as she looked back at me. Unfortunately, that would be the last time I ever saw Rhonda Brown. In 2017, Rhonda Brown passed away at the age of 33 due to health complications.

The comments on social media about Rhonda in the wake of her death expressed how she was a loving and kind person to everyone she met. So many people commented about how they would miss her smile and how it would light up the room. Reading the comments stirred up a fusion of emotions for me considering my history with her. I never knew Rhonda as the loving and kind person they described, but I wish I had known that version of her. The version of

Rhonda that I knew left me with mental and emotional scars that stuck with me for years.

Now that I am much older and have experienced life on a grand scale, I understand that we all have some sort of baggage that we carry with us from the hurt and pain inflicted upon us by others. We have all been hurt, and we have all hurt someone. Rhonda was no exception. As I looked at her on the floor that day at the Galt House, I knew that she was carrying with her a lot of hurt and pain from her past that had built up over the years and made her look for peace in a bottle. I do not know if she ever found the peace she was looking for while she was alive, but I pray that she has found it on the other side of life and that all her friends and family find peace in the meaning of her life.

[23]

THE GREATEST FEELING THAT I NEVER FELT

For the first time in a long time, I was happy. I would wake up happy, go to work happy, and go to sleep happy. I wish I could say that I had my life back, but that was not the case. The life I was living was a life that I never knew could exist. I was finally out of the darkness and living life to the fullest. A few months prior, I was pessimistic about my life and the future. I believed I would never get past the lowest point of my life.

Evangelist Billy Graham said it best. "Mountaintops are for views and inspiration, but the fruit is grown in the valleys." So after being buried in the valley of life and springing forward new fruit, I had finally ascended to the mountaintop. But the old saying, it is lonely at the top, is true.

I was content in my career and knew that I was right where God wanted me to be as an LMPD officer. I managed to turn around my job completely, regain the respect I had lost, and change my reputation. I continued to delve into my career and plan the next steps in my evolution as a police officer. I lived to be in my uniform, sitting behind the steering wheel of my cruiser. The adrenaline rush of driving with lights and sirens to an emergency gave me much satisfaction. But after the sirens and adrenaline receded, I would go home to the big empty house I had bought with Michelle, hoping that one day we would raise a family in it, but that never came to pass.

I still had a strong desire to have a family and be married, but I was already a two-time marriage loser, and I was afraid that I would become a three-time marriage loser. My desire to have that special someone in my life was overridden by the fear of rejection upon her learning about my relationship/marriage history. Who would want to marry someone like me? Being divorced twice by the time I was 26 was demoralizing. Had I still been in the military, this behavior would have been completely acceptable. No one would have thought twice about it. It was not uncommon for young soldiers to have multiple marriages at a young age. The police force was not too far behind with its high divorce rate. I had already contributed to the divorce rate in both of my professions, and I did not want to add to those numbers. I told myself that I would never get married again and that I would be OK being single for the rest of my life, but deep down, all I wanted was my own.

In the time I was single, I took the time to learn more about myself but also more about God. I found a new church to attend and become more active. The more time I spent in church, the more my love and reverence for God grew. When I was younger, I viewed God as the angry, fun-killing man in the sky. But after all my battles and me coming to learn more about God for myself, as opposed to what I was taught in my adolescence, my view of God had changed. I had known of God my entire life, but I never had a relationship with him. I no longer viewed him as the great terror in the sky watching over me, ready to smite me down and cast me into hell. I truly saw him as my spiritual father who loved me and wanted nothing but the best for me. His rules did not exist to hurt me but protect me and increase my quality of life.

I had my friends that I would hang out with from time to time. We would go out to the bars, drink, and have a good time when I was off. But at the end of the night, I would come home and be extremely lonely. I would try to imagine the sound of children running and playing and calling out to me. I pictured myself coming home from work and being greeted by my loving wife and kids after a long day of work. It was a dream that I wanted to become my reality, but I was not sure if I could ever love or trust other women after what I had been through. It would have to be a very special, truly God-fearing woman to make me want to try marriage a third time. I did not think that women existed, but apparently, I had known her since 7th grade, and she had been hiding in plain sight.

As I scrolled through my Facebook feed, I saw an encouraging post from Christina Powell: "If you are reading this, I just want to encourage you that one day this too shall pass. No matter what you are going through, the Lord will see you through, and you will have a great testimony. Believe, trust, and know that the best is yet to come. God bless!"

Her post was so encouraging and spoke to my soul. She still appeared to be the same God-loving saint of a girl that I had known since 7th grade. I recalled briefly running into her at the bank in Radcliff while I was home on convalescent leave from WRAMC. I figured that I would reach out to her and thank her for the encouraging message. I decided to ask her for her number as well so that we could chat from time to time.

We talked on the phone for weeks. I soon found myself making the one-hour and thirty-minute drive to Bowling Green just to see her for a few hours just to be in her presence. Christina was different from any other woman I had met. She was pure and innocent and had a heart of gold. At times I felt that I did not deserve to be in her presence because of the life I had lived, but she never judged me for any of it. She was beyond understanding and supportive, and encouraging of me.

Christina and I built our friendship upon our love for Christ and the church. The more time I spent with her, the more time I started to develop feelings for her. I knew how I felt about her, but I was not sure how she felt about me, and I did not want to rush things. One day I worked up the courage to tell her how I felt about her.

"Christina. I really like you, and I can see us being together." I told her softly.

"I really like you, Dexter, but technically, you are still married. When you get your divorce papers and show them to me, maybe we can start talking about a relationship." She said this with a "matter of fact" tone and did not hesitate.

Michelle and I had been separated for months and were in the final stage of our divorce proceedings. Christina was a true woman of Christ, and she would not entertain the thought of talking about being in a relationship with me until my divorce was final. Even then, she had such high standards and expectations, and I was not sure that I could live up to them. A grunt like myself, who had lived a harsh and deceptive life filled with a multitude of sins, did not deserve such a virtuous and genuine woman like Christina in my life. And she would not let herself be deceived by me or any man.

Once I had my divorce papers in hand, I showed them to her as she requested. It was the first time in my life where I had to pursue a woman and be persistent to win her heart. My efforts finally paid off on Thanksgiving Day of 2011, when we officially became a couple. Christina was sure to let me know that I would not be reaping any sort of extra benefits as her boyfriend and that she was saving herself for marriage. Once again, I felt like an unclean heathen being around her. I did not think that women like her still existed.

As our relationship continued to flourish, I tried to fight the feeling of falling in love. I cared about Christina so much, but I was afraid to fall in love again. I had promised myself that I would never love again or fully trust and give my heart to another woman, but Christina was breaking down my wall of protection that I erected to protect myself. I tried so hard not to fall in love, but her charming, thoughtful, and innocence continued to tug on my heartstrings. I saw myself having a beautiful family with her. Before I decided to give marriage a try for the third time, I got down on my knees and prayed and asked God for clarification and if this was the real deal.

Before I went all-in with Christina, I wanted to know what my mom's family thought about her. My auntie Allie was very much like my mother and had amazing discernment. My mother had warned me about Michelle, and I did not listen. I paid dearly for not heeding her warning. I was not going to make the same mistake twice. My mom was no longer here, but my Auntie Allie had stepped into her place to be that motherly figure to me. If she got a good vibe from Christina and gave me her blessing, I planned to ask Christina to marry me.

"Dexter. She is just lovely. She genuinely loves the Lord, and I can tell that she really cares about you. She is such a wonderful woman. If your mom were still here, she would love her." My Auntie Allie said to me.

My auntie gave me her blessing. Not only did my auntie give me her blessing, but the rest of my family did as well. On the Lake Michigan pier in Milwaukee, I asked Christina for her hand in marriage, and she gladly accepted. On August 11, 2012, Christina and I tied the knot in a small wedding ceremony at her family's church in Elizabethtown, Kentucky.

Eight days after our wedding day, I was contacted by the Radcliff Police Department. They called to inform me that they had completed the investigation into my mother's death. Christina and I drove down to the police station in Radcliff to talk to the lead detective. He informed me that my mother's death would be classified as a suicide and that my father would not be charged. They showed me the forensic reports that revealed that she had gunpowder residue on her right hand from where she pulled the trigger of the pistol that she pointed to her head.

I was given a summary of the report, and they released my mother's gun and the box of 9mm ammunition that they had taken for evidence. Looking at the gun that my mother used to take her own life jarred my soul. Even worse was looking at the box of ammunition.

I gazed at the 50-count box of 9mm rounds. As I pulled out the sleeve from inside the box that held the rounds, that one single bullet was missing. Forty-nine rounds instead of 50. Looking at the empty slot and the gun sitting next to the box reopened the still fresh and healing wound of my mom's death.

Later that night, Christina I drove to the Ohio River waterfront in downtown Louisville. I stood on the edge of the bank of the Ohio River as the moon sat high in the sky and reflected off the rugged surface of the waterway. I took the 9mm handgun and the box of ammunition and cast them into the Ohio River, where they sank to the bottom of the muddy riverbed where they would never be able to take another life.

There was no favorable outcome to the investigation of my mother's death that would have made me feel better. My life would not have changed, no matter the conclusion. God had given me ample peace about the outcome, and I was ready and willing to accept the findings of the investigation without argument. I had to accept the findings of the investigation so that I could continue on with my life.

Before we got married, we had an in-depth conversation about our lives and planned out the details of what our plans and goals were as a couple. First, we wanted to pay off some debts, do some traveling, then we would start a family a few years down the line. We were in no rush to have children, but apparently, she and I were having too good of a time and slipped up in the early months of our marriage.

In December of 2012, Christina shocked me when she told me that she was pregnant. I was stunned and speechless. This was part of our plan, but not this early in the game. This was going to throw our entire plan off track. Usually, when people find out that they are having a baby, it is a joyous occasion. That was not the case for me.

I had dreamed of being a father, but when reality hit, I did not think that I was ready to do what the job entailed. I realized that I still had traces of selfishness embedded in me. My concern had shifted from not having money for a child to all the things that I would not be able to do anymore.

Our first child was due towards the end of August of 2013, according to the doctors. I was too stressed out to enjoy the pregnancy. I was focused on paying off as much debt as possible to help get us some breathing room. At our first ultrasound appointment, I remember looking at the screen and seeing the little spec in Christina's belly moving around.

"That's your baby!" The doctor said to us,

Christina fell instantly in love. She smiled and cried as she squeezed my hand. I felt like I was turning into my father. I sat silent and emotionless. I felt nothing.

"All my friends that had kids told me that once my child was born that all my fears and worries would go away once, I held my kid for the first time and how overpowering the feeling of love for my first child would be. I was still having trouble showing and feeling the love I had for Christina due to my PTSD. How was I supposed to do this with a child?

On August 24, 2013, at 2053 hours, Christina gave birth to a healthy, beautiful baby girl. We named her Brooklynn Idella-Rosa Pitts. As her cries filled my ears and I cut the umbilical cord, I waited for that overpowering sense of love that everyone told me about, but it never came. As I held Brooklynn in my arms, I looked at her and felt like I was holding a stranger's child. I had no connection to this precious little bundle of joy. I wanted to have that connection, but there was nothing there.

"What is wrong with me?" I thought to myself.

I knew I was damaged from all the many traumas that I had suffered in life. I did not want my baby girl to suffer because of my life's experiences. That was not fair to her. She deserved better, and I hoped to give her better, but I was off to a bad start. As I sat holding her, I started to think about my mom.

"One day Dexter, you are going to be a father. I cannot wait to be a grandma. I am going to be the best grandma ever. I am going to spoil that child so much." My mom would tell me.

I had imagined that day for so long. Now that day had come, but the other half of the equation was absent. I tried to picture my mother's face as she looked at her first grandchild. Three days later, I was strolling the aisles of the grocery store shopping for baby formula. As I stood in front of the baby formula shelf, it was as if someone flipped a switch and all the absent feelings and emotions at the birth of my daughter hit me at once. An overabundance of love flowed out of my heart, and a strong sense of duty to protect and provide awoke in me.

My sole purpose for living and breathing was this beautiful little girl. I never understood what drove my mom to get on a plane in the middle of the night to fly to be by my bedside as I cried out for her. Now that I had created a life, I understood and felt the love that motivated her. I only wish that she would have been presented to see me as a father holding my little girl.

The birth of our daughter brought Christina and me even closer, and it made me a better man and a better officer. I had more compassion and understanding dealing with people, and I became wiser when it came to officer safety. Getting my partners back home in one piece to their families was of the utmost importance, but also making sure that I got back home to my little family became a top priority for me as well. I had more of a reason to be smarter and fight harder to get back home.

When I joined the police department, one of my goals was to become a TFO (Task Force Officer) with the USMS (United States Marshal Service) on their fugitive task force. In 2013, I was selected by the USMS to serve on their fugitive task force.

"Pitts. Do you realize that you are the first black officer in the department to get that position? Do you know how big of an accomplishment that is?" A fellow black officer told me.

When I was told that I had been selected for the position, I was happy because it was something that I had dreamed of for quite some time. My dream was not to be the first black LMPD officer on the USMS fugitive task force; my dream was to just be selected. Color had become irrelevant to me. But it was loud and clear that the color of someone's skin still held a lot of weight for some. I was focused on doing my job well and becoming a good TFO, not being the best "black" TFO.

During my time in the USMS Fugitive Task Force, I had the opportunity to work on some major cases in which I was the lead investigator. My investigations into the whereabouts of murder and robbery suspects lead to multiple arrests in other states. In 2014, I and the USMS responded to Fern Creek High School in response to an active shooter situation at the school. After we secured the building, we worked alongside the LMPD fugitive unit to track down the school shooter and were able to take him into custody.

Of all the cases I worked on, the naked suitcase Nazi was my favorite case that I assisted with. TFO's Sutton and Madya were Probation and Parole officers for the state of Kentucky. They had been looking for a fugitive suspect for months that kept evading them. They had received a tip that he was staying at a hotel by Interstate 264 and Goldsmith Lane. As they showed me his picture, the first thing I noticed was the giant swastika tattoo on his chest.

"He is not going to like seeing you, Pitts," John said to me jokingly.

We pulled up to the hotel and went to the room where we believed he was staying. We knocked on the door, but there was no answer. We could hear shuffling around on the inside.

"We know you are in there, open up the door, or we are coming in." FTO Sutton shouted.

A half-dressed female with blonde hair came to the door. I could see her face through the crack of the door. Her face was covered with spots and sores. It was evident that she was a hardcore drug user.

She invited us into the room and consented to us searching. As we walked into the room, the stench of body odor populated the room. The place was filthy. You could see the remnants of their drug use all over the room. Uncapped needles, tin foil, cotton balls, spoons, and lighters sat on the table. We searched the room, and to our surprise, we did not find him. As we stood in the room trying to figure where he could have gone, TFO Sutton tapped me on the shoulder and pointed to a suitcase by the window. The red suitcase had an unnatural bulge. As we focused on the suitcase, we noticed a small patch of pale, white flesh that was not covered by the zipper.

"He's in the suitcase," Sutton Whispered.

TFO Madya walked over to the suitcase and started to unzip it.

"Show me your hands!" I yelled!

We found our fugitive, curled up in a ball with his knees to his chest, completely naked, wedged into the suitcase. He uncurled himself, got to his knees, and held his hands in the air. The swastika tattoo on his chest verified that he was the person we were looking for. We placed him under arrest and his girlfriend as well for outstanding warrants.

"I love you, baby! I am sorry! I will see you when I get out!" He yelled to her as we put him in the rear of one of our cars.

"I will wait for you, baby! I love you too! You're the best thing that's happened to me!" She yelled back at him as I placed her in my car.

Being on the Marshals Fugitive Task Force was exhilarating. I did not take my position for granted. My tour with the USMS was only a two-year deal, and I would be going back to patrol, and I did not want it to end. That was when I made the decision that I was going to pursue my dream of becoming a federal agent. I refused to live with the regret of not having at least attempted to become a federal agent.

[24]

BLIND TO MY BLESSINGS

I STARTED to explore my options for working as a federal law enforcement officer. I looked into the FBI, ATF, DEA, and a few other three-letter federal agencies, but none of them appealed to me. That was until I heard the story of USBP Agent Brian Terry, who was shot and killed in the line of duty on December 15, 2010, by drug smugglers near Rio Rico, AZ. He was a former marine and police officer who then became a Border Patrol Agent. Hearing his story inspired me, and I fixed my eyes on becoming a Border Patrol Agent.

I had been out of the valley and sitting on top of the mountain, enjoying the many blessings God had rained down upon me. God had spoiled me. Everything that I prayed for fell into my lap. God's favor was truly shining upon The Pitts family. But life is a rollercoaster, and no one can stay on top of the mountain top forever. And I slowly started my descent back into the valley so that God could grow and develop me further.

Seventeen months into my two-year tour with the USMS, I started to have issues with my left arm. I had increased the intensity of my workout routine and started lifting heavier weights. I was in full pursuit of becoming a federal agent, and I wanted to be ready when the opportunity arose. Unfortunately, with the increased intensity in my workout routine came new pain. I soon discovered that the titanium plate on my left arm was starting to come loose.

In June of 2015, I underwent my 13th operation on my left arm. Unfortunately, the pain that I had endured in 2005 had returned. Waking up from surgery, the familiar burning and stinging of my incisions sent me down memory lane of me at WRAMC. Thankfully, I would not have to endure six months in the hospital or therapy.

Aside from the pain, I was enjoying being off and spending time with Christina and Brooklynn. We had just moved into a tiny two-bedroom, two-bath courtesy apartment a few months prior in an attempt to speed up paying off our debt. We were cramped in our apartment, and things were about to get even more cramped. Christina and I found out that she was pregnant with our second child.

With me being on the USM Fugitive Task Force, I was on call a lot. With being on call, it was challenging to plan weekends and spend time with the family. With Christina being pregnant and us jumping from one to two children, we concluded that it was best for me to leave the fugitive task force and go back to patrol for a more stable and predictable schedule. Having the opportunity to be on the Marshals Fugitive Task Force was a fantastic experience and a true blessing. I would miss running around wearing my USMS gear and badge, but my family and what was best for them was my priority.

I was beyond excited to learn that our next child was a boy. However, 2015 would not let me enjoy the excitement for too long. In early 2015, me and my basic training battle-buddy, Cody Wilson, were making plans to meet up and hang out for the first time in 12 years. Unfortunately, we would never get the chance to meet up because he unexpectedly passed away in 2015. To add to my grief, I learned that my high school friend, Cameron Ponder, a Kentucky

State Trooper, had been shot and killed on Interstate 24 near Lamasco, Kentucky, on September 13, 2015.

Cameron's funeral had the greatest impact on me of all the funerals I attended over the years. Seeing Cameron lying lifeless in his casket wearing his Kentucky State Police uniform was a cold dose of reality. We were two kids from the same area, the same age, attended the same school, played on the same football team, and chose the same path in life, choosing to serve in the military and the police force. But for some unknown reason, his life was cut short, and he died a hero's death in the line of duty.

When my life was not of any value to myself, I submitted my will to live over to death and tried to die a hero's death shift after shift, but death never accepted my offer. Instead of coming and taking me, death continued to consume those around me year after year. I could hear death laughing and pointing at me, saying: "you're next."

The honeymoon period in police work lasts three to five years. In the first three to five years, you believe that you are a superhero and can save the world. You eat, sleep, and breathe police work. Then, you become addicted to the easy money, the power, the adrenaline, and the fun of your job. The pay, benefits, and politics are not a factor in those years. You just want to chase and catch the bad guys. Nothing else matters.

I had been a police officer for five years. And for the first time, I started to wonder if the sacrifice that came from putting on the uniform and badge every day was still worth it. I loved my job and had an immense sense of pride in my chosen profession. However, the profession of policing and being a selfless community servant comes at a high cost. It withdraws large sums of your soul and humanity and rarely redeposits anything. Your emotional bank account is constantly overdrawn, and with every call you respond to, you go further into debt.

A police officer's badge only weighs a few ounces physically, but the true weight of the badge cannot be weighed in ounces or pounds. Instead, the burden and weight of the badge are weighed in the haunting memories of gruesome homicide scenes with blood covering the area like a Picasso painting. Scenes like the many fatal car accidents involving innocent families killed by a drunk driver, the stench of decomposed bodies, and the looks on the faces of injured and dead children.

My senses are still haunted by the first homicide scene I responded to in 2010. My field training officer and I responded to a shooting in the south 600 block of 44th Street in front of a row of apartments. As we approached, a white female in her early 20's lay dying on top of a three-foot-tall concrete barrier that sat at the head of the parking lot. She had been shot dead center in her chest. Her blood gleamed under the officer's lights as it poured out of her body and cascaded down the concrete barrier, and pooled at the base.

"Please don't let me die! I don't want to die!" She cried out to us, begging us to save her life.

Officers worked frantically performing first-aid on her to try and prolong her life until the EMS arrived. As I stood there, the metallic smell of her blood invaded my nose. I could hear the high pitch whaling of EMS sirens off in the distance rushing towards the scene, but it was too late. She started coughing up blood, and I could hear the death gargle coming from her mouth. Her cries for help ceased as she died right before our eyes. EMS arrived moments later and tried to revive her, but their efforts were futile as she was beyond help.

There was also the issue of politics and the frustration of people with no police experience telling you how to do your job and what you should have done while they criticize you from behind the safety of their phone. More than anything, the stress of the racial divide between the black community and the police department and being caught in the middle as a black police officer left me feeling like I was being forced to choose between being black or being a cop.

"Race traitor! Boot licker! Slave catcher! House nigga! Uncle Tom! You coon ass nigga!" Black people from the neighborhood would yell at me as I stood guard behind the yellow crime scene tape.

There I stood on yet another homicide scene where a young

black man lay dead after being shot to death in broad daylight with no witnesses. The gut-wrenching cries of his mother rang through the air and into my eardrums as she tried to muscle her way through the crowd of officers, past the crime scene tape, to get to her son.

"Lord, Jesus! They done killed my child!"

Friends and family try to hold her back and comfort her, but there is no comfort for her as she stares at her son's lifeless body in the middle of the street on display for everyone to see. The anger and frustration of the neighborhood then turned to the police and blamed us for the loss of the young man's life.

"Where were you all!" "This is all your fault!" "You all don't care about us!" "One less nigga for you all to worry about, huh?"

"Did anyone see anything? Does anyone have any information that can help us?" I asked.

"Screw y'all! I don't talk to the police! I ain't no snitch!" Someone yelled out.

I was there to help the deceased and his family get answers, get justice, and find the person responsible for this family's grief. I knew why we were there, but the perception of the neighborhood as to why we were there did not coincide with ours. This type of incident was not unique. It was a recurring theme where I worked. The only things that seemed to change were the names and location, but the faces of all those involved and the horrific cries became indistinguishable.

The struggles of black police officers working in black neighborhoods are just now starting to gain attention in the light of the 2020 protest. However, the struggles that black police officers experience policing in black neighborhoods is not new. The divide between the police and the black community was deep and wide and growing wider. As a black officer, I wanted to help bridge the gap, but I was starting to see that it was too big of a gap to bridge on my own.

I sat in a restaurant at 34th and Market Street in Louisville's West End, eating lunch with my black partner Officer Williams. As we sat in the restaurant, a black mother and two young black children no more than five walked into the restaurant. As the mom stood at the counter ordering their food, the kids were focused on the 50-cent machine and wanted a toy. So I took it upon myself to give the kids some change from my pocket to get a toy from the machine. Their faces lit up like it was Christmas as they retrieved their toys.

When the mom finished placing their order, she turned around and noticed them playing with the toy.

"Where did you get that from!" She scolded him.

The kids pointed to me as I sat eating my lunch. Then, their mother snatched the toy from their hands, walked over to me with attitude, and slammed the toys down on the table in front of me.

"We don't need a damn thing from you." She screamed at me.

She grabbed her food in one hand and snatched her kids with the other, and stormed out of the restaurant. I was left dazed and confused, trying to figure out what I had done wrong.

Not only was there strife between black officers and the community, but there was also an internal battle between other black police officers and me. As I became more comfortable and confident with my identity and political beliefs as a conservative, I became more opinionated and outspoken about racism and politics. The old me would have been silent and agreed just for the sake of getting along and being accepted by everyone. However, I was no longer that person. I knew who I was and what I believed. I did not need the approval of black officers or the black community to validate my beliefs. Instead, I gained the reputation amongst some of my fellow black officers as being a sellout and an Uncle Tom. Some black officers believed that I hated black people because of my views and opinions on black issues and my perception of what people considered "black culture."

The assumption that I hated black people was insulting. I was born black, grew up in a black family with a strong black lineage. I had a black wife and black children. I policed in a black neighborhood by choice. But since I spoke out against the ills of black culture and the lack of accountability and personal responsibility that haunts the community, many folks looked down upon me.

"Why are you always defending them (white people)? It feels like you are always against us (black people). Remember, when you are out of uniform, you are just another black man to them." A black officer's wife wrote to me in a FB message.

"You are just a lost soul, and there is no hope for you," a black officer once wrote to me in a social media debate.

Seeing those messages and hearing how some of my fellow black officers viewed me grew my resolve and made me stand more firm on God's word and my beliefs as a conservative. I had been on the far-left side of the argument years prior and played the poor black victim, and I went nowhere fast. It was not until I embraced being conservative and embracing my Pitts Principles that I could break the bondage of black victimhood that I was able to free myself and become the man/officer that God designed me to be. I did not need anyone's opinion or approval to do so.

Being a police officer, you quickly learn that people you once considered your friends can soon become your enemies. My strong opinions and stubbornness cost me some lifelong friendships. When I was not a cop and agreed on most things, everything was OK between us, but when I put on the uniform and became my own person and had a dissenting opinion, trouble started brewing.

"I hope one of my west-end peeps shoots you in your face!" A former friend of mine who I had known since 7th grade direct messaged me.

On February 23, 2016, at 0115 hours, Christina gave birth to our son Dexter Jameson Pitts, or as we have come to call him, DJ. Shortly after carrying a small stuffed animal that she wanted to give to her new baby brother, Brooklyn came into the room. She was so excited about being a big sister and would not stop talking about her little brother in her mommy's belly. She placed the stuffed animal next to DJ and grinned at him. We then took DJ and put him in Brooklynn's arms.

"Hi, DJ. I am your big sister, Brooklynn." She said in her squeaky three-year-old voice.

My heart melted as I gazed at my two beautiful children. My heart was full, and I was bursting with joy. I had a job that I loved and a beautiful family. I was living the American dream. Yet, looking at Brooklynn holding her new baby brother made me think about the strained relationship between Celeste and me. We had not talked in five years. Although my mission in life as the father of these two beautiful children would not be to only love and provide for them, I was determined not to let the many tragedies that had unfolded in my life take root in their lives.

We were truly living the good life. We were debt-free and were practically living for free in an apartment where I was the complex courtesy officer. Christina and I were ready to plant some roots and buy our first home together. In my mind, we were in Louisville for the long haul. I was going to be with LMPD for the next 15 plus years. I had a solid position on DAP (Downtown Area Patrol) with a phenomenal schedule and worked with some incredible officers. Every day, I would go to work smiling because of the amount of fun I was having getting paid to ride four-wheelers and Polaris RZR's around downtown and on the waterfront. Life was nearly perfect, but the election of President Donald Trump soon changed that and gave me a golden opportunity to accomplish a dream that I had been chasing for five years.

Under the Trump administration, the USBP wanted to increase the number of agents patrolling the border. To increase their numbers, the USBP exempted military veterans with law enforcement experience from taking the entrance exam. I could hear the voice of God telling me, "Yes! This is for you, my child!"

I informed Christina about the opportunity that had arisen. To my surprise, she was not as thrilled as I expected her to be. When we built our beautiful home, I told her that we were done moving and that this would be our home for many years to come. She had her mindset on that. We were living a comfortable life and had the world at our fingertips. There was nothing we wanted that we couldn't have. We were living a life that people dream about living. We were not rich, but money was not an issue. For me, I was not only looking at the glory of being a federal agent, but I was looking at the financial aspect of it as well.

She was not sold on the idea and had many reservations about me taking this giant leap of faith into the unknown to chase a dream that I had been tenaciously in pursuit of for years. I had enough regrets in my life, and I did not want to have to live with another regret. I at least had to try and give it a shot.

I listened to and understood her concerns, but I was doing this regardless. I had missed out on one too many opportunities in my life to make others happy, and I was not willing to miss out on this once-in-a-lifetime opportunity. I was no longer a young man. I was now 33 years old and had a ton of responsibilities. And the older I got, the harder it would be for me to make the transition. It was now or never.

In October 2017, I submitted my application to CBP for the USBP.

"Pitts. Are you sure you want to leave? You are in a good spot here with LMPD?" My lieutenant reminded me.

"It's 100,000 dollars a year to run around in the desert carrying a rifle chasing people. I did that in Iraq in the army for a lot less money, sir." I replied to him.

When I was a rookie officer and single, I did not have to worry about pay, benefits, and things such as saving for retirement and my children's college. Now that I was a husband and a father of two young children, those things started to matter to me. As much as I wanted the job to protect our country and boast that I was a federal agent, I saw the Border Patrol as a way for me to provide a better life for my family and for me to spend more time with them as well. The pride of calling myself a federal agent was just the cherry on top of it all.

LMPD has been a blessing to my family and me for so many years. LMPD was my home. So many people had poured themselves into me and did so much to help raise me from my struggles and grow me into the man/officer I had become. I never saw myself leaving LMPD, but I started to feel as though I had outgrown LMPD; I needed more. I need more money. I needed more of a challenge, and I needed more purpose. LMPD had become the minor leagues, and I was ready to be called up to play in the major leagues.

I was so confident that I would get the job that we stepped out on faith and sold our brand-new home in September of 2018. Two months later, I received a phone call from CBP telling me that the USBP had officially hired me. I would be part of USBP Academy Class 1110. I chose the Brian A. Terry Border Patrol Station in Naco, Arizona, as my station. I was scheduled to EOD (Enter on Duty) on November 5, 2018, at the Tucson Border Patrol Station.

The thought of me going away for six months for training while she was left at home to care for our children on her own did not sit well with her. Kentucky was our entire life. This is where our family resided. We would be uprooting our whole lives and moving across the country with no family support to live in a border town. Even more of a risk was that we would have to pay for our own move out west. It was a lot for her to take in, but my excitement overrode all my fears and anxiety. I only saw the positives, not the negatives. People thought I was crazy. And I could understand why. Taking a big risk and jumping into the unknown is hard.

People grow accustomed to living in a state of comfort, and it is hard for them to detach and take risks. There is no growth in comfort. Life had taught me that lesson the hard way. Being with LMPD for nine years, I also realized that people grow accustomed to being miserable and just settle. For nine years of my career with LMPD, I would have to sit and listen to salty veteran officers and entitled rookies complain about how horrible of a place LMPD was to work and how they hated their jobs. Yet, they never quit and always came to work and spread their pessimism. I did not want to become that disgruntled officer.

After eight years on the job, my perspective on many things had changed. I had lost sight of my initial reason as to why I became a police officer. I was blind to all the blessings I had in my life. Comfort started to set in, and my position and career began to grow stale. The red, hot, internal fire that once burned in my soul drove me to serve the community and confront the evil in this world started to fade. I wanted and needed a new challenge, and the USBP was what I needed to reignite that flame and passion inside me to serve my country again.

After I turned in my letter of resignation, I went around saying my goodbyes to all the friends I had made over the years with LMPD. Everyone was supportive, encouraging and wished me the best of luck.

The day before I shipped out, I was at the LMPD Academy gym getting in one last workout before I flew out the following morning. As I was working out, Dee Dee walked into the gym.

"What's up, Sunshine! I am so happy for you, and I am so proud of you. I remember how big you used to be. You do not even look like the same person. I hate to see you leave, but I am so happy for you. Make us proud." Dee Dee said to me.

Dee Dee gave me the biggest hug and went about her way. She was well on her way to having a spectacular career. She had recently moved from patrol to the detective offices, and I was just as proud of her.

Christina and the kids drove me to the airport and escorted me inside. My flight was not for a few more hours, so we decided to have one last family breakfast. As we sat eating our meal, DJ looked at me with a mouth full of food and asked, "Are you going on a plane, daddy?"

"I am, buddy."

"No! You can't leave, daddy! You can't leave!" He said to me.

Brooklynn came and sat next to me and cuddled under my arms. She did not have to say anything to me. Instead, her facial expressions said how she was feeling.

"I don't want you to go, daddy." She said with tears collecting in her eyes.

Christina's face was blank as she sat eating her breakfast.

When I deployed to Iraq in 2004, I only had a wife to be concerned with, and that was hard enough. I was not going to war but having a 5-year-old, and a 21-month-old made it a lot harder than I imagined it would be to leave for six months. I did not realize the sacrifice, and what it took for all the soldiers I served with who deployed and had children. We shared one last family hug before I checked into my flight. I looked back at my family as I made my way down the terminal, and I could see the tears glistening on their faces. It was going to be hard being absent, but I was doing this for them. I was doing this for my country. Six months was a minor sacrifice for 20 plus years as a federal agent.

[25]

CHASING DREAMS CATCHING NIGHTMARES

I LOOKED out my window at the brown and barren landscape of the Arizona desert. The lush green hills and trees of the eastern U.S. had transitioned to dirt and rugged mountains. The Arizona terrain reminded me of photos of Mars.

"I finally made it," I said to myself as I stepped off the plane.

After three days of processing at the Tucson Border Patrol station, it was time for Class 1110 to start its six-month academy. At 34 years old, I was the 4th oldest in the class. I was officially the old guy.

Being that I was older, I knew that the USBP Academy was going to be physically and mentally demanding, but I underestimated just how tough it was going to be and over-exaggerated my abilities. Not only did I have to battle my physical handicaps, but I was also battling against my age. I quickly realized that I was not a 19-year-old kid going through army boot camp. My bedtime snack consisted of 1000 mg of ibuprofen and stretching.

On top of the heavy physical demands were the academic rigors of the USBP Academy. Constitutional law, immigration law, naturalization law, BP operations, and of course, Spanish were the true stressors. When I was not getting hammered in PT, I was buried in academic studies, especially Spanish. Eighty percent of my class was Hispanic and grew up speaking Spanish, so they did not have to worry about Spanish. I and the other non-Spanish-speaking recruits had to dedicate every second of our free time to learning Spanish.

In my downtime, I would listen to Spanish YouTube videos for kids to help me learn the Spanish alphabet, the days of the weeks, and the months. When I was not listening to that, I would constantly study the Spanish flashcards that I made. Time management was critical to survival, but there did not seem to be enough time in the day. I considered myself a tough guy, but after the first few weeks in the academy, I did not feel so tough and cocky.

I was only a few weeks in, and I was ready to quit and go back home. I started to have doubts that I was going to survive the next five months and make it to graduation in April of 2019. I leaned on my classmates for support, and I did my best to do the same for them.

In early December of 2018, we learned that we were being furloughed due to the government shutdown. I flew home on December 23. I had only been gone about seven weeks, but it truly felt like a lifetime. As I walked to the terminal, DJ and Brooklynn rushed me to give me a hug. Hearing their little voices scream "Daddy" instantly recharged my mentally and emotionally depleted mind. I had to report back to the academy by December 26th, so my stay would be brief, as I had to drive 19 hours across the country to be back in time.

We awoke on Christmas Eve on December 24, and the kids ripped into their gifts like feral animals. The smiles on their faces were so big, and the cheer in their voices made it hard for me to want to hit the road in a few hours. I wanted to stay in this moment with them forever. As I continued to watch them open their gifts, my phone rang. It was my good friend Beth calling to tell me the bad news.

The morning of December 24, 2018, Detective Deidre Mengedoht stopped a vehicle for a traffic violation on Interstate 64 in the eastbound lane. While she was seated in her vehicle, it was struck by an MSD (Metro Sewer District) semi-truck and burst into flames. She was killed instantly.

I got in my truck and drove to the FOP lodge to be with my fellow officers in this horrific moment. We had gathered at the FOP lodge two months prior to saying goodbye to our beloved LMPD Homicide Detective Joh Lesher, who passed unexpectedly. Nineteen months prior to that, we gathered to grieve the loss of our brother Officer Nick Rodman who was killed in the line of duty on March 29, 2017, in a vehicular assault. The tears of grief-stricken LMPD officers littered the floor of the FOP lodge.

"They are getting ready to transport Dee Dee's body, and we need cars to help with the escort."

Officers got up from their seats and walked outside to their cruisers to help. I impulsively reached for my keys in my pocket, thinking that the keys to my police cruiser were still there as though my police cruiser was parked outside in the parking lot. I was no longer part of the LMPD family. I was merely a guest at the lodge, and I had forfeited my right to escort my fallen sister and former partner. I had exchanged my LMPD uniform for an opportunity to chase a dream. I knew I had made a mistake leaving. I felt like I had betrayed them. I wanted to stay here with my brothers, but I had to hit the road. I drove back home, grabbed my bags, and prepared to hit the road.

"Dex! Please don't go! You are in no condition to drive right now! Look at yourself!" Christina pleaded with me.

I was already stressed out and in so much physical pain from only two months at the academy. I was on the verge of just throwing in the towel and returning home before this incident. Seeing my fellow officers crying was hard enough. But seeing Christina crying and the kids begging me not to leave on top of Dee Dee's tragic loss conflicted my heart. Quitting on the spot and returning back to my old life was so tempting, but I had worked so hard and prayed so many prayers to

God to get hired on with the USBP. I could not just quit and walk away so easily.

I kissed and hugged my wife and kids and drove off. I sat in my truck downtown on the waterfront as the sun was starting to set. I heisted to get on Interstate 64 westbound because I would have to drive by Dee Dee's crash site. The sun was starting to set, and I could see the red and blue lights from the crash site as they were still working on the investigation. I finally worked up the courage and drove up the Interstate 64 westbound on-ramp. As I drove by and stared at the carnage of the wreck that took the life of my former partner, tears flooded my eyes as I drove by. I spilled tears all the way from Louisville to Oklahoma City, where I stopped to rest for the night.

I was two hours away from the academy. I was tired and struggling to focus due to not getting enough sleep. As I was driving through the small town of Clovis, NM, I briefly looked at my GPS. As I put my eyes back onto the road, I noticed that my light was red and slammed my brakes, but it was too late. My truck tires screeched as I slid into the intersection.

Shards of glass flew into my face—pain shot through my left shoulder. I was dazed and confused. The accident happened so fast. My door was crushed, and I had to climb out of my car through the passenger door. I found my cell phone on the passenger side floorboard and called Christina to tell her that I had been involved in an accident.

"I told you not to leave. I told you that you were not in the right mindset to drive, Dex. Are you OK?" She cried to me.

I looked at my truck and saw where the car hit me directly on my door. How I survived without a scratch, and only some shoulder pain was beyond me. I knew that Dee Dee was looking out for me from up above. There was no other explanation.

When I got back to my room, I started to pack my bags. I was done. My classmates tried to convince me to stay, but I was ready to call it quits. This was clearly a sign from God that I was not supposed to be here. There was a knock on my door, and I answered it. It was my other class coordinator, Border Patrol Agent Benjamin. She reminded me of Dee Dee; she was tiny but possessed that same attitude. As I was being driven back to FLETC, I called her and told her that I was going to resign and go back home.

"I know you are a man of faith. How about you pray about it tonight and decide in the morning. You are not in a good mental space to make such a decision right now." She suggested.

I spent the night in my room in deep thought. I thought about what Dee Dee might say to me if she were alive and found out that I quit. I can say for sure that she would not have wanted me to quit on account of her death. She knew how hard I had worked and seen my transformation over the years. She would have given me a large dose of her big attitude and a stern talking to for quitting. I knew I had to stay the course and graduate from the academy. I did not want to dwell on the past and what it used to be. My classmates needed me; I did not want to let them down. I needed them just as bad, if not more, to help me not only survive but thrive.

I knew if I quit, I would wake up with regret and be forced to wonder "what if" about something I was so passionate about and chased after for many years. Walking away was easy, but staying the course and fighting through all the pain, stress, sadness, and doubt would take tenacity, and I had plenty of it.

As you are reading this, I am sure you are waiting for the dramatic moment where I bounced back from the circumstances and plowed my way through the rest of the academy with vitality and ease. There was no second burst of energy or great awakening. I had to battle the urge to quit every day. I had dug down deep within me to keep going. The daily grind of the USBP Academy continued to push my classmates and me to our physical, mental, and emotional limits.

On April 29, 2019, after six months of pain, stress, struggle, and anxiety, USBP Academy Class 1110 stood proudly before our family members and our class instructors dressed in our green Class A uniform, complete with our Stratton campaign hats and shined Justin boots. As my graduation picture was displayed on the screen and my name was called to come and receive my certificate, I swelled with satisfaction.

As I stood on stage receiving my certificate, DJ burst forward, ran up on stage, and hugged my legs. I patted him on the head as he looked up to me, and the crowd clapped and cheered. I saw Christina and Brooklynn at the edge of the staging, both smiling and clapping for me as well. If only my mom was still alive to see me at this moment.

Towards the end of the ceremony, my name was called, and I was summoned to the stage once more. To my surprise, my classmates voted amongst themselves and selected me to receive the Director's Leadership Award. The Director's Leadership Award is awarded to the recruit for exemplifying the highest standards and embodying the leadership characteristics of a Federal Law Enforcement Officer as one who positively influences others; serves as a role model; is responsible to themselves and others; does more than expect, and puts others first and is team-oriented.

I always tried to avoid the spotlight and being in leadership positions because I never saw myself as a leader, and I never wanted to be a leader. My goal was to be a contributing member of the team, not the head of the team. But time and time again, I found myself being forced to lead. Clearly, my classmates saw something in me that I did not see myself. I still have trouble seeing what they see. I never strived to be a leader. I strive to be a good person and take care of and help others. I strived to live out my Pitts Principles.

I have done a lot of tough things in my life but making it through the USBP Academy tops the list for me. In the BP recruiting commercial, they say that the title of Border Patrol Agent is not given but earned, and they are not exaggerating. I wore my BP uniform and badge proudly. I will forever be proud to have been a part of USBP Academy Class 1110.

Not only had I accomplished my dream of becoming a federal

agent, but I also accomplished something that meant even more to me. I achieved my dream in front of my children, which helped me set an example for my kids and what it meant to live up to our last name and the principles attached to it. DJ was almost four, and Brooklynn was six. They might not have completely understood everything I went through and why, but they knew that I had done something big. I wanted them to remember this moment and think back to it when they are in the midst of their struggles as they chase their dreams and say, "Daddy did it, so can I." I had a list of reasons and excuses as to why I could have quit, but I never let the excuses win, and I want my kids to possess that same attitude and drive.

After a four-day drive in a 26-foot Penske moving truck with Christina following behind me in her car with the kids, we arrived in our new home of Sierra Vista, Arizona, on my birthday. Arriving in Sierra Vista was the perfect gift, and I instantly fell in love with Arizona. The mountain views were breathtaking, and the weather was perfect. The small-town atmosphere of Sierra Vista was calming. Living next to the Fort Huachuca army base made me reminisce of growing up on Fort Knox, and I wanted my kids to experience that same type of upbringing.

I reported to the Brian A. Terry Station on May 13, 2019, where me and my classmates, Stephen Stewart and Johanny Sanchez, were introduced to our FTO, Border Patrol Agent Boudreaux. We loaded into the scratched-up BP Chevy Suburban and traveled down the bumpy road into the Naco, Arizona desert north of Naco, Sonora, Mexico. We were still on American soil, but it felt like I was in a third-world country. The Arizona heat reminded me of being on patrol in Iraq in 2004. Looking at tattered homes and buildings through the border wall closely resembled Abu Ghraib. The border wall was constructed of rusted steel beams and soared 25 feet into the air, and had barbed wire strung across the top of it.

I had dreamed of and given chase to this moment for so long. I was ecstatic to be here, and I was ready to get into the action, but I had a lot to learn, and I had to prove that I could operate safely in this rough environment and learn the basics of being a Border Patrol Agent.

"We just had five bodies jump the fence by Sierra Delta!" The camera operator's voice came across the radio.

We were close to the area sped towards Sierra Delta, just in time to see a group of UDAs (Undocumented Aliens). They saw us and immediately turned around and ran back south to the border wall. Stew and Johany were able to apprehend two out of the group. I watched as the others scaled the border wall back to safety in Mexico. I could hear them taunting us from across the border fence.

"Screw you guys!" They shouted at us in broken English through the border wall.

Every group of UDAs we caught was all dressed the same. They wore camouflage over their clothing to hide from us and our cameras as they trekked through the desert for miles. They wore booties over their shoes with carpet on the soles to help mask their tracks to make it difficult for us to cut signs and track them. They were very crafty.

We would stroll through the southern Arizona desert under the blazing sun carrying our AR-15 for extra firepower in case we were ambushed by drug mules. We would hike through the demanding terrain traversing the rocky soil as we descended down into the dry washes tracking groups of UDAs. We would track for hours, and it seemed as though we were chasing ghosts in the desert. At times we would receive assistance from the BP Mounted Patrol as they rode their horses or the BP Air Unit known as Omaha would direct us to where there was a group of UDAs hiding near us.

At nighttime, we would post up on a hilltop under the star-scattered sky and use the FLIR (Forward Looking Infrared) Recon to see into the darkness and detect bodies of UDAs hiding under cover of darkness.

"Pitts. Your mission tonight is to man this post using the recon." Border Patrol Agent Bordeaux informed me.

Border Patrol Agent Bordeaux, Stew, and Johanny got into the suburban and drove off into the night. I watched as the glow of the red brake lights disappeared into the darkness, and I was left alone out in the desert. The only light was from the moon and the stars. I sat in the darkness of the desert for hours alone, hearing the bushes around me ruffle and my mind telling me that I was about to be attacked by some large desert creature.

I was living my dream of being a Border Patrol Agent, but my dream soon turned into a nightmare. I soon found myself dreading getting up in the morning and going to work. The BP recruiting commercials, like with any good recruiting commercial, only showed the fun side of the job. They purposely left out the not so glorious parts of the job, such as working in the detention and processing facility or the camera room. I felt more like a jail guard as I sat dazed and confused, looking at my computer screen and the never-ending files of legal paper. There was also the mind-numbing boredom of watching the border fence rust.

Spanish was not my native language; therefore, I struggled to ask the proper questions and get the proper response back from the UDAs I had to process. I passed the USBP Spanish class with an 85 average, but I continued to struggle to grasp the Spanish language enough to process the UDAs quickly and effectively. I would sit and stare at my watch, waiting for the end of the workday.

I thought back to when I was a rookie cop on LMPD. Even being the new guy, I never hated going to work, I never hated any assignments I was given, and I never dreaded going to work. From the first day, I put on my uniform and hit the streets; I loved my job. It was now the exact opposite for me with the BP. I was making great money as a GS-9, and I would soon be moving up to a GS-11 which would have put me just under 100,000 a year, but the paychecks did not make me happy. I had sold my soul for money, and I was paying the price for it. I would go home after work and dread having to put on my uniform and make the 45-minute drive through the desert the next day.

I missed the fast pace of being a big city cop. I missed the interactions I had with the public. Most of all, I missed actually helping people, not just arresting them. I was constantly reminded that I was an immigration officer, not a police officer, and it rubbed me the wrong way. I had become a miserable person to be around, and Christina took notice.

"I've never seen you this unhappy, Dex," Christina said to me.

I was unable to say anything back to her. My mind was blank as I thought about my options. I had moved my entire family across the country away from our family and friends. I felt stuck. I was fortunate enough to have a retirement check coming in from the VA, and we had some money saved. I was not worried about paying bills, but I needed to figure out my next move. I was so miserable and unhappy, and it was starting to affect my family life. That was when I made the decision to resign from the Border Patrol.

I spent 11 months of my life with BP, and I had no regrets. I had put in the hard work to earn the title of Border Patrol Agent and proved that I was more than capable of doing the job, and I left on my own terms. The 11 months I spent with BP was some of the most challenging, rewarding, and memorable months of my life. Even though I am no longer a Border Patrol Agent, I will forever be proud to have been a part of USBP Class 1110.

[26]
THIS IS SUPPOSED TO BE HOME

In December of 2019, I was hired by the SPD (Sahuarita Police Department) in Sahuarita, Arizona. Even though I had almost a decade of experience as a street cop and just shy of a year as a Border Patrol Agent, I had a lot to learn about small-town policing. Policing in Sahuarita with a force of 50 officers was vastly different from policing in Louisville with a force of more than 1200 officers.

Even though I was focused on building a new life with my family in Arizona, I always kept up with everything back home in Louisville. The streets of Louisville were becoming increasingly dangerous due to the anti-police sentiment sweeping the nation due to politics, protesting, and misleading media coverage. In addition, LMPD, like other major cities, was hemorrhaging officers due to retirements and officers resigning because of the hostile work environment and lack of support. The more I focused on everything going on back home, the more disconnected I felt from my new life in Arizona and, strangely, my family.

The joy and peace that I once had going to and coming from my shift at LMPD had escaped me. I had assumed that simply becoming a police officer again would give me that energy, drive and passion that I once had to serve the community, but I could not manage to find that spark to relight that flame. I loved Arizona. I loved Sahuarita. This was supposed to be home, but it felt like an alternate universe.

I was grappling with trying to make a new life for my family and me in Arizona, but I soon found myself slipping into a deep, dark depression in which my PTSD led the charge. Christina and I always had a solid marriage, but we hit a colossal snag even after eight years of a great marriage. The stress of moving across the country was enough, but to move from Sierra Vista to Sahuarita only eight months later and me struggling to adjust to yet another new job and Christina trying to get the kids settled was more stress than we realized. The anxiety and uncertainty started to reveal each of our deficiencies.

I continued to put my emotions aside to function and focus on the many tasks in front of me. But with the hassle of being a 35-year-old police officer and trying to adjust to the many changes in my life puts an enormous strain on my mental health. I soon wanted to avoid the one place where I was supposed to have complete peace: home.

While trying to relax at home, DJ and Brooklynn started arguing, and DJ had a complete meltdown and started crying. DJ's cry has always sounded like a high pitch sonic boom and could pierce the soul of any man. The verbal sparring back and forth between my two children and DJ's air raid siren of a squeal triggered something inside of me, and I snapped: I shut down emotionally. All the pressure and unfortunate events of the last year pushed me to my breaking point. I went into a trance and was on autopilot.

I would come in from work, not looking at or speaking to Christina and the kids. Instead, I would go straight to my office and keep to myself. I asked a question; I would respond in an inaudible mumble or shrug my shoulders. I was emotionless. Sleep soon became rare, and when I did manage to fall asleep, nightmares of Iraq and the many horror scenes I had come across in a decade of police work started replaying in my dreams. It felt like my soul was being held hostage by an invisible force, and I was trapped inside my mind, unable to break free.

Further into the depths of my misery, I descended. I moved out into the garage away from my family. My spending habits became spontaneous as I purchased random big-ticket items without telling my wife. The look on Christina's face was unforgettable when she came home and saw the brand new 65-inch TV I bought for my space in the garage.

A week passed by, and no matter what I did, I could not seem to set my mind free from the mental prison where I was captive. My kids would hug me and tell me how much they loved me, but I could not return to them the loving gesture they gave me. I saw how my struggle impacted my family and was concerned as my mental health spiraled out of control. I did not want to feel like this, but it was beyond my control. The invisible force continued to grip my mind. I could not even pray. I grew desperate for help, and I drove myself to the Tucson Veterans Affairs office (VA). The VA told me that they did not have anyone to assist me with my issues at that time.

"Please. I just need help." I begged them.

I was sent home with a brochure of phone numbers to call and a bottle of Trazadone to help me sleep. I could not feel much emotion, but I felt the disappointment and frustration of being turned away by the government entity whose motto is "To take care of him who shall borne the battle." I had borne the battle for my country, but where was my care? I had heard the horror stories of the VA turning away veterans in need of mental help. I always assumed that those stories were over-exaggerated until it happened to me. I did not want to harm myself or anyone else. I just wanted to be myself again. I started to believe that I would be stuck in this state of mind forever and that I would never be myself again.

In a rare instance where I actually forced out more than a few words and a mumble, I told Christina to leave me and take the kids because they deserved better.

"I am not leaving you, Dex! I love you! The kids love you! We need you! I am going to continue to pray for you until whatever this thing is you are battling is done." She said to me with tears pouring down her face.

She reached out to hug me, and I walked past her outstretched arms and retreated to my layer, where I sat in the dark for hours on end. For four weeks, I suffered silently as I drowned in hopelessness, believing that I was doomed to wander the earth for the rest of my days as an emotionless zombie. I was sitting on my futon in the garage when the dense brain fog and numbness suddenly turned off. Whatever it was that had a grip on me released its hold, and I instantly felt like myself. I ran into the house, and I hugged Christina and the kids as tight as I could. I could feel their love, and I could feel my love for them. I was so relieved. I spent the next week apologizing to Christina, telling her how sorry I was.

My wife, being the loving and kind person that she is, understood. She knew that the person living in the garage who refused to talk and acknowledge her and the kids was not her husband. She did not cease praying for me until I had a breakthrough.

"Just give it some time, and you will get used to the way things are around here." Seasoned SPD officers told me.

The same thing was said to me about BP. Give it time, and it will get better. I did not have the patience or the time to wait for things to get better. I had come out of my month-long funk, and I felt like myself again, but the enjoyment and peace of going to work continued to evade me. Policing with SPD felt like work. I never felt like I was working with LMPD.

I came to Arizona chasing a dream and continued to strikeout. Everything about our lives in Arizona was perfect. It was everything we had dreamed and hoped it would be. Everything about Arizona felt like home, but that single, missing, important piece that made me tick, get up out of bed and smile going to and from my shift was not here. Without that key piece, I had no peace, and nothing else really mattered. If I could not enjoy my work, I could not enjoy life.

I contemplated leaving police work altogether and just getting a normal 9 to 5 job and staying in Arizona. I was going to be a normal person and live a normal life. But there was one problem. A normal job would not suit me. There was nothing normal about me. I knew what I had to do.

On May 26, 2020, I watched the city of Minneapolis go up in flames and burn in a fury of hate and outrage at the hand of rioters following the tragic death of George Floyd at the hands of a thoughtless police officer. I watched in disbelief as a Minneapolis police station was burned to the ground, and the Minneapolis Police battled to take back control of the city, but they were outnumbered. My attention then immediately turned from Minneapolis to Louisville and my comrades of LMPD. Large groups of protestors started to form in the streets of downtown to protest the unfortunate death of Breonna Taylor. Breonna Taylor was shot and killed by an LMPD detective while serving a search warrant. During the serving of the warrant, Taylor's boyfriend fired a shot through the door, striking a detective in the leg, which led the detectives to return fire in self-defense. During the volley of gunfire, Breonna Taylor was struck multiple times and died in the apartment hallway, not her bed, as the media falsely reported.

I watched the media coverage, and multiple live streams as hordes of rioters proceeded to destroy downtown Louisville and try to set it ablaze. I was in dismay as someone smashed the window of the DAP office where I had worked just over a year prior. Storefront windows shattered as they were stuck with rocks and baseball bats. The shattered glass littered the sidewalks and reflected the streetlights as it was trampled upon by the feet of Antifa and BLM members dressed in their all-black attire with their faces hidden.

The mob then started launching fireworks, bricks, frozen bottles of water, gallons of milk, bleach bombs, Molotov cocktails, and bottles filled with hazardous materials and human waste at Louisville's finest, KSP troopers and Kentucky National Guard troops as they held the line trying to protect the city. Officers launched tear gas, pepper balls, and flashbangs to help disperse the crowds, but they repealed the ordnance being fired at them using picnic tables, leaf blowers and umbrellas, gas masks, and goggles. I watched ghastly as flaming shopping carts rolled towards officers holding the line downtown. I never imagined that I would be seeing this type of unrest in the streets of Louisville.

Local stores and shops in the downtown area had not only been destroyed but were also being looted. Fourth Street Live, Louisville's premier downtown tourist attraction, and hangout spot were ravaged. The Kroger grocery store at 28th and Broadway had been broken into, and the shelves were almost bare. I looked on as rioters tried to break into ATMs and attempted to get into pawn shops where they would have access to an abundance of firearms and ammunition.

As I continued to watch the chaos unfolding in downtown Louisville, a group of voracious rioters attempted to tip over an LMPD prisoner transport vehicle as the red and blue lights flashed. The vehicle rocked back and forward as the rioters tried to tip the vehicle over onto its side but were unsuccessful. As the rioters and the large crowd of protestors swarmed the area, a series of 10 gunshots rang out as someone indiscriminately fired into the crowd of protesters and struck seven people. Without hesitation, the courageous officers of LMPD's SRT instinctively ran towards the gunfire, placing themselves directly in harm's way to protect the wounded without care for their own safety. I watched proudly as the familiar faces of my SRT brethren tended to the wounds of the people who only moments before were yelling obscenities at them, spitting at them, and wishing death upon them.

"I should be there!" I yelled at Christina as I sat in bed, watching the anarchy continue to unfurl.

As I continued to watch from my phone, I wished that there had been a way for me to jump through my iPhone screen and into the action and stand side by side with SRT in their finest, yet most daunting moment. History was being made without me, and it wrenched my gut. Seeing the streets that I patrolled for almost ten years descend into chaos and unrest stirred my emotions and my soul. I had the same feelings 13 years prior as I watched the news about the 10th Mountain Division in Iraq in 2007 while I sat comfortably and helplessly in my home, longing to be part of the fight.

The unrest in Louisville carried on for days. Photos of exhausted LMPD officers laying on the sidewalk and resting against buildings trying to soak up what little bit of rest and peace they could before they dove back into the chaos dominated my newsfeed.

Rioters grew bolder as the chaos ensued. I watched as gunshots echoed through downtown and rounds were hurled towards LMPD officers and the SWAT team. I then made the decision that the Pitts family would be returning to Louisville, and I would be returning to my original blessing: being an LMPD officer.

I resigned from my position with the SPD immediately and started the rehire process with LMPD. I was due back in Louisville on June 12th of 2020 and was sworn back in on June 15th. I was grateful for the opportunity that the SPD gave my family and me, but it was time for the Pitts family to return home.

[27]

UNCLE TOM AND THE CALM IN THE STORM

*NOTE: *I have included explicit and graphic language as witnessed first-hand from the Louisville riots and protests in this chapter.*

After 19 hours of driving, I took the 9th Street exit into downtown Louisville. I wanted to see the devastation caused by the riots. Seeing the destruction on the live stream from my phone did not prepare me for seeing it in person. Seeing downtown absent of people gave me chills. The boarded-up buildings and graffiti that read "Fuck 12," "ACAB" (all cops are bastards), and "the only good cop is a dead cop" reminded me of the movie "The Purge," where anarchy was the law for 24 hours. Anarchy had been the law in Louisville for weeks.

I drove past Jefferson Square Park at the intersection of 6th and Jefferson, where BLM and ANTIFA had set up camp and established a foothold in the heart of the city across from the mayor's office. They had desecrated the fallen police officer memorial in the park with spray paint and snuffed out the eternal flame on top of the memorial. When I left Louisville nineteen months prior, this place looked different; this wasn't the same city.

On June 15, 2020, I was sworn in and returned to duty at

LMPD. I was assigned to patrol in the First Division as a patrol officer on the night shift in the downtown area. While I was excited to be back in patrol, I wanted more than anything my spot back on the SRT.

After a brief conversation with the SRT commander, I scrambled to gather enough gear so that I could rejoin SRT on the frontline. Like every other officer in the department and other specialty units, SRT worked around the clock since the riots to maintain order.

I reported to SRT the following day and joined them for their detail on standby as an ORF (quick reaction force) in case more pop-up protests and civil unrest started. As I approached them, I saw the weariness on their faces and their voices dragged with exhaustion as they spoke to me.

"Pitts! You are crazy for coming back here!" "Have lost your mind coming back to this place." "You seriously left the Border Patrol making 100,000 a year to come back here and be crapped on with the rest of us?"

SRT had worked 120 hours of overtime in just over two weeks. They noticed a significant increase in their paychecks from the forced overtime. Their paychecks was significantly larger, but what they were forced to give up in exchange were things that money could not buy: peace, time with family, and their health.

I listened to all of their experiences having to deal with the riots.

"I felt like I was back in Fallujah the first three nights of the riots," one of my fellow SRT brothers explained to me.

I sat with SRT the next few days in our staging area, waiting for things to flare back up, but all was quiet thus far. So I sat eagerly waiting for my chance to stand firm on the thin blue line next to my brothers and sisters in defense of the city and the citizens.

"All SRT members report to the Clark Memorial Bridge!" I read in a text message. I put on my SRT uniform and drove as fast as I could downtown. Protestors took over the 2nd Street bridge, hung up a giant banner, and completely stopped the traffic flow by parking cars on the bridge.

As I drove downtown towards the Clark Memorial Bridge, scores of people started to come into view. Some held signs that read "No Justice No Peace," "Defund the Police," and "Arrest the mother fucking cops." "How do you spell racist? LMPD!" What was different about this protest from the ones in the past was the number of armed protesters. They stood on the streets with their AR-15's and AK-47s at the low ready position and their handguns holstered on their hips while wearing body armor.

"Pitts! Replace somebody on the line at the base of the bridge," my sergeant instructed me.

I tapped one of the SRT officers on the shoulders who had been standing on the line, letting him know that he had been relieved. Then, as I took my spot on the line, the protestors instantly noticed me and converged in front of me.

One protestor looked at me with pure hatred in his eyes and said to me, "Look at this big, black, faggot ass, Uncle Tom ass nigga right here!"

I stood my ground and smiled at him as he continued with his verbal assault directed at me. Then, like a pack of wolves, his fellow protestors joined in with bullhorns and proceeded to say some of the vilest and most disrespectful things one human can say to another human.

Some of the things they said to us, I was reluctant even to repeat it here. But I want you to know what happened and the hypocrisy of some folks. I want you to know the hatred we were dealing with regularly. But, unfortunately, this is the type of treatment, so many law enforcement officers deal with daily, and specifically what we dealt with during the riots.

"You ain't black!" "Suck my dick, you faggot ass nigga!" "Yeah! I bet you love sucking that white dick!" "You're a fucking traitor to your people and deserve to die!" "You are a sellout! "I bet you are a good ol' nigga and do everything them white boys tell you!" "How do you live with yourself having black skin and wearing that uniform?" "Why do you work for your oppressor!" "You hate your own people. I bet you hate having black skin. I bet it pains you that you don't look like them white boys!" "I hope one of these white officers rapes your daughters."

As I stood before the angry, hate-filled mob of protestors and listened to their hateful comments, I thought back to my time riding the bus in the 7th grade and all the hurtful things said to me and how the other black kids dehumanized me. This was the same scenario but in a modern-day setting. But this time, I was not the scared, self-conscious kid afraid to stand up for himself or say anything back. I refused to live in fear and be offended as they pelted me with their indigent words, unable to penetrate my resilient psyche and elicit the negative response that they desired. I stood resolute amid a diabolical category five storms of scorn, mockery, evil, and hostility. Even though I was engulfed in this storm, I was calm, unphased, and at complete peace. I was home. I was where God had intended me to be all along. My purpose in life was not down on the border in Arizona, patrolling the border for $100,000 a year. God did not create me to police the picturesque streets of Sahuarita. He brought me back home for this moment, for these people and the city of Louisville.

"If you are really black, take a knee before us and show us that you are with us," one black protestor said to me with his bullhorn.

I responded to the protestor, "I will not kneel before you, but I will pray with you. So take my hand and pray with me."

What was his response to my gesture of peace? He said, "No! If I touch you, you are going to say that I assaulted you and arrest me!"

"How about we bow our heads and pray together?" I once again suggested.

He bowed his head, and I proceeded to pray. As I prayed, cameras closed in on us. After the prayer, the protester went about his way. Most of the protestors left me alone once they realized that they would not break me and get under my skin. After standing under the blazing sun in the thick humidity, sweating out our uniforms for hours, the crowd of protestors finally called it quits for the day and retreated to their camp at Jefferson Square Park. SRT headed back to our staging area to do a debrief and go home.

Not only did I have the peace of God to hold me together during this stressful time, but I also had something that a lot of my fellow officers did not have which was the perspective of working for another agency. I had the luxury of working on the federal level and the opportunity to work in a small department in another state. Due to that experience, I was able to appreciate working for LMPD. LMPD had its fair share of issues that needed to be addressed like any major organization. Despite its issues, LMPD was home, and it fits within the scope of my life and my family's life.

I could have gone to any other federal law enforcement agency or a smaller agency in the surrounding area with my credentials and resume, but I had no interest in either. I had already stepped out of God's will not once but twice before, and I paid for it dearly, and I was not going to do it again.

Before the grand jury trial and the charges brought against the detectives involved in the Breonna Taylor case, The NFAC (Not Fuckin Around Collation), a heavily armed, black separatist militia group, had recently emerged. The NFAC previously had a show of force in Stone Mountain, Georgia. They marched in formation dressed in all black with their faces covered, carrying an assortment of weapons, and announced their outrageous list of demands, such as creating their own black nation within Texas. They were now ready to march on Louisville demanding justice for Breonna Taylor and wanted the investigation into the incident expedited.

"NFAC is here! I bet you punk ass pigs are scared now! Try some bullshit today! They're going to kill every one of you boot lickers! We are coming to your front doors, and we are coming for your families! Now what!" An armed protestor screamed at us from across the barrier.

NFAC had assembled at Boone's Park at 20th and Duncan Street to start their march downtown to Metro Hall. Before they could even begin their march, they encountered multiple casualties from their members' lack of experience with handling firearms and the sweltering heat.

"Shots fired at Boone's Park!" Dispatch announced over the radio waves.

An NFAC member had an negligent discharge with their weapon and fired off a round striking two NFAC march participants sending both to the hospital with bullet wounds. On top of the negligent discharge, NFAC members were passing out due to their lack of physical conditioning, dehydration, and the all-black they were wearing in the almost 100-degree summer heat.

Our SRT squad stood in a line formation at the intersection of 5th and Jefferson Street wearing our full SRT uniform and gear. Due to the potential for violence at the event, a lot of us wore double body armor. We wore our level IIA soft armor as usual, but we took it a step further and wore our issued IIIA strike plates on top, which would protect us from larger high-velocity rounds like .223 rounds fired from an AR-15 or a 7.62 mm fired from an AK-47. The extra weight of the armor combined with our helmets and gun belts tortured us as we stood in formation on the asphalt under the fierce sun and oppressive humidity. Officers not on the line constantly walked around the formation handing out water and snacks to those standing so that we could replenish ourselves and be ready for whatever task might arise.

Not only did we have to remain cautious of NFAC and its supporters, but we also had to stay alert due to a local "3 Percenter" group known as the Oath Keepers who came to counter-protest the NFAC. Most of them were not hostile towards law enforcement, but the concern was the opposing factions clashing and sparking a significant gun battle. NFAC was given permission to have the west side of the street directly in front of Metro Hall, where their leader would speak after the march. The Oath Keepers were given the area east of the intersection. SRT held the north and south corners of the intersection between each faction. If a firefight broke out between the groups, we would be caught directly in the crossfire. We were heavily outnumbered and outgunned, but we had to live up to our oath as police officers and protect the Constitutional rights of both parties, ensuring that their freedom of speech, freedom of assembly, and their right to bear arms was not infringed upon despite their anti-police rhetoric. Our feelings and personal opinions could not supersede the Constitution, and they did not on that day. So we stood firm and carried out our sworn duties as professional and well-trained law enforcement officers in the face of hatred and potentially death.

"If shots start getting fired, we are falling back to cover behind these dump trucks, and we are going to saturate the intersection with smoke to conceal us as we fall back and to stop the gunfight hopefully," our squad leader informed us.

The dump trucks he referred to were massive trash and salt trucks that the city put in place at key intersections to keep vehicles from entering the protest area to avoid a Charlottesville-type scenario; that was a horrible situation where someone drove their car into a crowd of protestors, killing one and injuring others. If a gunfight broke out, it would be a one-block mad dash to get to cover behind the vehicles.

We continued to brave the brutal heat as protestors made their way to the barricade closest to us so that they could heckle us and hurl insults at us for their daily entertainment.

Under the physical challenge of the intense heat, another protestor said, "Suck a dick and die slow, you fucking whores! I hope every last one of you fucking pigs die today!"

A loud cheer erupted through downtown as NFAC marched down the street to Metro Hall. The tension downtown grew thicker, and you could feel the potential for a massive altercation brewing. Many local protesters walked around the block to circumvent us and the safety barricade, walked into the 3 Percenters protest area, and started antagonizing them. They say it only takes a spark to burn down the forest. We were standing in the middle of a giant, dried-out forest, and there were hundreds of potential tiny sparks ready to set the entire place ablaze.

"These white boys don't care about you! When it comes down to it, they are going to put themselves before your black ass every time. Look at what they have done to our people!" A protestor yelled at me.

He was alluding to the white boys, and white girls who did not care about me were the same white boys and girls I had worked with and watched for almost ten years, keeping the black community from plunging into complete chaos. It was the same white boys and girls who I watched time after time again driving code 3 to a scene where the life of an innocent, young, black child was hanging in the balance after being struck by a stray bullet in a drive-by as the child sat at the table playing on his tablet. The white boys and girls that he claims did not care about me were the same ones who took care of me in my darkest days and gave me another chance to prove myself and keep my job. I had seen the white boys and white girls that he was talking about putting their lives on the line for the black citizens of Louisville time and time again for little money and hardly any recognition. While the protesters tried to shame them for being white and me for being black and standing next to them, I stood prouder than ever to be wearing my LMPD uniform next to my brother and sister officers in this historic moment.

Thankfully, the NFAC event ended peacefully, and we were all able to return to our homes and to our families safely without any extra holes in us. The NFAC protest was just one of many protests that occurred in the city. It was a daily occurrence, and SRT was always at the forefront, ready to stand on the skirmish line to hold the city together as the protestors continued to block streets and cause chaos downtown.

"Put a white body in front of a black body right now! All white people to the front of the line! It is time for all of you white folks to atone for your sins and your privilege!" A black protest leader yelled into a bullhorn.

The protestors set up tables in the middle of the east 600 block of Market Street and proceeded to have a cookout. They also brought a trampoline and games to entertain themselves as they ate and protested in the middle of the street, stopping all traffic and harassing people walking in the area. SRT had been called to restore peace, order, and the rights of the citizens of Louisville to be able to drive freely on the road.

SRT surrounded the group, and the SRT commander asked them to leave the area multiple times using the LRAD. All the black protestors got up from the table and made their way to the sidewalks, and as instructed, the white protestors stayed to be arrested to "atone" for their sins and white privilege. SRT arrested 76 protestors. I stood guard watching a small group of the protestors when a very woke, middle-aged, white male that had been arrested was agitated by my presence and me being a black police officer.

"You're an Uncle Tom! Look at you! Of all the things you could have done with your life! You could have been a teacher, a doctor, a lawyer! You could have been anything, and you choose to become a fucking pig and oppress your own people! You race traitor!" He yelled to me as he sat on the ground with his legs crossed and his hands cuffed behind his back.

My tolerance and patience were starting to run low, and I could no longer just sit and be yelled at without saying something back. So, I used their own woke principles and beliefs against him.

I told the group of protestors, "I do not think it is appropriate for you all as white people to call me an Uncle Tom. I would appreciate it if all of you would stop yelling at me. I am a POC (person of color), and you all are using your white privilege to yell at me. I do not appreciate that at all."

Their eyes widened, and their mouths dropped to the floor. I could see the wheels turning in their heads and thought that their brains had exploded inside of their skulls as I used their own ideologies and beliefs against them. I triggered the entire group, and they were outraged. They stumbled over their words as they tried to yell at me and process me having turned the tables on them.

"That's fucking bullshit! And you know it!" One of them yelled as his face turned bright red.

The protestors continued with their child-like behavior and tantrums. One night in front of the park, they became enraged and dumped piles of trash in the streets and set them ablaze. SRT was called out to handle the problem. The constant callouts, threats of death, and violence to not only us but our families started to wear on all of us. Not only did we have to contend with the threats, but the protestors continued to grow more brazen in their interactions with us.

On more than one occasion, I found myself and a few other SRT members trying to arrest someone, and we found ourselves being surrounded by armed protestors. I can recall seeing two SRT officers trying to arrest someone in the middle of the street and two white Antifa members (one male and one female) with their faces covered carrying AR-15s rushing to where the officers were making an arrest so that they could interfere. I was able to put myself in between the arresting officers and the armed ANTIFA members trying to stop the arrest.

Leading up to the grand jury verdict for the officers involved in the Breonna Taylor killing, the tension continued to multiply in the city. More large-scale protests continued to grip the city as the protestors marched in the streets demanding justice day and night. Our anxiety awaiting the AG's (Attorney General) decision on the case was made worse by the fact that there was not a specific date or time when he would make his announcement. The rumor mill was in full swing, and we were going mad as we waited.

We knew that things were about to come to a head when we saw concrete barricades and fences being erected around downtown in preparation for the verdict. The city of Louisville was caught off guard during the initial start of the riots and was not prepared. That would not be the case this time. The city knew that a second round of protest was probable if the grand jury verdict was not in favor of the Taylor family. We also learned that a citywide curfew would be in place starting at 2100 hours.

On September 23, 2020, the grand jury charged one of the three

LMPD detectives with three counts of wanton endangerment 1st. No other charges were filed against the other detectives involved in the case. Once we heard the announcement, we knew that the protesters were not going to be happy and that we were going to be in for a long and rough few days.

"Double-check your gear and make sure that you are ready to go at a moment's notice!" The SRT commander announced.

We had gathered in a parking lot just south of Broadway and only a few blocks from the heart of downtown, where thousands of protestors had gathered. With us in the parking lot were members of the Kentucky National Guard, who were tasked with providing critical security infrastructure in the downtown area. KSP had mobilized their SRT unit to help assist us and beef up our numbers. The LMPD and KSP helicopter circled above us, monitoring the downtown area. I had that same feeling in my gut that I had before I would go on patrol in Iraq.

"Check out this video that someone just posted," someone yelled.

Everyone pulled out their phones and watched a video of a U-Haul truck pulling up in the downtown area. The back door of the U-Haul rolled up, and protesters proceeded to pull dozens of giant, hastily constructed shields that had an assortment of messages on them: "protect black women," "Las Vidas Negras Important," "Charge the police," "Abolish the police."

"They do not want to protest. They want to fight." Someone in the group said.

We watched the live stream view from the news helicopter as the crowd of protesters continued to increase. We were ready to head downtown and hold the line but were thrown for a loop when the SRT commander told us to load up in our vehicles and head to the Highlands on Bardstown Road, where another large group of protesters had gathered and were blocking the street.

"Face shields down!" An officer yelled as loud as he could, trying to make sure we could hear his command over the sound of police sirens and the angry voices of protesters.

I lowered my face shield and put on my Mechanic gloves as we marched in formation towards the ruckus on Bardstown road. As we marched down the road, we soon found ourselves encircled by the angry crowd thirsting for justice and revenge.

"You fucking Nazis!" "Fascist pricks!" "We want justice!" "How would you feel if that was your daughter or family member!" "Eat shit and die, you fucking pigs!"

With every step I took further into the crowd and deeper into the bedlam, the more it felt like I was patrolling the bizarre in Abu Ghraib. My eyes fluctuated back and forward, scanning the crowd for threats. The negative energy from the coward and the looks upon their faces was the same that I had experienced patrolling the Abu Ghraib bizarre. I could feel that same pair of invisible eyes from Iraq 15 years prior that stalked me all day before trying to kill me. That same pair of eyes had somehow followed me to the Highlands of Louisville from Iraq to finish the job it failed to do.

We were at a tactical disadvantage walking down the middle of the street. If someone started shooting at us, we would have no cover to protect ourselves. My eyes and my mind were now pulling double duty, searching for not only threats in the crowd but also my next and nearest cover. I thought about the 2016 Dallas PD ambush in which 12 officers were wounded, and five were killed by a lone gunman during a BLM protest. I did not want to be caught out in the open with no plan if someone took aim at us.

The SRT LRAD then started emitting its message to the protesters.

"This is the Louisville Metro Police Department. In accordance with KRS 525.050, this assembly has been declared unlawful. Please leave the street and move to the sidewalk immediately."

The message blasted from the LRAD multiple times, but the protestors stood unwavering, refusing our command. We slowly encroached upon the large group in the street as we marched at a half step, yelling "move back" in sync with our riot sticks in hand. We were roughly 10 yards from the massive crowd when the tension reached its peak, and the bubble finally burst. The crowd chucked multiple objects at us. SRT dashed forward and clashed with the violent protesters in the crowd who wished not only to fight but do us harm. Skirmishes broke out between officers and protestors.

Due to ongoing legal battles as a result of this event which I named "The Rumble in The Highlands," I am unable to go into further detail about the event and the arrest that followed shortly after. Once the conflict was over, SRT had arrested multiple people who had been involved in the fray. In the middle of the street was a large pile of trash that consisted of shields, clubs, banners, sticks, bottles, and many other items the protesters used as weapons against us.

My adrenaline was still raging after we left the area and returned to our original staging location to await the next volley of madness. It was still early, and the sun was still shining bright. We tried to enjoy the peacefulness of the moment, call our friends and family members to give them an update on our status, and let them know that we were doing OK. We sat in the parking lot, monitoring the radio and social media anxiously waiting for our next call. The sun started to set, and darkness fell over the city, but downtown was still full of life as the protest continued.

"We have eyes on a large group of protesters heading towards the intersection of Brook and Broadway." RTCC (Real-Time Crime Center) notified us.

SRT loaded up into the back of pick-up trucks that had been assigned to us so that we could be more mobile and respond faster. My squad loaded onto an LMPD charter bus and headed east on Broadway towards the intersection to get ahead of the large group of protesters. Our convoy of vehicles came to a halt just west of the Broadway and Brook Street intersection under the I-65 overpass, where we started to unload from the bus and got ready to go to work. My hands gripped my baton as I stepped off the bus. The day had been a mixture of boredom, pandemonium, and adrenaline, and I was intoxicated off of the concoction that provided me with a natural high.

We walked down the sidewalk towards the intersection as we moved out from under the overpass. To our right (south of the sidewalk), there was a large, empty parking lot that stretched roughly 64 yards to an alley that ran east to west, where there was an assortment of people standing. After spotting the group, SRT proceeded to march south towards the group. I had just walked past the last concrete support beam when I heard the all too familiar sequence of gunfire.

"Get to cover!" I yelled.

I dashed back to the concrete beam that I had just walked past. I reached out and grabbed the officer in front of me by the back of his outer vest and yanked him behind cover with me. The gunshots ripped through the night and echoed under the overpass. I drew my weapon and started scanning the alley south of me, looking for the shooter.

"We got officers down! Major and D are hit!" Someone frantically screamed.

My stomach flipped inside of me, and cold chills ran throughout my body, hearing the two most horrifying words that an officer can hear in their career: "officers down." The squad of officers that were to my left as we got off the bus and started making their way across the parking lot had been caught out in the open with no cover when they were ambushed.

"Get them in the trucks! Let's go!"

SRT grenadiers fired smoke grenades towards the area where the shots came from to help conceal the officers as they carried our wounded to the awaiting pick-up trucks that would escort them to the UofL ER. I watched as our Major and D were loaded into the trucks. I prayed for them both and asked God to spare their lives. We had no clue where they had been shot or how severe their wounds were. They were in God's hands, and all we could do was pray for them.

For the first time since I had come back and had been dealing with the unrest and protest day in and day out, I was scared. My greatest fear was that we would end up in a Dallas PD-style ambush, and it came to pass. I enjoyed the chaos and the adrenaline that came from dealing with these high-stress situations, but I did not enjoy seeing my brothers being gunned down or the looks of concern and sadness upon everyone else's faces.

My cell phone started to buzz and light up. Every time it would finally stop, there would be a break for a few seconds and start again. News of the officers being shot in downtown Louisville spread quickly. The people in my life that I love and called my friends were reaching out to me because they wanted to know if I was OK. But this was no time for me to have my nose buried in my phone. We still had a dangerous suspect at large downtown, and that suspect had already proven that he was not afraid to shoot it out with us.

We moved to the north side of the street between two buildings and set up a security perimeter so that we could collect ourselves and figure out what our next plan of action would be. I looked around at everyone, and I could see the flame in their eyes. We were ready to get back into the fight.

"Why are we just standing here! We should be out there! Someone just shot two of our guys!" Someone yelled.

We were eager to hit the streets, but SRT was not equipped to handle such events. We did not possess the armor, weaponry, or practice the tactics needed to handle this type of incident. This was a job for SWAT and their Bearcat (armored personnel carrier vehicle). With a tip from a nearby witness, SWAT was able to locate the subject in the area of 1st Street and Broadway and take him into custody without further incident.

As we stood in a security hold, our dispatch advised us that a large group of protestors was seen heading towards the hospital where our two wounded officers were en route. Two weeks prior, two LA Sheriff's Deputies were ambushed while they were sitting in their marked police car. After the deputies were shot, they were rushed to the hospital, but a group protestor had arrived at the hospital ahead of the wounded deputies and proceeded to block the emergency entrances preventing the deputies from getting medical attention. Hearing that a group of protestors were heading towards the hospital, we believed that they were going to try and do the same.

We were unable to access our vehicles at the time because they were a part of the crime scene, so we decided to head towards the hospital on foot. We were four blocks away and had to go another four blocks north. We opened our strides as we marched to help us cover more ground quickly. I was surrounded by heavy breathing, and the sound of heavy-footed SRT officers weighed down by their gear trampling the asphalt. We were only a few blocks into our movement when we encountered a group of five to ten protesters. We were not sure if they were the group that RTCC was referring to, but they were in the general area, and they were out past the established curfew. We moved towards the group, and they scattered. We were able to round up most of the group and placed them under arrest. We sat with a prisoner waiting for a prisoner transport vehicle to come to our location. We then received an update on our fellow wounded officers.

"Both of them are going to be OK."

"Thank God!" Someone replied.

I let out a giant sigh of relief, knowing that they were going to be OK. The road to recovery was going to belong, but I was happy that they were still with us and that we did not have to plan two police officer funerals.

Once I had a moment to catch my breath, gather my thoughts and make sure that we were not in danger, I pulled out my phone and called Christina to let her know that I was OK. She had been at home watching the live stream when the shooting happened.

"Do me a favor. Please stop watching this live stream. It is not healthy for you. It is going to worry you sick." I requested.

I hung up the phone and looked at my text alerts. I had dozens of text messages asking me if I was OK. I did not have time to reply to each message, so I hopped on my Facebook account and made a quick and simple post: "I am OK." That would have to do for now because there was still work to be done. We were ready for our next mission for the night, but we were informed that we were done for the night and that we needed to decompress. We were transported back to our staging area and told to sit down and relax. We were all flustered, knowing that there was still work that needed to be done and justice needing to be served, but we had been sidelined. We were excited. Too amped up and command thought it would be best to have us stand down and decompress so that we did not make any harsh or rash decisions out of anger which would have done us more harm than good. Even though we did not like it, we understood. We circled up in the parking lot and said a quick prayer for the Major, Des, and the city.

We lounged in the parking lot discussing the day's events and monitoring the ongoing events downtown. The day seemed unreal, and this was just day one. We expected more action the next day. We were eventually released from our detail for the evening and told what time to return the following day. As I drove home, my paranoia was high. I scanned and monitored everything around me. Instead of going straight to my home, I stopped at a few places along the way and circled the parking lot to make sure that I had not been followed. When I was a few blocks away from my apartment complex, I turned off my lights to conceal my movement and drove through the dark. I parked my police car on the opposite side of the complex and walked to my apartment.

I walked into my apartment, and it was dark and peaceful, but inside of me, inside of my mind, the chaotic events continued to play on a continuous loop. Christina heard me come in and greeted me at the door with a hug and a kiss. I went into my children's room. They were already asleep, but I needed to see them. I stood in their room and looked at them both as they slept peacefully and soundly unaware of the day's events. Everything in their young and innocent world was perfect. I leaned over and gave each of them a kiss. I then prayed over each of them before I left.

I downloaded my gear and climbed into the shower to cleanse myself of the day's filth. The hot water cascading over me felt good and helped to relax me. As I washed the dirt and sweat off of my skin, I wished that there had been a way for me to wash my mind and forget about the terrifying events that had transpired hours prior. After showering, I sat on the couch in the living room next to Christina and poured my heart out to her as she comforted me.

I was still more than happy to be back with LMPD, and I still had peace, but I was starting to feel the frustration of fighting a political battle in which politicians and the media stacked the deck against my chosen profession. Two of my brothers had been shot fighting this battle and sacrificed themselves in defense of Louisville and its citizens. I felt hopeless fighting this battle, trying to bridge the gap between the police, protesters, and the community.

I eventually fell asleep; however, as soon as I closed my eyes, it seemed as though my alarm had gone off, and it was time to put my uniform and armor back on and head back into the pandemonium. I was ready to get back to doing what I did best, but first, I had to take a moment to pray with my family and ask for God to protect me and the rest of the officers holding the city together and from plunging into complete disarray.

I got down on one knee and my kids towards me, and I held them in my arms. They were young and did not understand the circumstances behind everything, but they were old enough to know the difference between good guys and bad guys. They knew that daddy was the good guy and that he had to go and catch the bad guys. They looked into my eyes and could tell that I was tired. It felt like they were reading my thoughts.

"Please don't go, daddy. Please stay home. I don't want you to get hurt." Brooklynn begged me.

"Yeah, daddy. Please stay. I love you." DJ said to me.

My heart had been made hard, and my emotions had been taxed from having to deal with the constant protest response, long hours, the adrenaline dumps, and the countless hours sitting around waiting to be called to squash any unlawful protest, but my kid's words cut through the jumbled mess in my mind, my emotions, and fatigue and hit me directly in the heart. I knew they loved their daddy, but I could feel how much they loved me by how tight they held onto me. I could hear the stress and concern in their voices. I knew they could feel the tension radiating from me and the tension permeating from the city.

We formed a circle in the living room, held hands, and went before God in prayer as a family. Christina prayed to God and asked him to send a legion of his angels to watch over the rest of my fellow officers and me heading back into the eye of the storm. We all took turns praying.

"God, please protect my daddy and his friends. And I hope they lock up all the bad people, Amen." DJ prayed.

"God. Please let my daddy make it back home safe, and please take care of him and all his police officer friends. Amen." Brooklynn prayed.

I shared one last hug and kiss with them. I savored the hugs and kisses more than usual because less than 24 hours ago, someone literally tried to kill my fellow officers and me simply because of the uniform we wore and the badge on our chest. None of us knew what the coming hours held. But if God decided to call me home during this next protest detail, I needed my family to know how much I truly loved them. I wanted my last interaction with them to be one that would give them comfort going forward in my absence, leaving no doubt that they were at the center of my life and that I loved them dearly. Not even death would be able to keep my love from living on with them.

I closed the door behind me and walked to my police cruiser at the opposite end of the complex. I continued talking to God as I walked. I sat in my seat, turned on my car, and turned on my police radio. As I got ready to put my car in drive and head downtown, I realized and acknowledged my fear for the first time. I had more than enough close encounters with death in my 36 years, with 13 of those years carrying a gun. The danger of my chosen profession was awfully familiar to me, but I realized now more than ever what was at stake-my family's future without me. And that scared me.

Once again, SRT had amassed in our staging area at the Fairgrounds, awaiting the day's mission. I looked around the room at everyone. I was sure that everyone went home after being released from the last detail and that they all held their families a little tighter. I knew that if I was, but that is what made us unique. That is what made me proud to be a part of SRT. Despite the night's previous events, we were back and ready to do our jobs yet again without hesitation. The fear was there, but our dedication, loyalty, and love for each other surpassed the fear. If anything, we were even more eager and motivated to take back the streets and serve up justice to those wanting to destroy the city, people's business, and property.

As we sat awaiting our daily briefing, Major limped into the room wearing a pair of cargo shorts and a hoodie. He had been shot in his hip less than 12 hours prior, yet here he was to address his officers. He was one of the most respected leaders in the department, and he was showing us why because he was leading from the front. I had previously worked for him in the Second Division, where he was my Lieutenant, so I was not surprised seeing him walk in because I knew the type of man that he was.

Major stood before us and thanked all of us for taking care of him after the incident. He also thanked us for our continued service as SRT members because SRT is a volunteer team. The major updated us on D's condition. D had undergone surgery immediately after he had been shot in the gut. He was stable, but he had a long road to recovery ahead of him, but he was going to be just fine. After being briefed, we all enjoyed a nice meal that had been catered for us, but before we could even digest our food, SRT had been called upon once again to save the city.

I felt like I was going on a combat deployment as I walked out of the fairgrounds and onto the awaiting transport bus waiting to take us downtown. A large group of protestors were marching east on Main Street, blocking traffic. Our vehicle convoy stopped at the intersection of East Market Street and South Hancock Street, where we offloaded. We would then march north on South Hancock Street to intercept the group.

"Squads one, two, three, and four form the line!" An SRT commander shouted.

We formed a skirmish line extending from east to west across South Hancock Street and started to march forward towards the crowd. The first thing I noticed as we moved forward towards East Main Street was that we were once again at a tactical disadvantage. We were wedged between a building on our east side and the steep, foliage-covered, I-65 expressway embankment on our west. We were in a fatal funnel with zero cover, and the major concern on this day was rioters and protesters feeling emboldened to attack us and try to kill us once again.

"This is a great spot for an ambush," I said to the rest of the officers on the line.

Officers then rushed forward and climbed up the embankment, and started to clear the overgrown, grassy area making sure that there was not a shooter lurking in the tall grass. I scanned my sector, looking for any threats. It was an uncomfortable and unnerving feeling moving closer towards the hostile crowd, not knowing their intentions for us on this day. As I pushed forward, I felt a large presence behind me and heavy footsteps. It was Officer Tyson. He and a few other officers with military experience had been assigned to SRT as our lethal cover. Knowing that Tyson had my six and was looking over us gave me some comfort and confidence.

"How does it feel now to be the hunted, you fucking pigs!" A protestor yelled at us.

"I heard two of your friends got shot last night! What a shame!" A protestor pointed at us and laughed hysterically.

I expected to hear such disrespectful and hateful comments from the protestors concerning our two officers who had been shot. It was no surprise. Deep down, I was angry, but I refused to let them get to me. I was the professional, and I was in control, not them. I held my tongue, unwilling to give in to the rage inside of me. I was also expecting to hear gunfire aimed at us any moment as the hostility reached its pinnacle.

Not only did I have to keep my cool to maintain control and not escalate the situation, but the eyes of the world were on Louisville at this very moment, and SRT was front and center on the world stage. It was our time to shine and show the world who we were. We continued to scan the crowd for threats as we stood before them. LMPD and SRT commanders spoke to the leaders of the protest, trying to de-escalate the situation. After reaching some sort of agreement with the protestors, we tactically withdrew from the area and returned to our staging area south of Broadway. We sat in the staging area for hours and the entire day passed us by quickly. There was no way that this day was going to come to an end without some carnage and destruction of property occurring. The day had been quiet. Too quiet, and we all knew that trouble was afoot. As soon as night fell over the city, the static sound of our radios filled the silence of the night.

"All units be advised. We have eyes on a large group walking around downtown. They smashed the windows at Jeff Ruby's Steakhouse." Dispatch advised us.

The radio went silent for a few minutes, and the dispatcher's voice reemerged.

"That same group just spray painted a TARC (Transit Authority of River City) Bus." She reiterated.

"SRT! Grab your gear and load up!" A voice rumbled through the staging area.

We loaded onto the bus and convoyed down the street as the dispatcher kept us in the loop with up-to-date information as it came in.

"That group is heading southbound on Fourth Street! They just broke out the window at the library and tossed a flare inside!" Dispatch notified us.

"They are trying to burn down the library!" Someone screamed.

We had come across some intel that informed us that the rioters were planning on seeking refuge at a Unitarian Church at the intersection of Fourth Street and York Street. We downloaded from the bus close to the area and moved in on foot, and were able to intercept the group and arrest 20 individuals. While we were occupied arresting the group of 20, another large group made their way around our location and onto the church grounds, where they proceeded to taunt us.

"One, two, three, four, five, six, seven, eight, nine, ten, eleven, fuck twelve!" They screamed at us in unison from the church property.

They had a speaker with them and blared rap music with curse words and violent and explicit lyrics as they danced in front of us on the church grounds as well.

"Ha! Ha! You fagots can't touch us! They taunted us.

I was sickened at their audacity and lack of respect for the holy ground that they were standing on. We were at a stalemate, and command withdrew us from the location. As we were preparing to leave the area, we heard an explosion southeast of our location. We headed to the area and saw giant flames reflecting off of windows of surrounding buildings.

"They just firebombed a car in the parking lot of Spalding University." Someone announced over the radio.

"Does anyone else feel like we are fighting an insurgency?" I said, referencing the tactics being used by the rioters.

"Yeah, no shit, man! This is the same I saw in Iraq and Afghanistan." Some reiterated.

Regardless of all, we were dealing with at work, I still loved putting on my uniform and going to work, but it was starting to feel more like I was going on a 12-hour deployment as opposed to a work shift. By the time 2020 came to an end, I had worked 321 hours of

OT on top of working my normal shift. I was so entrenched in everything going on at work that the lines between work and home life started to blur. Anxiety, stress, and paranoia from the continuous exposure to the volatile work environment started to bleed over into my at-home life. I started to become irritable, moody and my sleep cycle was off because of having to work the graveyard shift on top of SRT callouts. I was not aware of what was going on with me, but it took my precious daughter to help me realize where I was going wrong.

"Daddy. Can you get off of your phone and play with me, please? You are always on your phone." Brooklynn would ask me.

"Brooklynn! I am looking at important stuff for work! You are too young to understand, but daddy is talking to his friends and discussing important issues facing our country." I snapped back at her.

"OK. I'm sorry, daddy." She said to me as she hung her head low and walked off with her heart crushed after being rejected by the man she loved and admired.

After she walked off, I would continue to stare at my phone and scroll through social media, reading article after article about the current state of policing in America. After reading the articles, I would go further down the social media rabbit hole and read the negative and hateful comments, which would suck me in further and throw fuel on the fire of anxiety, stress, and paranoia in my life. I would then furiously type my response and argue my point of view and opinion with strangers who I would never meet in my lifetime. I found myself constantly having to defend my post, my beliefs, and the entire police profession. It was exhausting.

Not only did I have to contend with negativity from the public and the media, who had no clue what it was like to walk in our shoes and carry the weight of the nation on our chest. There was also the issue of low morale amongst officers. Their attitudes were pessimistic, and their complaints were never-ending. I had never seen so many disgruntled and cynical officers on the PD before. LMPD was hemorrhaging officers like a shotgun slug round through the femoral artery. The lack of support and political pressure from city leadership in light of the protest pushed many officers into retiring early to safely escape the hostile witch hunt of an environment with their pensions secured. Officers were fleeing LMPD to other agencies in the surrounding areas for better pay, benefits, support, less stress, and the feeling of being appreciated. Not only was LMPD losing officers, but we were also losing some of our best and most experienced officers.

I listened to my fellow officers' complaints and read all their negative comments on social media, and I completely understood and shared their frustration. I had many of the same thoughts, feelings, and concerns regarding all the issues plaguing the city, the department, our careers, and our personal lives. Soon, their dissatisfactions and negativity slowly started to bleed over into my mind and poison my thoughts. I started to lose focus of my purpose and why I decided to return to LMPD. I found myself starting to agonize over the things that I could not control, such as decisions made by city and police department leadership that impacted all officers. I was starting to lose my peace that had carried me through the riots and all the challenges that came with being on the frontline. My smile was starting to turn into a frown as I wasted all my energy scrolling through social media and engaging in heated discussions that would not change my mind or the other person's. I had lost sight of what was truly important in my life and the blessing that LMPD had been to my family.

I love and care about my LMPD brothers and sisters more than they will ever know, but despite my love for them, I could no longer afford to be influenced by some of their personal feelings and experiences that led them to become the negative and unhappy people that some of them were. The experience I was having being back with LMPD during this stressful time was the same experience I had with the Buffalo Soldiers in Italy in 2007. I was living in an echo chamber filled with the voices of my brothers and sisters in blue who shared many of the ideologies and political leanings. With every post I made and read, every comment I responded to, and emoji I posted, I was being influenced by their personal experiences and life circumstances, not my own. I am not saying that my fellow officers are horrible people or that I hated being around them. That was not the case. I love being around them, laughing and joking; they are some of the best people I know. However, I had to consider my life, my family, and our circumstances when it came to working with LMPD and enjoying my job, and being happy when it was time to report to my shift.

As I stated before, I shared many of the same gripes and complaints as everyone else who worked for LMPD, but I had to shift my focus from all the negative things that were beyond my span of control and focus on what I could impact and control in my immediate reach. I had to boost my own morale and find my own meaning and reason to get up and smile every morning. I never considered the power of an organization to give you higher morale and give you happiness, and also the power to take it away. But if you find your own morale and happiness, and it lives within you, there is nothing they can do to take that away from you because you personally own it.

My eyes were connected to my phone every second of the day. My mind was constantly linked to the pessimism and the calamity of politics, police work, and unrest affecting every police department in the nation. I spent countless hours looking at my phone as opposed to focusing on what was profoundly more important in my life, my family. I knew what I had to do, but I resisted because I had to be in the know and at the forefront of everything happening in America, Louisville, and the PD.

I could see Christina and the kids starving for my love and attention and me slowly slipping back into that dark void where I was for a month, and I could not let that happen. I had to get ahead of the problem and cut it off at its source. I deactivated my Facebook account and made the conscious decision to stop watching and reading the news. Facebook and the news had become a second job to me that I willingly worked for as a volunteer in my free time, and it drained me of my peace, my morale and robbed my family of their time with me. Once I put down my phone and turned off the news, my anxiety started to decrease, and my morale increased. My peace returned to me when I stopped concerning myself with external circumstances that I did not control. Ridding myself of the anxiety-inducing and panic persuading social media apps and the news gave me a fresh breath of air and a positive outlook. I realized that the sky was not falling, and it was not the end of the world. I took advantage of my spare time and started getting more involved in my children's lives and spending more quality time with Christina, and my personal life began to flourish.

2020 was a bizarre and hectic year for the entire country as we endured wave after wave of unforeseen happenings from Covid-19 and all the disorder that came with it, nationwide civil unrest, protest, and of course, the ongoing saga that is American politics. Even though all of these major life-changing events impacted me just like they did everyone in the country, the most bizarre thing I encountered in 2020 was me praying, dreaming, and rushing to get back to the place where it seemed everyone was trying escapee-LMPD. Even though 2020 was an unsettling year, I was able to smile through it. Now that 2020 is behind us and the future remains uncertain, I want my life and the way I live it to spread joy, encouragement, compassion, reasonableness, forgiveness, and most of all, hope for a better tomorrow for all those I meet. Instead of being influenced, I want to be the influencer shining my light into the darkness and helping lead the way to a brighter future for us all.

[28]

THE FUTURE

IT HAS BEEN JUST over a decade since my mother's tragic death. Even though I have peace about the situation, there were still pieces of the puzzle missing, and I needed to find them. I wanted closure. I could not get that closure from my sister because she and I have not communicated since 2011. I spoke to my father three times over the years, and each time I tried to talk to him, he reminded me why I chose to keep him out of my life. I would find no closure with him.

It was time to close this dark and hurtful chapter of my life finally and put it away for good. And if I was going to get the closure I desired, I had to go directly to the source-the Radcliff Police Department. On January 12, 2021, a light and fresh blanket of snow had fallen during the night. The snow crunched under my tires as I reversed from my parking spot and started the 45-minute trip down I-65 southbound and the Joe Prather highway to the Radcliff Police Department (RPD).

Weeks prior, I had talked to my friend from high school who was an RPD sergeant about obtaining a copy of my mother's death investigation file. Like the other officers at RPD, he did his best to talk me out of getting the file to protect me. They knew just how gruesome the crime scene was and all the intricate details of the case.

I heard their plea's for me to reconsider getting a copy of the file, and I understood. I had been in their shoes as a police officer on the scene of many homicide scenes as grieving family members wanted to tear down the yellow crime scene tape to see their deceased loved ones. Not only did we hold them back to preserve the scene, but we held them back to protect the grieving family members from the grisliness of the crime scene. For me, I had already seen the worst of the situation as I stood by my mother's bedside in the emergency room.

Although I had continued with my life after this unfathomable tale of events, I still needed to know what exactly happened between my parents on that August day. I took possession of the thick manila file jacket. It was cumbersome. The weight of the file signified the complexity and seriousness of the investigation into the final moments of mother's life. When I arrived back home, I sat in my recliner and started to read through the vast reports and interviews. They painted a vivid picture for me of the events of that day. I then took one of the CDs, placed it on the laptop, and scrolled through the many images. Bloodstains throughout the home, blood spatter, bloody handprints on the wall, and my mother's car further helped me put the pieces of the puzzle together.

I spent hours looking through the file, trying to make sense of everything. Due to privacy concerns and out of respect for my mother's family and my father's family, I will not go into any more details about this horrific event. But I can and will say this. My mother, although very strong and resilient, was a battered woman and reached her breaking point. She carried with her 50 years of pain and unresolved issues stemming from her childhood. Piled on top of that was 28 years in a marriage filled with physical, mental, and emotional abuse. On August 29, 2010, all of her demons converged in my mother's mind and overpowered her in her darkest moment, which led her to pull the trigger of her 9 mm handgun while it was pressed against her head. While the investigation might have exonerated my father of murder, he was complicit in her death by how he treated her and will have to stand before God one day to answer.

I cannot stand in judgment of my father, mother, or sister without standing in judgment of myself. I am no angel, and I cannot abstain from any wrongdoing. I have done and said things that I am not proud of in the heat of the moment and take personal responsibility for those things and the pain I might have caused family members. I have been hurt, and I have hurt people, but I do not want the hurt I have felt or the pain that I have caused to be my legacy. I refuse to let the darkness in my life guide, dictate, and shape my perception of the world and how I am perceived. Instead, I choose to be the light that shines through the darkness as a beacon of hope and guidance for all those who have suffered, feel smothered, and overpowered by darkness.

As America moves forward through these tense, uncertain, and perilous times, we are faced with deciding who we will be as a country. Political dissonance, left vs. right, black vs. white, the poor versus the wealthy, law enforcement and military having their honor trampled, the erosion of law and order, reasonableness, and misleading media headlines have left America crippled, divided, and splitting at the seams into opposing factions. I believed that we were living in Dr. Martin Luther King Jr's dream at one point and time. Dr. King dreamed of America living up to its creed that all men are created equal. He dreamed of sons of slaves and former slave owners sitting at the table of brotherhood. He dreamed that his children would be judged by the content of their character and not the color of their skin. The America I grew up in was Martin Luther King, Jr's dream turned into reality. The men who fought next to me in Iraq and the men and women I have served with for the last 12 years as a police officer and Border Patrol Agent are the ones I sit with daily at the table of brotherhood in defense of the Constitution and our nation.

Dr. King envisioned a country where his children would be

judged by the content of their character, not the color of their skin. But somehow, after all the hard work, sacrifice and ground gained during the Civil Rights movement, 57 years later, we are reverting back to where we fought so hard to escape. The color of a person's skin now carries more weight than who they are at their core. The color of a person's skin is now being weaponized to put them in one of two categories: victims or oppressors. Instead of keeping our nation's history at the forefront where we can learn from our mistakes, we are now sanitizing our history to adhere to woke culture standards and protecting people's feelings. The America that I signed up to fight for and defend is now unrecognizable. The America we are currently living in is not the America that I desire for my children or future generations of the Pitts family. So much of what is going on in America is beyond my control. Instead of constantly stressing and fretting over things beyond my control, I have found peace accepting and learning that the only thing I can control is my reaction, attitude, and looking to the future.

When I say the future, future is my acronym for how America can move forward as a unified country past our union's current state of decay. Future stands for forgiving, understanding, transforming, unplug, respecting, and educating.

Forgive - One of the greatest lessons I want people to walk away with from this book is the power of forgiveness by showcasing the many personal struggles in my life and how learning to forgive those who hurt me enriched my quality of life. If it worked for me, I know that it can for anyone else and for America. There is a lot of pain, bloodshed, and distrust attached to the United States of America and the flag because of the misdeeds of America's past and our forefathers. They were flawed men with a vision of a nation that was so unique that no other place at that time existed. America today was born out of a foundation built on violence and the attempted irradiation of the Native American population, the evils of slavery that my ancestors endured, the silencing and mistreatment of women, the greed of wealthy men, and war. Despite the many atrocities that have stained our nation's history, a beautiful country arose out of such ugliness. But at what point do we as one nation under God take the advice of his son, Jesus Christ, as he was being persecuted and hung on the cross and say, "Father, forgive them, for they do not know what they are doing."

Despite being unfairly persecuted, Jesus Christ forgave those who targeted him for death without just cause. True healing can only happen in our resegregated country if those who feel persecuted forgive America of its shortcomings. Why should people today be held responsible for the decisions made by those who are no longer alive? Imagine having to serve a life sentence in prison because of a crime that your grandfather committed before you were born. America is truly the home of free, but true freedom cannot be achieved and experienced in the bondage of unforgiveness. Forgiveness is the only key to unlocking the chains of resentment that keep people from experiencing freedom and liberty, as our founding fathers pledged for all men. Forgiveness does not mean that we simply forget the transgressions of the past, but we go forward with grace and understanding that none of us are perfect and that we have all fallen short of the standards set by God. And in failing to meet that standard, all of us would like to be extended grace and forgiveness by those we might have hurt. Forgiveness does not exist to set our oppressors and offenders free; it exists to set us free.

Understanding - A key element missing from American society today that is hindering us from being a united body is understanding. In today's culture, every issue we encounter revolves around politics and results in us going down the road of never-ending debates where the only objective is total victory. The truth is, there is hardly ever a winner in these debates that seem to drag out. No one's mind is changed, and no one's perception is altered. The only thing that occurs is people retreat to their echo chambers to be patted on their back and be told, "Yeah! You showed them!" Yet, the issue that caused the debate is still there. Instead of arguing our talking points, shaming the other person into submission, and trying to "win" the debate, try to understand the other person's point of view.

Life in America is different for every community and the individuals who make up that community; therefore, the perception of America is unique for every community and its individuals. And because of that, our individual perceptions are not in alignment with others' beliefs about America. It does not mean that your vision of America is wrong, but it does show that there is a disconnect and lack of understanding between communities which is being exploited by special interest groups, the media, and politicians with an agenda to divide us. There are certain issues in which it is an issue of right and wrong. There is good, and there is evil. In the end, what is good, what is right and what is just must win out; however, in the world in which we live, there is a lot of grey area where there is no right or wrong, but our personal feelings and perspective drives us to believe that only our version of the issue is the only correct one.

The old saying, "walk a mile in my shoes," comes to mind when I think of two different people talking to each other from two very different walks of life. Instead of trying to make someone see the world through your eyes, put yourself in someone else's shoes and imagine what it might feel like to be that young black kid in the hood who feels like he is being unjustly targeted by the police or followed in a store. Put yourself in the shoes of a white cop who has served with honor and integrity all of his career, yet he is constantly accused of being a racist even though his record is spotless, and there is no evidence to support such derogatory claims. Taking to the time to listen and understand someone is not a sign of weakness or defeat. It is a sign of strength, confidence, and humanity.

Transform - If we are going to live in the brilliance of Martin Luther King Jr's dream, we have to transform our hearts and minds from thinking about what only benefits ourselves, our families, and our communities and become selfless servants and transformational leaders in pursuit of equality and unity for all just as Martin Luther King Jr was. Even though Martin Luther King Jr was an advocate for the black community during the Civil Rights Movement, Martin Luther King Jr was a man of God who encompassed all people. He did not desire black dominance or separate but equal accommodations. He wanted what was best for everyone, not just his family. Until we learn to live by God's second commandment, "You shall love your neighbor as yourself," we will never move past these trying times to overcome our current societal issues.

Unplug - Even though social media is a key component in today's culture, we must unplug from time to time and take a healthy break. Technology is humanity's greatest strength but has also proven to be our greatest weakness and source of division. Social media has made it possible for us to connect no matter where we are in the world, but the same technology that connects us causes so much strife and brings out the worst of us. Anytime we log onto our social media accounts and scroll our feeds, there is a potential to be dragged into pointless war or words and dulling ideologies. Think of all the lifelong friendships, relationships, and careers that have ended because of what someone posted. I can personally attest to the chaos that social media can bring to your front door and destroy relationships. There is also an abundance of misleading articles written with a slant in favor of someone's political party or personal agenda. After a while, it all gets too overwhelming, exhausting, confusing, and frustrating, having to argue with strangers, friends, family members, and trying to decipher truth from fiction. That is why I believe it is important that we unplug from the deception and madness of social media at times.

Social media has led to many of us becoming detached from reality and estranged from real human interaction. We construct our own world to support our own beliefs and expect everyone to abide by the rules we set in our imaginary world. To combat this, I suggest we unplug from social media at times and go outside and talk to people in real-time. Social networking makes us believe that people only exist in the extremes and never in the middle. Many of us would be pleasantly surprised if they put down the phone and struck up a conversation with a random person. We would all come to learn that most of us have more in common that unites us than separates us.

Respect - Respect is a small word that carries enormous weight. Ask different people what respect means to them, and you will get a blended array of answers. The best definition of respect comes from the Oxford Dictionary and defines it as due regard for the feelings, wishes, rights, or traditions of others. Respect is so important that it is mentioned in the Holy Bible 36 times. Unfortunately, the lack of respect has taken root in America and has permeated and overtaken American society. America suffers from culture rot due to the lack of respect between those who call the US home. And social media has made it too easy and convenient to be comfortable being a disrespectful person and not suffer the consequences of the things that come out of our mouths.

If we want to reclaim our country and live up to our country name, "The United States of America," instead of our current name, "The Divide States of America," we have to start respecting our differences. The best way to repair the fracture between our fellow countrymen is living by what some call the golden rule, but to us Christians, we refer to it as Matthew 7:12 "So in everything, do to others what you would have them do to you, for this sums up the Law and the Prophets." We can easily mend the divide by living by this simple principle. But to do that, we have to be willing to come to the table and accept the fact that we are all different and be OK existing and living in a country with such a diverse population. We do not have to like, accept, or agree with someone's culture or way of life, but we do have to respect it.

Educate - Education is one of the most important pillars of any successful nation. In America, our education system has taken the approach of teaching people what to think and not how to think. Critical thinking and original thoughts have been replaced by memes and Tik-Tok videos. Instead of encouraging diverse thoughts and ideas, our schools are factories of linear thinking producing mindless robots ready to do the bidding of government and politicians.

The lack of education and knowledge of our nation's history has made it possible for political organizations and individuals to come in and rewrite history according to their agenda. With curriculum like CRT (Critical Race Theory) and the 1619 Project indoctrinating America's youth, the disenfranchised and the uneducated believe America is evil and needs to be dismantled from top to bottom. The only way to reverse the current trajectory of America and bring us back from the brink of destruction can be found in 2 Timothy 2:15, "Study to show yourself approved unto God, a workman that need not to be ashamed, rightly dividing the word of truth."

Aristotle said, "It is the mark of an educated mind to be able to entertain a thought without accepting it." When you are educated, grounded in the truth and factual information, not feelings and propaganda, you cannot be swayed into the divisiveness and predatory practices and beliefs of extremist and political organizations that need droves useful idiots and helpless victims to power their movement in the pursuit of absolute power and influence. It is not enough to simply hear a flashy and charismatic leader's views and interpretation of history and current events and believe it as gospel. An educated mind knows not to believe everything they hear. It is an educated mind that knows how to think independently and can arrive at its own conclusions. An educated mind is not easily coerced or persuaded by misinformation campaigns and the overly emotional and irrational mob. Education is the key to America's future and preserving the American way of life and crushing the Communist/Marxist utopia illusion.

It has been a long, challenging, stressful, adventurous, and fulfilling 37 years of life, and I would not change anything. I have made many mistakes in my journey, and I have learned many lessons, but the greatest lesson I have learned that I want to pass is this. Life is whatever you make it. The same thing can be said about living in America in this current time. So when I think of life and living in America being whatever you make it, my mind reverts to Matthew

7:7, "Ask and it will be given to you; seek and you will find; knock and the door will be opened to you," (NIV.)

I truly believe that we find whatever we are looking for; If you seek out and sow chaos, destruction, hate, bitterness, and division, you will find it, and it will consume you. If you seek out and sow love, peace, reasonableness, understanding, grace, and mercy, it will inundate your life and be returned to you. If you search for the worst in people, you will easily find it. If you seek out the best in people, you will uncover it. If you look for a reason to hate America and label it a racist and evil country, you can find countless examples to validate your beliefs. But suppose you, like me, believe that America is one of the greatest nations to have ever existed and see America as a beacon of hope, liberty, freedom, and prosperity. There are endless examples that speak to America's excellence. And I am proud to have my life story be one of the examples.

It was not until I read Proverbs 23:7, "For as he thinketh in his heart, so is he." That I realized that no matter what I said or what evidence I presented, some people's minds were made up and set in stone, nothing I presented to them would change their train of thought. In some people's hearts and minds, they are genuinely victims of America and "the system." They are unable to envision a life beyond the circumstances that have befallen them. In my heart, I know I am free and live in the privilege of being an American citizen every day. And because of my life experiences, I do not take that for granted. I wake up free, go to work free, come home free and sleep soundly, knowing that neither my family nor I will have to endure the hardships that others in the world have to live with daily. So instead of arguing with people and trying to change their minds and win them over, I focus on living my life in a way that will inspire others. I want to show people that if I can overcome the many obstacles in this life and live out my purpose daily, there is hope for a brighter future for everyone. It is not a change that happens overnight or in an instance, but it starts with fixing your focus on what you can control and changing your mindset from that of a victim to that of a victor.

In life, people will try to tell you what to be, who to be, where to go, what to believe, and what to think. The truth is no one can tell you who you are. External forces and pressures will try to influence, guide, mold, and force you to bend a knee to their will for your life. But they can only do that when you willingly submit yourself to them and cave to the pressure. And if you do not know who you are and what you believe, you will be their next victim. I am a father. I am a husband. I am a Christian. I am a veteran. I am an American. I am a police officer. I am a conservative. I am Pitts. But above all things, I am a child of God. I know who I am. Who are you?

ABOUT THE AUTHOR

Dexter Pitts is a proud Purple Heart recipient and medically retired U.S. Army veteran. He proudly served in Iraq with the 10th Mountain Division and is a graduate of American Military University with a bachelor's degree in Criminal Justice. After serving his country in a time of war, Dexter exchanged his military fatigues for a police officer uniform. He has continually served his community as a law enforcement officer for over a decade and a one-year tour of duty as an agent with the United States Border Patrol on the southern Arizona border.

Raised as a Christian in a military family, Dexter starts to question his faith in the wake of his mother's unexpected suicide while he is on duty. Having struggled all of his life trying to find his own identity, Dexter became submerged in the battle between his conservative values, black skin, and PTSD (Post Traumatic-stress Disorder).

Despite the obstacles that have befallen him, Dexter stands unshakable in his faith and identity as a proud American patriot who believes in the promises of America. Dexter's faith and values are tested once more as civil unrest consumed America in 2020. In defense of his profession, his community and the U.S. Constitution, he stands shoulder to shoulder with his brothers and sisters of the thin blue line on Louisville's embattled streets.